WRITING T

Poetics and ...ics in
Social Science Discourse

COMMUNICATION AND SOCIAL ORDER

An Aldine de Gruyter Series of Texts and Monographs

Series Editor

David R. Maines, Wayne State University

Advisory Editors

Bruce Gronbeck • Peter K. Manning • William K. Rawlins

David L. Altheide and Robert Snow, **Media Worlds in the Era of Postjournalism**

Joseph Bensman and Robert Lilienfeld, **Craft and Consciousness: Occupational Technique and the Development of World Images** (*Second Edition*)

Valerie Malhotra Bentz, **Becoming Mature: Childhood Ghosts and Spirits in Adult Life**

Herbert Blumer, **Industrialization as an Agent of Social Change: A Critical Analysis** (*Edited with an Introduction by David R. Maines and Thomas J. Morrione*)

Dennis Brissett and Charles Edgley (*editors*), **Life as Theater: A Dramaturgical Sourcebook** (*Second Edition*)

Richard Harvey Brown (*editor*), **Writing the Social Text: Poetics and Politics in Social Science Discourse**

Norman K. Denzin, **Hollywood Shot by Shot: Alcoholism in American Cinema**

Irwin Deutscher, Fred P. Pestello, and Frances G. Pestello, **Sentiments and Acts**

Bruce E. Gronbeck, **Rhetoric and Socioculture**

J. T. Hansen, A. Susan Owen, and Michael Patrick Madden, **Parallels: The Soldiers' Knowledge and the Oral History of Contemporary Warfare**

Emmanuel Lazega, **The Micropolitics of Knowledge: Communication and Interaction in Work Groups**

David R. Maines (*editor*), **Social Organization and Social Process: Essays in Honor of Anselm Strauss**

David R. Maines, **Time and Social Process: Gender, Life Course, and Social Organization**

Peter K. Manning, **Organizational Communication**

Stjepan G. Meštrović, **Durkheim and Postmodernist Culture**

R. S. Perinbanayagam, **Discursive Acts**

William K. Rawlins, **Friendship Matters: Communication, Dialectics, and the Life Course**

Vladimir Shlapentokh and Dmitry Shlapentokh, **Ideological Trends in Soviet Movies**

Jim Thomas, **Communicating Prison Culture: The Deconstruction of Social Existence**

Jacqueline P. Wiseman, **The Other Half: Wives of Alcoholics and Their Social-Psychological Situation**

WRITING THE SOCIAL TEXT

Poetics and Politics in
Social Science Discourse

Richard Harvey Brown
EDITOR

ALDINE DE GRUYTER
New York

ABOUT THE EDITOR

Richard Harvey Brown is Professor of Sociology and Affiliate Professor of Comparative Literature at the University of Maryland, College Park. His first career was in social planning and international development, and he continues these activities as President of the Washington Institute for Social Research and through writings on the cultural aspects of state formation and economic growth in India, East Asia, and Latin America. Richard Brown's works in social theory include *Structure, Consciousness, and History* (1978, with Stanford Lyman), *A Poetic for Sociology* (1977/1989), *Society as Text* (1987), *(Social Science as Civic Discourse* (1989) and *Discourse and Domination* (1993).

Copyright © 1992 Walter de Gruyter, Inc., New York
All rights reserved. No part of this publication may be reproduced or transmitted in any form or by any means, electronic or mechanical, including photocopy, recording, or any information storage and retrieval system, without permission in writing from the publisher.

ALDINE DE GRUYTER
A division of Walter de Gruyter, Inc.
200 Saw Mill River Road
Hawthorne, New York 10532

The paper used in this publication meets the minimum requirements of American National Standard for Information Sciences—Permanence of Paper for Printed Library Materials, ANSI Z39.48-1984.   ∞

Library of Congress Cataloging-in-Publication Data

Writing the social text : poetics and politics in social science
    discourse / Richard Harvey Brown (editor).
        p.   cm. — (Communication and social order)
    Based on two conferences held at the University of Maryland in
1989.
    Includes bibliographical references and index.
    ISBN 0-202-30386-1 (cloth : alk. paper). — ISBN 0-202-30387-X
(pbk. : alk. paper)
    1. Social sciences—Methodology.   2. Humanities—Methodology.
3. Rhetoric.   4. Discourse analysis.   I. Brown, Richard Harvey.
II. Series.
    H61.W86   1991
    300'.1—dc20
                                                                    91-19147
                                                                    CIP

Manufactured in the United States of America

10   9   8   7   6   5   4   3   2   1

CONTENTS

v

LIST OF CONTRIBUTORS

Jon Anderson
Department of Anthropology
Catholic University of America
Washington, DC 20064

Charles Bazerman
Department of English
Georgia Institute of Technology
Atlanta, GA 30332

Richard Harvey Brown
Department of Sociology and
    Program in Comparative
    Literature
University of Maryland
College Park, MD 20742

Walter Fisher
Communications Arts and
    Sciences
University of Southern California
Los Angeles, CA 90089

Joseph Gusfield
Department of Sociology
University of California
    at San Diego
La Jolla, CA 92037

Michael Herzfeld
Department of Anthropology
Harvard University
Cambridge, MA 02138

Julie Klein
College of Humanities
Wayne State University
Detroit, MI 48202

David Leary
Faculty of Arts and Sciences
University of Richmond
Richmond, VA 23173

Carl Milofsky
Department of Sociology
Bucknell University
Lewisburg, PA 17837

Jacques A. Mourrain
    (aka Renée Denūvo)
Social Science
University of California
Irvine, CA 92716

Paul Sites
Department of Sociology and
    Anthropology
Kent State University
Kent, OH 44242

Hilkka Summa
Aameryontie 14c
SF-02210 Espoo
Finland

PREFACE

The "rhetorical turn" has become an important intellectual movement in the human sciences. In response to rising distress with objectivist canons, scholars from many disciplines have reconceived their activities in rhetorical terms. In seeing scientific disciplines as rhetorical constructions, such scholars also have undermined foundationalist notions such as the correspondence theory of truth, scientific language as a neutral mirror of reality, and verification and falsification as criteria that demarcate true, objective science.

This turn toward rhetoric has intensified critical attention to the language and logic of the human sciences. For example, there have been attempts at "decentering" and "defamiliarizing" scholarly texts and a greater practice of what Ricoeur called the "hermeneutics of suspicion." Structuralists and formalists have called attention to the tropological character of language, and to the influence of discursive and even prediscursive linguistic forms on both thought and expression. Following Foucault, other scholars have sought to reveal institutionally imposed constraints on rhetorical choices, constraints that are themselves made up of discursive practices.

At issue in these and other parallel debates is not only the status of scientific claims, but of objectivity itself, whether it be in history of hematology, etymology or entomology, philosophy or physics. Seen poetically and politically, these bodies of knowledge are not mirrors of an independent reality, but the result of social negotiation, rules of procedure, literary tropes, and stratagems of persuasion. Thus, in the emerging metalanguage of the human sciences, we may speak of behaviors, cultures, and entire historical epochs as texts, scientific data and theories as symbolic constructions, mathematical proofs as rhetorical tropes, and scientific communities as ongoing conversations.

The present volume is part of this broad intellectual movement. Hence, we take it for granted that social and cultural reality, and the social sciences themselves, are linguistic constructions. Not only do we view society as a text, but we see scientific texts themselves as rhetorical constructions. In such a view, the distinctions between fact and fiction become blurred, since both are seen to be the products of, and resources for, communicative action; both are viewed as projections of reality that also protect the interests and values of various group.

These challenges to foundationalist conceptions of science and society clearly are not the province of one discipline alone. For example, anthropologists have led in deconstructing our images of the cultural Other; sociologists have applied critical interpretive methods to statistical-deductive studies of modern societies; literary theorists have provided key tools for cultural criticism and disciplinary self-reflection. Interventions from all these perspectives are represented in the present volume. Across our several disciplines, we realize that we are part of a shared conversation, a conversation that has much to contribute to intellectual and social life.

The volume opens with overviews of the intellectual developments mentioned above, focusing on poetics and politics, or language and power, in social science discourse. Section II concerns rhetoric and truth in the social sciences. The question of the epistemological status of the social sciences is discussed from a rhetorical or textualist perspective, and the status of this perspective iteself is reflexively considered. Section II, on social science as political discourse, carries the discussion in a more practical direction. The essays here consider the use of social science as political rhetoric in contexts of professionalization, social policy, and colonial domination. Essays in the final section of the volume pose and assess challenges for the rhetoric of the social sciences itself, and how these challenges might be fruitfully exploited or surmounted.

The volume grows out of two conferences held at the University of Maryland in 1989: "The Rhetoric of the Social Sciences," and "Writing the Social Text." I sincerely thank the University of Maryland for its support, as well as my co-organizers Jeanne Fahnstock, James Klumpp, Mark Leone, and Joan Vecchia. Critical guidance also was provided by David Maines and other members at the University of Iowa's Symposium on Narrative, Summer 1990. Other volumes that issued from the Maryland conferences are special numbers of *Sociological Theory* (1990) and *Revista Colombiana de la Sociologia* (1992), and *Le retour de la rhetorique* (1992).

PART I

Language/Power in the Social Sciences

Chapter 1

Poetics, Politics, and Truth: An Invitation to Rhetorical Analysis

Richard Harvey Brown

In recent decades we have witnessed profound challenges to our ways of understanding the world. Widespread experience of radically changed social orders has undermined confidence in the adequacy of our means to describe and interpret social reality. Thus, in every contemporary field whose subject is society or human sensibility, there are attempts to reassess the styles of theory and modes of representation inherited from "classical" thinkers and to reorient inquiry toward new directions.

Against a backdrop of rising dissatisfaction with objectivist beliefs, scholars from a variety of disciplines have once again been reconceiving what they are about in rhetorical terms. Significant objections have been raised in recent years to such foundationalist notions as the correspondence theory of truth, the mind as a knowing essence, scientific language as a mirror of reality, and verification and falsification as demarcation criteria for science (Simons 1990). At stake has been not just the validity of particular truth claims from one or another discipline, but of the status of the scientific enterprise itself.

These debates over the nature of social reality and how we can know it are not new to the Western intellectual tradition. Instead, they replay the conflict between those who hope for a natural science of society and those who say that people must be understood differently than nature. Even more deeply, current conflicts can be seen as an extension of the ancient debate between philosophy and rhetoric, expressed today as a conflict between modern science and postmodern theories of textuality and deconstruction. In both the ancient and the current versions, there is distress and confusion about how we are to make knowledge present through our representations of social reality. Thus, both debates are about how an emergent postclassical or postmodern world is to be represented as an object for social thought in its various disciplinary manifestations (Marcus and Fischer 1986:vii).

For over a century most Western thinkers held that knowledge could be gained with certainty through empirical observations and logical deductions. In their view, there is a world of objective facts governed by causal laws. The discovery of these causal laws permits the theorist to map reality accurately for purposes of prediction and control. Thus, reality was seen as independent of the thinker, who through systematic observation may develop testable propositions. Those propositions that survive empirical tests and are able to predict real events come to constitute the body of knowledge.

This view of knowledge has eroded in recent decades. Many disparate voices have converged to question the positivist account and even to reverse its assumptions of facticity and causal sequence. In this alternative view, theories do not mirror reality; they are products of human artifice, which themselves shape what we take as real and true. This view draws on the ancient Sophist conception of reality as molded through discourse. It is a return of rhetoric.

This resurgence of rhetoric has been resisted. Modern science and its philosophies abjure their own rhetorical practices and contend that the figures of language are not suitable for scientific discourse. For example, in the spirit of Bacon and Sprat, modern analytic philosophers have attempted to rid language of ambiguity and thus make it a suitable tool for science. For them, the figures of language invite ambiguity because the interpretation of tropes is open-ended, capable of supporting several logical interpretations. This contrasts to the desired univocality of scientific writing, in which the author ideally conveys one meaning and only one meaning in what he or she says. Thus, an ideal scientific language should be as impersonal, transparent, and exact as mathematics.

Since positivism aspires to objectively valid and universally applicable knowledge, that is, knowledge without a human point of view, it also must eschew more personalized modes of expression. Thus figures in scientific writing are resisted not only because of their polyvocality, but also because they violate the proper role of the writer in scientific prose. Figures can add individuality and personality to a writer's style, but scientific writing requires the author to subordinate his or her individuality in favor of objective and impersonal expression. For example, the writer of science should remain in the background by using the passive voice or the collective "we."

Contrary to many of its advocates, however, science is not just objective knowledge gleaned from logic and observation. No synthesis could ever be achieved, no models postulated, no paradigms established or advanced, if science relied wholly upon logic and observation. Model-building requires inductive leaps that exploit the power of metaphor. Such models are themselves metaphors of their domains of application, guiding the choice of experiments and the interpretation of data in a realm of thought that is outside the literal world.

Neither the ancient nor the modern condemnation of figures has been successful in eliminating these devices from scientific prose. Tropes exist because science must build models; schemes exist because these models must be explained and understood. Aristotle's criticism of the sophistic use of figures was based on the excessive use of schemes, yet Aristotle recognized the power of metaphor and was its first major theorist. Later rhetoricians such as Cicero and Quintilian elaborated the judicious use of figures in prose. Even Bacon, the father of modern scientific writing style, did not practice what he preached; his own style was highly figured. Thus, condemning figures proves to be easier than eliminating them.

Despite protests to the contrary, science has and does rely on rhetorical devices. Even those discourses of the philosophy of science that explicitly eschew figuration inadvertently demonstrate its pervasiveness by using figures to defend their rejection of them. Descartes, Bacon, Locke, and others used rhetorical tropes to develop their anti-rhetorical positions. Descartes's epistemology, for example, elaborates the image of the knower alternately as traveler and as builder. Similarly, though Locke claimed that figurative language breaks the direct connection between an idea of a thing and the thing itself, his very concept of *idea* comes from the Greek *eide*, meaning light. Descartes and Locke both tried to exclude metaphorical language from epistemological discourse, yet both constructed their discourse with metaphors (Brown 1989; Shapiro 1989:8).

Thus, if the texts of science are to be analyzed rhetorically, Aristotle's limitation of rhetoric to political and judicial setting must be removed. Moreover, whether, after rhetorical analysis is completed, there will be left in scientific texts any constraints not the result of prior persuasion, any "natural" constraints, must remain, for the moment, an open question. In the meantime, as rhetorical analysis proceeds unabated, science may be progressively revealed, not as the privileged route to certain knowledge, but as another intellectual enterprise, an activity that takes its place beside, but not above, jurisprudence, literary criticism, history, and rhetoric itself.

To update Aristotle's theory of rhetoric, the work of Chaim Perelman is essential. His masterpiece, *The New Rhetoric*, written with Madame Lucie Olbrechts-Tyteca (1969), sought to rehabilitate rhetoric as a discipline whose task is the analysis of persuasion in the humanities and the social sciences. A central concept in the new rhetoric is the "universal audience," an ideal public that can refuse a rhetor's conclusions only on pain of irrationality. In contrast to ancient rhetoric, the new rhetoric is concerned with discourse addressed to any sort of audience—a crowd in a public square or a gathering of scientific researchers, one person or all of humanity.

In such a rhetoric of science, the hegemonic claims for scientific logic are curtailed, and the scope of classical rhetoric is extended to the constitution of scientific texts. In this new rhetoric of science, everyday and scientific reasoning differ in degree but not in kind. No deductive logic is a closed system, all of whose premises can be stipulated; every deductive chain consists of a finite number of steps between each of which an infinite number may be intercalated. Likewise, no inductions can be justified with rigor: all commit the fallacy of affirming the consequent; hence, all experimental generalizations illustrate the rhetorical procedure of reasoning by example (Gross 1990). Because logics of science and ordinary language differ only in degree, both are appropriate objects for rhetorical analysis.

In extending classical rhetorical ideas of style, arrangement, and invention, we do not need to apply them point for point to scientific texts. The key notion is not that science is oratory but that, like oratory, science is a rhetorical enterprise, centered on persuasion (Gross 1990). We can use the long tradition of rhetoric and rhetorical analysis to elaborate this shift. At the very outset of this tradition, Plato and Aristotle tried to ensure the certainty of knowledge, whereas the Sophists regarded knowledge as human and changeable, as poetic and politic, as rhetorical. Thus, the contest over the relative scope and status of science and rhetoric began early in the intellectual history of the West. And then as now, a broad scope for rhetoric is not possible unless rhetorical analysis includes not only the style and arrangement of science, but also those of its features commonly construed not as rhetoric, but as the discovery of scientific facts and theories.

From this rhetorical point of view, scientific discovery is properly described as *inventio*, invention. To discover is to find out what is already there. But discovery is not a description of what scientists do; it is a hidden metaphor that begs the question concerning the certainty of scientific knowledge. To call scientific theories inventions, therefore, is to challenge the intellectual privilege and authority of science. On this challenge, discovery is an honorific, not a descriptive, term; and it is used in a manner at odds with the history and practice of science—a record for the most part of mistaken theories, errors, and misdirections, a history and practice of correcting data and revising theories. Invention, on the other hand, recognizes the historically contingent and radically uncertain character of all scientific claims, even the most successful. If scientific theories are discoveries, their unfailing obsolescence is difficult to explain; if these theories are rhetorical inventions, no explanation of their radical vulnerability is necessary.

These few observations are part of a wider rhetorical deconstruction of the presumption of ontological certitude, a priori meaning, and foundationalism in general. Critical legal studies, for example, have demystified the authoritative model of legal reasoning. Ethnographers and cultural anthropologists also have been reformulating the social sciences in rhetorical terms. Similarly, literary criticism has moved away from "new criticism," now viewed as a positivist argument for the internal coherence of literary text, toward the social, historical, psychoanalytic, cultural, and ideological contexts of text and the multiple responses of readers (Marcus and Fischer 1986:7–8; Klein, in this volume).

While no single term can adequately describe the multitude of interests and intellectual problems associated with the postmodern temper, the term *rhetoric* is being used increasingly to do just that. For some, rhetoric means traditional rhetorical analysis of tone and style, the tropes of argument, invocations of authority, and appeals to audiences. For others, it means the practice of interpretive approaches such as structuralism, hermeneutics, deconstruction, archetypal and genre criticism. For others, it overlaps with an expanding sociology of knowledge that investigates the social and linguistic constitution of truth. As a result, in the movement toward a new rhetoric for the social sciences there is not one privileged meaning but many meanings and many voices. Necessarily, then, as both rhetoricians and scientists, we are all engaged in textual problems and productions.

As an old word made rich but also ambiguous by a long history of inconsistent usage, the term *rhetoric* directs our attention to the discursive practices of the human sciences from a variety of perspectives. There are, for example, the various pejorative senses of rhetoric as pretense, display, "mere" rhetoric. There are the more neutral senses of rhetoric as persuasion or figuration. And there are the eulogistic senses of rhetoric as the study of how to inquire and to advocate on matters for which there can be no proof, and of "proof" itself as a rhetorical device.

Each of these conceptions of rhetoric has been productive. The most common focus is on a text or set of texts and their contextual relations. The most common awareness is that all truths are partial truths. However convincing, genuine, and empirically tested, however valid they are within an historically situated community of knowers, all texts remain open. There is no first foundation and no last disclosure. Yet, as society itself is seen as a text, social theory becomes a voice of significant authorial power.

References

Brown, Richard Harvey. 1989. *A Poetic for Sociology: Toward a Logic of Discovery for the Human Sciences*. Chicago: University of Chicago Press.

Gross, Alan G. 1990. *The Rhetoric of Science*. Cambridge, MA: Harvard University Press.

Marcus, George E. and Michael M. J. Fischer. 1986. *Anthropology as Cultural Critique: An Experimental Moment in the Human Sciences*. Chicago: University of Chicago Press.

Perelman, Chaim and Lucie Olbrechts-Tyteca. 1989. *The New Rhetoric: A Treatise on Argumentation*. Notre Dame, IN: University of Notre Dame Press.

Shapiro, Michael J. 1989. *The Politics of Representation: Writing Practices in Biography, Photography, and Policy Analysis*. Minneapolis: University of Wisconsin Press.

Simons, Herbert W., ed. 1990. *The Rhetorical Turn: Invention and Persuasion in the Conduct of Inquiry*. Chicago: University of Chicago Press.

Chapter 2

Text/Context:
The Rhetoric of the Social Sciences

Julie Thompson Klein

Rhetoric and Textuality

The titles of two international symposia held at the University of Maryland in 1989—"The Rhetoric of the Social Sciences" and "Writing the Social Text"—are important signs of an intellectual sea change. During the past two decades scholars have been paying increased attention to language and text to the point that conferences and publications on rhetoric in the social sciences are no longer considered bizarre. At the first symposium scholars from several countries examined the rhetorical construction of the social sciences as fields of study, delineating the logics and techniques of research, revealing the rhetoric of reason and epistemology, and defining the relationship among discourse, power, and truth. At the second symposium scholars from the social sciences and humanities joined in a closer examination of writing by defining relationships among social reality and textual truth; scholarly discourse, disciplinarity, and civic life; constructions of the self and the "other"; reason, culture, and reasoning about culture. The chapters in this volume reflect the rich diversity of their investigations, while sketching the broad outlines of rhetoric in the social sciences.

The current rhetorical turn in scholarship constitutes a "quiet revolution" in the same sense Susan Suleiman used the phrase to describe a shift in literary theory and criticism from attention to story to storyteller to reader and audience. Suleiman observed:

> Some revolutions occur quietly: no manifestoes, no marching and singing, no tumult in the streets; simply a shift in perspective, a new way of seeing

9

what had always been there. New words enter the vocabulary, old words suddenly take on new meaning. . . . Or they retain their meaning but their *position* changes: the peripheral becomes central, the walk-on becomes the hero of the play. (1980:3; emphasis in original)

The quiet revolution embodied in the rhetorical turn is larger than the field of audience-oriented criticism in the humanities, but it is not unrelated and has evolved, in no small part, from the borrowing of textual and rhetorical theory from the humanities. Like audience-oriented criticism, rhetoric is not a single field but, to borrow Suleiman's description, "a multiplicity of crisscrossing, often divergent tracks that cover a vast area of the critical landscape" (ibid.:6). The connecting link among these divergent tracks is the idea that language is the very condition of thought, not its one-to-one representative.

The implications of a language-based model of knowledge are many, though one of the most significant has been a reconceptualization of what constitutes "text." The idea of a text is no longer confined to a written representation of "reality" or, more narrowly, a work of litera-ture. Any statement of experience—any oral or written record, any theory or method, any natural or human science—is a discursive practice that can be "read." A text might be a mathematical model or statistical analysis, a novel or ethnographic record, a work of art or tool, a ritual or painting, a social action or public policy. This widened view of text has fostered a new metalanguage in the human sciences, which opens up behaviors, cultures, and even entire historical epochs to reading as texts: scientific data are being viewed as symbolic construc-tions, scientific descriptions and theories read as narratives, mathemati-cal proofs analyzed as rhetorical tropes, and the ongoing activities of scientific communities revealed as conversations (Simons 1989:5). In-deed, culture itself is seen as an "ensemble of texts" (Geertz 1973:452). Necessarily, then, we are all engaged in textual problems. Texts are no longer the province of English departments, metaphor the business of literary critics, or narrative the stuff of fiction.

Correspondingly, "meaning" does not reside within an autonomous text, locked inside a hermeneutic code waiting to be cracked by a learned scholar. Meaning, Charles Bazerman explains in "The Interpretation of Disciplinary Writing" (in this volume), arises from the "multiple hetero-geneous contexts" of a text. Historically situated and culturally embed-ded, meaning is constructed locally, "within the occasions of the text's appearance." Thus a single text is actually an intertextual network, "a kind of junction where other texts, norms, and values meet and work upon each other" (Iser 1987:219). Because texts have readers, Bazerman adds, meaning also evolves from the reader's response to a text. Both reader and writer draw upon their understanding and experience of their social, literary/linguistic, natural, and psychological worlds. Furthermore, because these worlds are not static, the conditions of meaning change over time. Thus a text is not a permanent fixture but "a temporary stable place."

These shifts in definition of text and meaning have not taken place within the confines of the humanities. They are part of a much wider critique of prevailing modes of representation, styles of theory, and the presumption that truth and certainty are only obtainable through empirical observation and logical deduction. The broader roots of this critique lie in modern revolutions in philosophy, the principle of uncertainty, and Godelian limits to mathematical axiomatization. Within the human sciences per se the critique has generated a "crisis of representation" that stems from uncertainty about adequate means of describing "reality" in the wake of declining support for grand theory, global systems, and the promise of unity held out by a number of synthetic theories, including Parsonsian sociology (Marcus and Fischer 1986:7–9). The rhetoric of crisis is marked by attacks upon received notions of objectivity, authority, neutrality, truth, law, explanation, logic, epistemology, positivism, essentialism, experimentalism, empiricism, operationalism, formalism, modernism, the fact or artifact that speaks for itself, and the notion that there is a single, final meaning. Correspondingly, the former walk-ons of the play are subjectivity, relativity, pluralism, polyphony, interpretation, description, case study, dialogue, the linguistic, the literary, and the rhetorical. Accordingly the ranks of the playwrights have been joined by the likes of Habermas, Gadamer, Wittgenstein, Barthes, Foucault, Derrida, Lacan, Kuhn, Perelman, Rorty, and Geertz.

The rhetoric of crisis has given a distinctly "postmodern" temper to contemporary scholarship. It is a time of postconditions defined, Marcus and Fischer suggest, "not so much by what they are as by what they come after." Challenges to prevailing orthodoxies have created a period of "postparadigm" in many disciplines, ranging from postcolonial perspectives in history and anthropology and poststructuralism in literary theory to post-Marxism in cultural and historical criticism and a generalized postmodernism in all the disciplines of the human sciences (1986:7–8). While no single term adequately describes the multitude of interests and problems associated with the postmodern temper—in fact, there are contradictions among them—the rhetorical turn is often linked with postmodernism because challenges to orthodoxy have intensified interest in the role language plays in the construction of knowledge. Gusfield (in this volume), in fact, places the linguistics revolution in the social sciences within the wider context of postmodernism. Thus the rhetorical turn in scholarship is linked with current debates on the adequacy of disciplinary representation, the validity of claims we make about the world, as well as the forms, arguments, and language through which we make them. Rhetoric is an ancient field whose focus and status, Richard Brown (in this volume) shows, have changed through the ages. The current "recuperation" of rhetoric, as it is sometimes called, reflects a movement away from association of the term rhetoric with artifice, elocution, ornament, and manipulative or propagandistic uses of language to a more general interest in persuasion in all human activities, including the ways in which academic disciplines function as communities of discourse. Inevitably the movement has also stimulated discussion of the role that rhetoric might play as a metadiscourse capable of articulating interconnections among social science, civic life, and the disciplines of the humanities.

As social scientists have used the term *rhetoric* they have done so in different ways. Some consider rhetoric simply a borrowed methodology, a set of tools for understanding how authors of texts employ the devices of tone and style, the tropes of arguments, metaphor, and imagery, invocations of authority, and appeals to audiences. For others, methodology and conceptual purpose cannot be separated so neatly. In their practices, rhetorical analysis is linked with a particular critical interpretive approach such as poststructuralism, deconstruction, hermeneutics, critical pluralism, Habermasian critical theory, archetypal and genre criticism, each with its own attendant assumptions about the nature of language, culture, and knowledge. For others the term overlaps with an expanding sociology of knowledge and rhetoric of inquiry, broader fields in which examination of the language and argument of communities of inquiry has revealed the interrelationships of author, text, discipline, history, and culture. As a result, there is not one rhetoric of the social sciences but several, and the term is being used synonymously with the terms *literary, critical, social constructivist, deconstructivist, reflexive,* and several varieties of *feminist, neo-Marxist,* and *neo-Freudian* critique. To talk about the "rhetoric of the social sciences," then, is to talk about a diverse set of investigations of how the traditional disciplines of the social sciences create, apply, transmit, and institutionally maintain knowledge in texts.

Through rhetorical analysis, Bazerman (in this volume) explains, genres, conventions, and styles of writing within the disciplines are revealed as regularities in the practice and organization of disciplinary knowledge, with major social and epistemic consequences. As the familiar features of texts emerge within disciplinary practices, disciplines reveal their sense of business, their ways of going about that business, and the ways people in the field relate not only to each other as colleagues but also to those outside the space of their literatures and professional practices. Thus disciplinary modes of writing are also records of action. In describing the kinds of studies he himself has been interested in, Bazerman is in effect sketching an overview of the kinds of rhetorical studies being conducted in the social sciences today as well, studies of:

- sequences of texts, to see how they evolve out of and act upon each other
- the formation of social roles, relationships, and norms across and within literate activity
- the emergence and evolution of historical genres, to see how standardized features of texts respond to changing rhetorical needs
- the emergence of single texts within and as part of a writer's professional activities
- the behaviors of writing and reading as parts of socialization
- the cognitive processes by which individuals construct meaning within specific contexts and their individual cognitive biographies
- additional phenomena that clarify how texts are located within and across our complex worlds.

Contemporary Practices

Growing attention to rhetoric and textuality in the social sciences is evident in a variety of concrete practices:

- the reading of culture and society as text (Geertz 1973; Brown 1987)
- analyses of the rhetoric in a wide range of disciplines and fields (Nelson, Megill, and McCloskey 1987a,b)
- discussion of problems of authority and representation in ethnography
- recognition of the role of language and meaning in psychology and psychoanalysis
- the creation of new poetics for sociology (Brown 1977), for history (White 1983), and for law (White 1985)
- the emergence of new methodologies and approaches, such as thick description, cognitive esthetics, and symbolic realism
- studies of public opinion and political ideology through the interpretation of of texts and rhetorical analysis of communication, reasoning, and symbolism (Nelson 1987b)
- explanations of the persuasive nature of data, sampling, regression analysis, formal language, experimental tests, thought experiments, metaphor and analogy, models, appeals to authority, and storytelling in economics (McCloskey 1985, 1990).

The essays collected in this volume likewise reflect a variety of practices and disciplinary contexts, in this particular instance focusing primarily on sociology, anthropology, and psychology. The essays are of several kinds. Some focus on individual texts and authors, though always situating those texts within their historical, cultural, and intellectual contexts. Others focus on the corpus of a particularly field or professional practice. Still others consider methodological issues raised by a rhetorical approach to social science, and several authors propose new theoretical perspectives. Walter Fisher proposes a narrative paradigm in "Narration, Reason, and Community," and Paul Sites, in "Human Needs and Control: A Foundation for Human Science and Critique," proposes a new grounding of social theory in four basic human needs, seen as analogs of primary emotions, as an invariant of agency. Individuals are thus given causal power in the production and reproduction of social order. The four needs are security, meaning, self-esteem, and satisfaction. Human needs, Sites argues, have been either implicit or explicit in many theoretical traditions. Richard Brown in his concluding essay also proposes ways to proceed beyond, or to exploit fruitfully, postmodernist dilemmas.

While the various authors come from different perspectives, they share a common concern for the ways in which language shapes the projects of a discipline, illuminating as well as obscuring questions in the field. This concern is especially evident in studies of the constitution of particular fields. Gusfield, in "Listening for the Silences: The Rhetorics of The Research Field," focuses on the field of alcohol studies. The corpus of the field consists of texts located in specialized journals, chapters of books, government reports, and conference proceedings. The prevailing rhetoric of the field has produced a "malevolence assumption." There are, in fact, several levels of rhetoric in the field. Construction of the "deviant" character of drinking and drunkenness has not only perpetuated identification of drinking and drunkenness as causes of damage and death, it has also shifted attention away from differences, diversities, and the social benefits of drinking. Drinking has not been conceptualized as a "natural" or "normal" activity and, consequently, the alcoholic as "ordinary" is not in the audience of the field. By shifting attention away from the study of drinking as a general activity and the drinker who is not alcoholic, alcohol studies has hidden an entire range of behavior. In the process other possibilities have been marginalized, including how drinkers actually manage to drive safely, ways that drinkers might diminish risks in driving, and alternative factors in driving accidents and fatalities such as the need for safer autos and alternative forms of transportation. The result is a "rhetoric of silence" that persuades us the drinker is always the villain, persuading by denying conflict and alternative perspectives. Merely failing to investigate a given area declares it unworthy of attention: if "presence" is a rhetorical figure, so too is "absence". Only recently have studies emerged with some attention to elements in the phenomena of drinking-involved driving that are not drinking-related. The major significance for social science research is that phenomena, emerging as they do from the activities of people and being open to change and alteration, are social constructions that can be affected by the ways in which they are imagined and are perceived. The frame in which research is enclosed sets the boundaries and, thereby, the perception of the field. Rhetorical analysis of the status of social problems, Gusfield concludes, is useful because it enables understanding of the ways public phenomena are social constructions as well as the ways authority is created and used in the area of public problems.

David Leary, in "Communication, Persuasion, and the Establishment of Academic Disciplines: The Case of American Psychology," is also concerned about the constitution of a field, in this case the turn-of-the-century effort to institutionalize a scientific psychology. The success of the effort is linked with proponents' skill in presenting arguments for the new field and the receptivity of American psychologists to arguments that told a more promising though, Leary cautions, still nascent "likely story" of what psychology ought to be. At the same time supporters were arguing for the New Psychology, they were also arguing against other constructions of the field, including Psychical Research, which not only had popular appeal but also was competing for the same institutional space. Discrediting Psychical Research as unscientific was a necessary action in their campaign for a new science. (Walter Fisher would label these efforts examples of an "affirmative rhetoric" and a "subversion rhetoric.") Into and throughout the 1890s a "silent process of appropriation" was underway as New Psychologists expanded their vision of the field and the language that advanced a scientific psychology in which measurement and experiment played a central role. Since they also had to discredit Psychical Research, proponents of the New Psychology altered their arguments to include a concern for atypical, nonadult, nonmale states of mind and action, and even nonconscious states of mind. New Psychology had an additional relationship to work out as well. Although the New Psychology, its theoretical language embellished with numerical calculations and references to experiments, often set itself up as a rejection of traditional philosophical psychology, it was actually an outgrowth of the older rational and empirical psychology. Leary describes the new language as an "emergent dialect of the old philosophical language," now refurbished with the terminology of basic physiological and psychological processes.

Though it sounded different, the new language was mapping out the same territory once occupied by the earlier philosophical psychology. "New languages," Leary concludes, "grow out of old ones." By the mid-1890s the new field had the institutional signs of an established scientific discipline, including laboratories, journals, professorships, graduate programs, a professional organization, and a major textbook in William James's *The Principles of Psychology*. Its progress was not unimpeded, however, by several forms of intellectual resistance and social demands, which modified presentation of the case for New Psychology. Nevertheless the new scientific psychology took hold as larger numbers of people were persuaded that it told "more likely stories."

When Leary writes of the believability of the story presented by New Psychology, he is acknowledging the role that familiar cultural categories play in the rhetorical construction of disciplines. In a society that places a high value on efficiency, Leary notes, metaphors of efficiency have been at the core of psychologists' thinking and their rhetoric. In a capitalist society, metaphors of productivity and exchange have had a prominent place in analyses of social behavior. And, in a society obsessed with technology, psychologists have used cybernetic analogs of both cognitive and neurological thinking. These metaphors have made their stories more believable, more likely to be heard.

Walter Fisher, in "Narration, Reason, and Community," proposes a narrative paradigm as a philosophy of human communication. The narrative paradigm envisions persons as narrative beings and their worlds as series of stories. The narrative paradigm is consistent with the rhetorical turn in that it implies human communication should be viewed both historically and situationally, as stories or accounts that compete with other stories and accounts constituted by good reasons. The stories are "rational" not only in terms of informal or formal logic but also the two basic principles of the narrative paradigm: coherence and fidelity. Stories, like rhetoric, are present in all forms of human communication.

Like Gusfield and Leary, Hilkka Summa, in "The Rhetoric of Efficiency: Applied Social Science as Depoliticization," is also concerned about the constitution of a field, in this case planning policy. In analyzing the field Summa traces briefly the replacement of a language of good governing of society with a language of managerial efficiency. This shift changed citizens into clients and policies into strategies, making the conceptual apparatus of managerial accounting, ends-means hierarchy, and rational coordination part of the "natural" language of public affairs. Although rhetorical figures and persuasive elements are not usually considered part of planning texts, Summa shows how there is in fact a special planning rhetoric in central government, a rhetoric that has arisen from historical shifts in the planning professions. This rhetoric became manifest in both the technical character of planning texts and increasing expressions of quantitative reasoning. Like Leary, Summa also finds a stock of believable metaphors, in this case mechanical metaphors, such as efficiency and equilibrium, that have become common in administrative writing. Ultimately the strategies of argumentation that are used in a bureaucracy, Summa concludes, create a "presence" for a particular totality of social facts, defining the range of possibilities and preferable states visible to participants in a policy process. Administrative rhetoric also influences civic discussion and the ways the demands of citizens are channeled by defining and limiting the vocabulary with which social phenomena are discussed. Thus a bureaucracy, through its dominant argumentative strategies, influences the arguments that are available both for and against particular policies. Rhetoricity, Summa concludes, is an "inherent quality" of any social inquiry.

Carl Milofsky comes to a similar conclusion in "Fact, Fiction and Factions: Scandal, Controversy, and 'Filemaking' as Social Theory." Milofsky focuses on two particular examples: Serge Lang's practice of filemaking and nonprofit research as the basis for considering the general conduct of social research. Milofsky has found that studying Lang's policy of keeping files on social scientists whose work he has attacked serves as an excellent pedagogical tool for teaching students how to read and respond critically to the arguments presented in sociological journals, arguments that they must disassemble, decode, and demystify in order to understand. Students, and researchers alike, need to know how to separate truth claims based on partisan interests from "real" claims about truth. Like Leary, Milofsky pays close attention to the rhetoric of scholarly authority, a rhetoric that casts research as value-neutral and authoritative rather than political, partisan, controversial, and open to criticism. The case studies of all four of these authors—Gusfield, Leary, Summa, and Milofsky—validate Richard Brown's assertion in his concluding essay that a rhetorically reflexive social science can illuminate the inseparability of objects, persons, and events from the processes of representation by which they are formed: "the *what* of any knowledge system," he maintains, "is radically entangled in the *how* of its writing and speaking".

The issues that are discussed by these authors are evident across the social sciences, though they have been particularly visible in anthropology. Marc Manganaro speaks of a new anthropology born out of "a coalescence of anthropology and current theories on discourse emerging from literary and other cultural studies." Characterized by an increasing reciprocity, modernist anthropology is part of a larger reciprocity and textualization of the social sciences (1990:4). Michael Herzfeld likewise recognizes that the literariness of an ethnological text is now an accepted device within anthropology, even a fashionable one. The rhetorical turn in anthropology, often dubbed a "literary" or "linguistic" turn, has had a major impact on the discipline. The once unquestioned authority of the field-worker has been challenged through rhetorical analysis of ethnographic texts: unmasking the role that argument plays in the representation of culture, revealing the interplay of personal and disciplinary components in modes of authority, demonstrating the extent to which culture is invented in the textual process, highlighting the polyvocality and multisubjective nature of culture, clarifying the contextual and contingent nature of cultural "truths," and, in James Clifford's words, illuminating the way in which ethnography functions as a "hybrid textual activity" that traverses genres and disciplines (1986a:26). The implications are profound. There is no final reading of culture, no neutral account. The scholarly enterprise thus becomes a "rigorous partiality," as the possibility of alternative interpretations and alternative constructions of the phenomena being studied is revealed. Anthropology's major tool, participant observation, has been "reformulated in hermeneutic terms as a dialectic of experience and interpretation," in a tradition leading from Wilhelm Dilthey via Max Weber to symbols and meaning in anthropologists such as Clifford Geertz (Clifford 1988:34). The effect has been to blur the traditional line between cultural theory and textual criticism, between representation and evocation, "explanation" and "understanding," the poetic and the political and, ultimately, the boundaries that separate art, science, history, language, and the dynamics of genre and institution.

Three of the authors in this volume deal directly with dimensions of the rhetorical turn in anthropology. Jon Anderson, in "Poetics and Politics in Ethnographic Texts: A View from the Colonial Ethnography of Afghanistan," examines the body of colonial ethnography of the Pakhtun tribal country of eastern Afghanistan and the northwest frontier of what is now Pakistan. This corpus consists of surveys, accounts of tours, memoirs, reports, compilations, composite handbooks, biographical dictionaries, gazetteers, and agency diaries. Variously incorporating romantic narrative, polemic, classified material, firsthand accounts, policy analysis and prescriptions, these records of frontier service, when analyzed rhetorically, reveal not only their mode of production but also modes of interpretation. The major topics of British interpretation included the notion of Pakhtun "character" and the drawing of genealogical connections in a composite reconstruction of Pakhtun history. "Character," though, was not a neutral category. It was a central concept in British self-conception. As it was applied to the Pakhtun, the concept of "character" operated to rationalize existing or projected boundaries in the Pakhtun region, just as genealogies served a similar local purpose under the influence of philological methods and dispersion-of-people metaphors. Over time the concept worked by generalization and abstraction to stereotype the Pakhtun. Because a significant number of British frontier officers were Scots, a clear Scots sensibility is also evident in the un-self-conscious and unproblematic application of the term *clan* to Pakhtun lineages. In reflecting on the interpretive categories, decontextualized assessment, encyclopedic composites, mix of purposes, collapsing of time and diverse settings, and taken-for-granted assumptions that he found in the corpus, Anderson shows how the complex interplay of social, psychological, and political rationalizations ultimately produced an intellectual technology, an interwoven set of interpretive ideas and practices that framed interpretations of the Pakhtun. Like Gusfield, Anderson is equally mindful of the silences in the record created by channeling nuanced, multiply determined, and even contradictory voices into a flattened model that takes a limited conversation as the model of conversation itself. "Something else," he concludes, "fills the space where inquiry does not go."

Michael Herzfeld, in "Textual Form and Social Formation in Evans-Pritchard and Lévi-Strauss," conducts a careful analysis of the sequential form of two classic texts: E. E. Evans-Pritchard's *The Nuer* and Claude Lévi-Strauss's *Tristes Tropiques*. Herzfeld shows how the two texts exemplify the analytical falsity of separating ethnographic observer from the object being described, as the two authors demonstrate the practical limits of anthropology itself. Both authors claim to address the underlying form that structures events, *The Nuer* through the political model of segmentation and *Tristes Tropiques* through an analogy between the experience of travel and the rite of passage. Yet both texts also are, or at least embody, what they purport to describe, the *Nuer* by expressing a segmentary view of cultural relations and *Tristes Tropiques* by actually becoming a rite of passage and adopting the segmentary worldview of *The Nuer*. Hence both texts are inscribed in a larger set of segmentary practices, the model becoming entailed within itself, not standing outside the ethnographic object. Evans-Pritchard's consideration of authority figures in Nuer political life and his use of diagrams wind up being subordinate to the imperatives of the segmentary system. (Anderson's discussion of character and clan come to mind.) The authors differ, in that Evans-Pritchard does show some awareness of the possible entailment of European powers in segmentary logic, but he lacks the reflexivity of Lévi-Strauss, who gives us a clear context for his intellectual and physical explorations, thus providing what Herzfeld calls "an exemplary text for the development of a semiotic consciousness." Lévi-Strauss's own voyage becomes emblematic of the role of anthropology in European society in general. Physical transitions in the tropics become tropic transformations in the text.

Any discussion of the rhetorical turn in anthropology should not end without acknowledging the controversies that surround it. The most obvious criticism is the opposition of empirical anthropologists, who have mounted challenges to the rhetorical turn in the journals and conference rooms of the profession. Renée Denüvo, in "No Anthro-Apologies: Der(r)idaing a Discipline," raises an additional critique. In reviewing two well-known books in the field, Marcus and Fisher's *Anthropology as Cultural Critique* and Clifford and Marcus's *Writing Culture*. Denüvo questions the status of the "literary turn" or "experimental moment" in anthropology. There is an unresolved tension, he finds, in the polyphony of voices expressed within the two books. When deconstruction is "summoned" to perform the task of demystifying reason, monophonic authority, textual coherence and closure, or the culture concept, it often appears in "arrested form," producing an account of modes of authority, genres of description, or forms of rhetoric and literary artifice without following through completely on the critique of underlying assumptions in ethnographic presentation. A number of the authors in the two books remain partially committed to representation, the presence of speech, the positive and centered character of meaning and symbols, the self-conscious subject, or its displaced though not decentered equivalents, intersubjectivity and intertextuality. Hence, he argues, they produce only "quasi-deconstructive" readings that remain at the level of textual exegesis or *explication de texte*, thereby succumbing to "hermeneutic seduction."

The Status of Rhetoric

Even as it is disputed, the rhetorical turn is having a clear impact on scholarship. To begin with, it has played a major role in generating new models of the scholar: Brown's new sociologist, alert to the ways in which reason itself is rhetorical; McCloskey's new economist, engaged in storytelling as well as empirical analysis; and Bazerman's new textual analyst, finding the ways texts function as dynamic operators within stories of events. The implications extend well beyond the disciplines of anthropology, economics, sociology, and psychology to the nature of scholarship itself. "It is not just theory or method or subject matter that alters," Clifford Geertz once wrote, "but the whole point of the enterprise" (Geertz 1983:8). Marcus and Fischer suggest what has happened in the case of anthropology is not that anthropologists have become "a strange breed of literary critic," nor have they given up the goals of a unified science that might encompass behavior as well as thought:

> rather that their attraction to theories, which pose the activity of interpreta-
> tion as a challenge to long-term goals of the social sciences, has led them to
> engage in wider-ranging critical reflections on their central practice of
> ethnography. Under the hegemony of positivist social science, this practice
> had been masquerading, relatively unreflected upon by anthropologists or
> others, as a method like any other. The attraction of interpretative
> anthropology at the moment is precisely its sophisticated inquiry into the
> nature of ethnographic reporting, which is not only the basis of all
> anthropological knowledge, pursued in whatever theoretical direction,
> but also one palatable source of inspiration for other social sciences in
> resolving their own predicaments, stimulated by the contemporary crisis
> of representation; historically, anthropology has been near to them in
> institutional definition as a social science, but far in the singularity of its
> subject and method. (1986:26–27).

Correspondingly there are also new metaphors of knowledge that challenge the privileging of the natural sciences. Stimulated by Richard Rorty's metaphor of knowledge as conversation, the metaphors of scholarship as conversation, negotiation, dialogue, and dialectic have gained prominence. Gadamer's concept of discourse as dialectic entailed a movement back and forth over the same ground, the same topic or subject. In fact when Gadamer spoke of the logic of the human sciences, it was "the logic of the question," a logic that is dialectical not propositional (Bruns 1987:253, 257). Not unexpectedly, the juridical metaphor has also found favor. Paul Ricouer (1988) has even suggested that a general theory of validation might emerge by treating juridical reasoning as a fundamental link between validation in literary criticism and validation in the social sciences. Ricouer's proposal acknowledges the polemical character of procedures of validation and the plurivocality of both texts and actions in conduct of the law, literary studies, and anthropology.

In these models knowledge evolves not on a linear track but in dialogic fashion. Modern ethnography, Marcus and Fischer remind us, underscores how much the growth of knowledge is a process of "creative rediscovery of older and persistent questions," raised now in response to the state of a discipline's practice in a world of unprecedented changes (Marcus & Fischer 1986:10). For this reason, of course, rhetoric and textuality themselves are also historically and culturally located within the context of contemporary relations among the social sciences and humanities. Not long ago Clifford Geertz was asked to comment on those relations. His reply—that they are increasingly characterized by "blurred genres"—has become a metaphor for the contemporary human sciences. Observing the borrowing of analogies from the humanities—particularly game, drama, and text—Geertz suggested the phenomenon of blurred genres is not simply another redrawing of the cultural map—"the moving of a few disputed borders, the marking of some more picturesque mountain lakes"—but an alteration of principles of mapping (Geertz 1983:20). The blurring of genres, he contends, is no longer anomalous but has become "the natural condition of things." However, despite the growing legitimation of rhetorical perspective, the rhetorical turn is neither natural nor universal. The contemporary social sciences have not embraced a new rhetorical paradigm but are, instead, beset by contradictory positions: Chomskyians versus Skinnerians, Cliometricians versus Hegelians, statisticians versus interpretationists, empiricists versus rhetoricians, positivists versus nonpositivists, and social scientists versus humanists. As a result even the most ardent proponents of the rhetorical turn often write in a tone of apologia.

The conflicts are real and the stakes are significant. Yet, despite the conflicts, there is a general trend apparent across sociology, psychology, anthropology, and the traditional humanistic disciplines of linguistics, literature, philosophy, rhetoric, esthetics, history, and art history. The trend is characterized by a reflexive questioning of traditional categories and assumptions through study of the role language and argument play in the construction of knowledge. This questioning, it must be said, assumes different forms in separate disciplinary quarters. The constellation of practices and beliefs that make up the rhetorical turn in scholarship are located at different levels of institutionalization: sometimes coalescing in schools of thought and networks of practitioners within disciplines; sometimes attaining material institutionalization in the form of conferences, publications, research projects, joint appointments, job listings, changes in the editorial policies of journals, and new curricula; sometimes becoming naturalized and canonized in mainstream disciplinary discourse; sometimes finding only begrudging recognition as an "alternative" approach. Even as they register differently in separate disciplinary quarters, however, the practices and beliefs that constitute the rhetorical turn overlap in the form of a new metalanguage that has connective power across the disciplines of the human sciences. This metalanguage is evident in shared questions about how reality has been represented, shared concerns about the way authority constructs and contains knowledge, shared texts, the forging of new disciplinary alliances, and overlapping uses of discourse theory.

On his essay in this volume, Gusfield himself writes of a "common meeting ground." The emergence of interest in rhetoric, he notes, "is part of the way in which humanistic disciplines, especially literature and philosophy, and social sciences, especially anthropology and sociology, have been developing common meeting ground." In an age of "postconditions" marked by heightened skepticism about global generalizations, synthetic methodologies, social and political metanarratives, and totalizing paradigms (Lyotard 1988), it is unlikely the result will be the formation of a new unity, master discipline, or epistemological hegemony, despite the imperialistic claims being made by some rhetoricians, semioticians, and textualists. The elevation of rhetoric to a "central discipline" that James Boyd White and others await seems less likely than the general increase of self-reflection in every field of inquiry, the vision of the "Iowa School" of the rhetoric of inquiry movement. Nelson, Megill, and McCloskey foresee rhetorical analysis becoming an internalized process in all fields, making researchers better aware of their own practices and assumptions, and thereby pluralizing theory and methodology (Nelson, Megill, and McCloskey 1987a:ix). In a similar vein, Marcus and Fischer observe, "The essence of holistic representation in modern ethnography has not been to produce a catalog or an encyclopedia (although the classic assumption supporting the authority of the ethnographic writer is that he commands this sort of background knowledge), but to contextualize elements of culture and to make systematic connections among them" (1986:23).

The rhetorical turn in the human sciences has taken rhetoric beyond the confines of a single discipline to the entire academy. "Rhetoric," Alan Gross points out, "is both a discipline and a perspective from which disciplines can be viewed. As a discipline, it has a hermeneutic task and generates knowledge; as a perspective, it has a critical, emancipatory task and generates new points of view" (1990:111). Dilip Parameshwar Gaonkar concurs with Gross. Writing in a recent essay Goankar notes a double movement in rhetoric's flight from pejorative status as mere rhetoric, as a supplement to other disciplines:

> This double movement simultaneously propels rhetoric on a vertical axis downward into its past to find itself a suitable history and on a horizontal axis sideways, to situate itself within the discursive practices of special "substantive" sciences, especially the human sciences. Rhetoric moves diachronically in order to discover for itself an alternative historical tradition that will free it from supplementary status, and it also moves synchronically to find itself in the discursive body (textuality) of other disciplines that will confirm its "presence." (1990:343).

There are two horizontal movements, Gaonkar explains, by which rhetoric attempts to confirm its presence in the discourse of other disciplines. The first is a revival of rhetoric's historical double, the sophistic tradition of which Richard Brown speaks in this volume. This first movement operates philosophically by decentering the epistemic question and historically by reconstituting the history of rhetoric as two histories, the manifest history of the "supplementary" tradition and the hidden history of the sophistic tradition (Gaonkar 1990:347–52). The second horizontal movement is the one that has concerned us here, the increase in rhetorical self-consciousness known as the rhetorical turn in scholarship, and sometimes also referred to as the "rhetoric of inquiry" movement. This rhetorical turn, Gaonkar adds, is actually two turns not one. The "explicit" turn consists of works that recognize explicitly the relevance of rhetoric for contemporary thought and also use rhetoric as a critical and interpretive method: in, for example, the works of the new rhetoricians, including Chaim Pereleman, Kenneth Burke, Richard McKeon, Paul de Man, Walter Ong, Northrop Frye, and Tzvetan Todorov. Their exercise of the explicit turn is not uniform, however: some view rhetoric as a general theory of discourse (a metadiscipline), others rely on it as a critical instrument for analyzing literary and social texts, while others use the term *rhetoric* randomly in their work. The second and more pertinent turn is the implicit turn, referring to texts whose authors may not even be fully aware of technical rhetorical vocabulary but who are turning toward rhetoric to analyze the tropological and persuasive aspects of disciplinary practice that hitherto have remained outside the mainstream disciplinary purview. The list of authors in the implicit turn is much longer, incorporating not only Kuhn, Feyerabend, Lacan, Gadamer, Habermas, and Foucault, but also, by extension, the authors in this volume, and, Gaonkar adds, practitioners of certain schools of thought that reveal a rhetorical orientation, including the sociology of knowledge tradition, symbolic interactionists, the dramatistic movement in anthropology and sociology, and a variety of philosophical positions that stress the role of language and language action. "The contemporary intellectual landscape," Gaonkar concludes, "is replete with signs of an implicit rhetorical turn" (1990:352–55).

Growing recognition that the social sciences contain an unavoidable rhetorical component has profound implications for the conduct of disciplinary inquiry. Rhetorical awareness calls attention to the inescapable role that communication plays in the construction of social knowledge, heightening our awareness of the interests that are being served by data and theory. In the wake of deconstruction there is concern about the negative ends of textual criticism, though rhetorical analysis of scholarly and social texts, Richard Brown points out, also has a positive constructive task, enabling us to imagine more adequate narratives, to affirm human authorship of social reality, and to undermine absolutism, thereby fostering broader tolerance for alternative perspectives. Reflexivity, Bazerman likewise concluded, need not end "in a world of unreliable appearances." The reflexivity made possible by the rhetorical turn can foster, instead, greater understanding and self-consciousness, enabling researchers to perform their work more effectively and self-consciously and, as they deem necessary, to reshape the projects of their disciplines.

References

Brown, Richard Harvey. 1977. *A Poetic for Sociology: Toward a Logic of Discovery for the Human Sciences*. Cambridge: Cambridge University Press.

———. 1987. *Society as Text: Essays on Rhetoric, Reason, and Reality*. Chicago: University of Chicago Press.

———. 1989. *Social Science as Civic Discourse: Essays on the Invention, Legitimation, and Uses of Social Theory*. Chicago: University of Chicago Press.

Bruns, Gerald L. 1987. "On the Weakness of Language in the Human Sciences." Pp. 239–62 in *The Rhetoric of the Human Sciences: Language and Argument in Scholarship and Public Affairs*, edited by John S. Nelson, Alan Megill, and Donald N. McCloskey. Madison: University of Wisconsin Press.

Clifford, James. 1986a. "Introduction: Partial Truths." Pp. 1–27 in *Writing Culture: The Poetics and Politics of Ethnography*, edited by J. Clifford and G. Marcus. Berkeley: University of California Press.

———. 1986b. "On Ethnographic Allegory." Pp. 98–121 in *Writing Culture: The Poetics and Politics of Ethnography*, edited by J. Clifford and G. Marcus. Berkeley: University of California Press.

———. 1988. *The Predicament of Culture: Twentieth-century Ethnography, Literature, and Art*. Cambridge, MA: Harvard University Press.

Clifford, James and Marcus, George, eds. 1986. *Writing Culture: The Poetics and Politics of Ethnography*. Berkeley: University of California Press.

Darnton, Robert. 1985. *The Great Cat Massacre and Other Episodes in French Cultural History*. New York: Vintage Books, Random House.

Gaonkar, Dilip P. 1990. "Rhetoric and Its Double: Reflections on the Rhetorical Turn in the Human Sciences." Pp. 341–66 in *The Rhetorical Turn: Invention and Persuasion in the Conducts of Inquiry*, edited by H. W. Simons. Chicago: University of Chicago Press.

Geertz, Clifford. 1973. *The Interpretation of Cultures*. New York: Basic Books.

———. 1983. "Blurred Genres: The Refiguration of Social Thought." In *Local knowledge: Further Essays on Interpretive Anthropology*. New York: Basic Books.

Gross, Alan. 1990. "The Origin of Species: Evolutionary Taxonomy as an Example of the Rhetoric of Science." Pp. 91–115 in *The Rhetorical Turn: Invention and Persuasion in the Conduct of Inquiry*, edited by H. W. Simons. Chicago: University of Chicago Press.

Iser, Wolfgang. 1987. "Representation: A Performative Act." Pp. 217–32 in *The Aims of Representation: Subject/Text/History*, edited by M. Krieger. New York: Columbia University Press.

Krieger, Murry., ed. 1987. *The Aims of Representation: Subject/Text/History*. New York: Columbia University Press.

LaCapra, Dominik. 1987. "Criticism Today." Pp. 235–255 in *The Aims of Represen-tation: Subject/Text/History*, edited by M. Krieger. New York: Columbia University Press.

Lyotard, Jean-Francoise. 1988. *The Postmodern Condition: A Report on Knowledge*. Translated by Geoff Bennington and Brian Massumi, with a foreword by Frederic Jameson. Minneapolis: University of Minnesota Press.

Manganaro, M. 1990. "Textual Play, Power, and Cultural Critique: An Orienta-tion to Modernist Anthropology." Pp. 3–47 in *Modernist Anthropology: From Fieldwork to Text*, edited by M. Manganaro. Princeton, NJ: Princeton University Press.

Marcus, George E. and Fischer, Michael M. J. 1986. *Anthropology as Cultural Critique: An Experimental Moment in the Human Sciences*. Chicago: University of Chicago Press.

McCloskey, Donald N. 1985. *The Rhetoric of Economics*. Madison: University of Wisconsin Press.

———. 1990. *If You're So Smart: The Narrative of Economic Expertise*. Chicago: University of Chicago Press.

McKeon, Richard. 1971. "The Uses of Rhetoric in a Technological Age: Architec-tonic Productive Arts." Pp. 44–63 in *The Prospect of Rhetoric*, edited by Lloyd F. Bitzer and Edwin Black. Englewood Cliffs, NJ: Prentice-Hall.

Nelson, John S., ed. 1983. *What Should Political Theory Be Now?* Albany: State University of New York Press.

Nelson, John S. 1987a. "Stories of Science and Politics: Some Rhetorics of Political Research." Pp. 198–220 in *The Rhetoric of the Human Sciences: Language and Argument in Scholarship and Public Affairs*, edited by John S. Nelson, Alan Megill, and Donald N. McCloskey. Madison: University of Wisconsin Press.

———. 1987b. "Seven Rhetorics of Inquiry: A Provocation." Pp. 407–34 in *The Rhetoric of the Human Sciences: Language and Argument in Scholarship and Public Affairs*, edited by John S. Nelson, Alan Megill, and Donald N. McCloskey. Madison: University of Wisconsin Press.

Nelson, John S., Allan Megill, and Donald N. McCloskey, eds. 1987a. *The Rhetoric of the Human Sciences: Language and Argument in Scholarship and Public Affairs*. Madison: University of Wisconsin Press.

———. 1987b. "Rhetoric of Inquiry." Pp. 3–18 in *The Rhetoric of the Human Sciences: Language and Argument in Scholarship and Public Affairs*, edited by John S. Nelson, Alan Megill, and Donald N. McCloskey. Madison: Univer-sity of Wisconsin Press.

Ricouer, Paul. 1988. *Hermeneutics and the Human Sciences*. Edited and translated by John B. Thompson. Cambridge: Cambridge University Press.

Simons, Herbert W. 1989. "Preface" and "Introduction." In *Rhetoric in the Human Sciences*, edited by Herbert W. Simons. London: Sage.

———, ed. 1990. *The Rhetorical Turn: Invention and Persuasion in the Conduct of Inquiry*. Chicago: University of Chicago Press.

Suleiman, Susan R. 1980. "Introduction: Varieties of Audience-oriented Criti-cism. In *The Reader in the Text: Essays on Audience and Interpretation*, edited by

Susan R. Suleiman and Inge Crosman. Princeton, NJ: Princeton University Press.

White, Hayden. 1983. *Metahistory: The Historical Imagination in Nineteenth-century Europe*. Baltimore: Johns Hopkins Press.

White, John Boyd. 1985. *Heracles' Bow: Essays on the Rhetoric and Poetics of the Law*. Madison: University of Wisconsin Press.

Willard, Charles A. 1983. *Argumentation and the Social Grounds of Knowledge*. Tuscaloosa: University of Alabama Press.

PART II

Rhetoric and Truth in the Social Sciences

Chapter 3

The Interpretation of Disciplinary Writing

Charles Bazerman

The reflexive rhetorical turn in knowledge-producing disciplines has called attention to the text, which is the medium through which knowledge is transmitted and is the matter in which knowledge is embodied outside the consciousness of any individual. Although text only gains meaning through the interpretive act of the reader, nonetheless text is the representation of knowledge that reaches beyond the mind of any individual. Text is knowledge that stands between people. Once attention is called to the text as the interpersonal, social realization of knowledge, many questions immediately arise as to what can and cannot be accomplished through a text, a purely symbolic artifact of human symbolic activity. Are these texts any more than arbitrary remnants of arbitrary signs? How can words and symbols, the shadows of transient mental concepts, embody any substantive knowledge of the physical world? How can language reach beyond the social beliefs and assumptions on which it is based and which it embodies? Even in purely social terms, is the intersubjectivity or apparent intersubjectivity on which language use is predicated of such a kind as to ensure fully shared meaning, univocality of expression, or even common understanding?

These are indeed puzzling questions that I have inevitably had to address in the course of my studies of scientific writing. But in addressing these questions I have gradually moved towards an interpretive stance where these questions no longer seem so troubling or important. The answers to the questions are not to be found by direct assault on epistemology, so much as by adopting an appropriate perspective on the interactions that occur through discourse. The questions as phrased all come out of a traditional hermeneutic perspective where the importance of a text is to be found in what it says, its meaning, as though essential meaning resided in the text, and all one

31

needed was the right method to read that meaning message correctly. Because texts exist between people, and only gain meaning in the individual acts of reading and the social acts of negotiating interpretation, such questions inevitably lead one down nihilistic paths of infinite regress and mirrored hallways with no end. I will argue here rather for an interpretive perspective that focuses on what a text does within local networks of activity, rather than on what it says. Such a perspective does not try to remove text and meaning from human symbol-making, but rather grants power and substance to the text as operationally significant in human affairs. Such a perspective takes language as neither essentially grounded nor irremediably insubstantial.

The beginning of traditional hermeneutics study is the text, the meaningful text, the sacred text, the text enbued with meaning by an extrahuman power. The aim of hermeneutics is to locate that meaning either in the correct reading of the surface of the words or more deeply within some underlying framework, metaphorical system, or secret decoding process. Hermeneutics takes the point of view of the reader confronting a text that is taken to be capable of revealing a correct and definitive meaning when interpreted by the skilled or knowledgeable reader. Despite the loss of universal belief in a divinity who guarantees that absolute meaning inheres in the word, the problem of meaning remains the central problem that activates and troubles most literary studies. The main activity remains, under many guises, developing a truer, deeper, more meaningful reading of various texts that are considered to yield up new secrets to hermeneutic gymnastics. The critic remains the primary intermediary between the unknowledgeable reader and the special meaning of the esoteric text, not unlike the role that some professors of literature take in the classroom, introducing students into the arts of literary reading and interpretation applied to the body of more meaningful, but difficult because so meaningful, texts that comprise the literary canon. This interpretive tradition, in which I was trained during its late-new-critical phase, has been transformed by the ideas of latter-day theory, which often attempts to show that texts mean nothing, that they are vapors of the moment, blown by political, ideological, cultural, or idiosyncratically personal winds. Yet meaning, or the lack thereof, remains the focus of literary attention. The daily practice of literary criticism, applied to texts deemed to be more meaningful, whether in a narrow traditional or broadly expanded canon, remains much the same. Thoughts of the evanescence of meaning, when addressed, are treated largely in the realm of abstraction and polemic, where these thoughts evoke either anarchic joy or outraged denial.

Of course, inherent in the idea of hermeneutics is the notion of difficult texts, texts whose meaning is not self-evident. When attention turned from divine, sacred texts, holding depths of wisdom beyond human understanding, to texts of human making, hermeneutics took for its domain those tricky texts written by clever authors who were thought to have greater wit or wisdom than the rest of us. This class of interesting texts was designated literature (along with several other classes of culturally valued texts), and was in most cases thought to be fictive, to be not responsible for conveying any state of affairs in the world in which we all live our daily lives. Texts that described that daily world were assumed to be mundane, and the familiarity of our own world made the meanings of such texts contemptuously easy to decode. Only by the free play of the imagination could writers create texts worthy of hermeneutics. Romantic versions of the self and the power of the imagination were crucial in institutionalizing this sacred role for literature and its interpretation.

The study of disciplinary texts as I practice it reverses all these assumptions. It is not hermeneutical; it is not primarily interested in drawing out a meaning taken to inhere in the text. It is in fact granted that these texts may be very easy indeed for the usual users of these texts (although not necessarily so, for philosophers and physicists and lawyers may devote many hours to drawing out the depths and crannies of a page). Moreover, it does not even assume there is a meaning that inheres in the text, although users may take the meaning as inhering unproblematically. Rather it considers the meaning to be constructed locally within the occasions of the text's appearance. Meaning is negotiated and accomplished between writer and reader across the text, both drawing on their understanding and experience of their social, literary/linguistic, natural, and psychological worlds, but does not exist within the text itself. It is within the art of writing to constrain potential meanings that might be imputed by readers from their likely frames of interests and interpretation to within the bounds desired by the writer. And it is within the art of reading to reconstruct out of the reader's own cognitive resources a meaning that might plausibly account for the words handed over by the writer. Lawyers and contending philosophers might hostilely test the bounds of the constraints of words within the relevant social context of linguistic practices, while poets and their readers might grant each other greater interpretive sympathy and leeway.

What I am interested in are the interactions and relationships established across the text, how the text conjoins things (people, words, memories, experiences, institutions, groups, actions, plans, literary traditions, conversations, and so on) within dynamic relations. The intentions and meanings attributed by writers and readers are only momentary events within the processes by which texts enter into the manifold dynamics of life. In this volume we are particularly concerned about the rhetorical dynamics of social science disciplines as they carry out their various activities of knowledge creation, application, and transmission as well as of institutional maintenance. The language is integrally part of the projects, activities, states of being, and foreseen and unforeseen consequences of disciplines.

The mode of interpretation I espouse situates texts within actions, and thus is fundamentally historical, placing texts as dynamic operators within stories of events. This general approach includes studies of sequences of texts to note how they evolve out of and act upon each other [such as my study (1988) of Newton's seven versions of his optical findings, which change in relation to the social circumstances of the presentation, contending texts of scientific opponents, and Newton's highly motivated search for compelling arguments to subordinate all other optical discourses beneath his own]; of negotiations within literate communities [such as Greg Myers's studies (1985a,b) of the social negotiation processes shaping the proposals and articles that are finally accepted by the relevant gatekeepers or Susan Cozzens' study (1985) of how discussions surrounding citations negotiate disciplinary beliefs about the primary conceptual message of an article]; of historical genre emergence and evolution to see how standardized features of texts respond to changing rhetorical needs [such as my studies (1988) of the invention and changing form of the experimental article from 1665 to 1800 and of the adaptation and codification of the experimental article in twentieth-century experimental psychology]; of the formation of social roles, relationships, and norms across and within literate activity (such as my study of the proliferation of social roles within the scientific community as a result of the development of specialized forms of discourse, the kinds of role conflicts that emerge within the social complex of scientific communication, and the development of normative attitudes towards scientific communication as conflict-mediating devices); of the emergence of single texts within and as part of a writer's professional activities [such as my study (1988) of A. H. Compton's drafting and revision of an article]; of writing and reading behavior as part of socialization [such as Berkenkotter, Huckin, and Ackerman's studies (1988, 1990) of changing literate practices of a graduate student or Cheryl Geisler's study (1990) of the differences in the way undergraduate and professional philosophers conceive of and use philosophic texts in their own writing]; of the cognitive processes by which individuals construct meaning within specific contexts and their individual cognitive biographies [such as my study (1988) of how physicists read physics articles]; and of any other phenomenon that will shed light on how texts are located within, reach out towards, and help realize the complex worlds we live in.

Even when looking at a text in isolation, I look at how the text reaches out beyond the page, what connections it makes with the reader, the ambient natural world, the ambient social world. I look at how a text defines or reorders relationships and implies activities, how it places itself within its multiple heterogeneous contexts and creates a temporary stable place within which the text exists and within which the reader may confront the text and construct a meaning.

Such an approach obviously treats the regularized literate practices of disciplinary discourse as more than arbitrary conventions or habits. Genres and conventions (not just within the text, but in how we handle the texts and how we act in response to texts) represent deep-seated regularities in the practice and organization of disciplines with major social and epistemic consequences. Within stories of the emergence of familiar features of texts we can find disciplines sorting out what their business is, how to go about it, how they should relate to each other as colleagues, and how to relate to various other groups and individuals that they cast as outsiders in the very acts of creating and enclosing the space of their literatures. In so doing they regularize modes of writing and thinking and of acting accountably with respect to their disciplinary material, for every statement implies a range of activity that comes before the writing and after the reading, all accomplished within expected disciplinary procedures.

Ultimately a study of these regularized practices returns us to a theory of meaning, or rather a theory of how meaning is accomplished within a range of variation sufficient for people who share a regularized disciplinary space to cooperate on their endeavor. Put more simply, with the regularization of practices we can see how people can come to understand one another well enough to get on with what they are doing. This social theory of meaning is local and dynamic; meaning is accomplished only as the regularized space is brought into being and only as part of the activity realized within that space. Within that space meaning is held accountable by the network of relations constructed within that space, including relations with material objects, so that empiricism need not be treated as a naive fiction (as it currently is by naive relativists).

That is, if a particular community incorporates regularized material activities within the same network of activities that includes text production and text interpretation, the material activities and the texts can become mutually accountable. The material activities become part of the processes by which texts are framed, understood, and evaluated just as much as the texts become part of the processes by which the material practices are framed, understood, and evaluated. The theoretical regularities of physics or chemistry are dependent on the experienced material regularities of physical and chemical experiments as performed by socialized members of those communities as much as those experimental regularities are produced within a context of theories and bench practices. This interdependence of experience and formulation within discourse communities holds particularly strongly in those discourse communities that make it a point to hold their formulations accountable to empirical experience. In such communities the very grounds of intersubjectivity depend on a body of material practices first introduced in laboratory courses and elaborated throughout the professional career. Of course, among other communities whose intersubjectivity is based on other kinds of communal experience, such as the group recitation of the Koran or the social practice of each individual retreating to a semiprivate space to contemplate the human spirit, the accountabilities that are used to frame, understand, and evaluate discourse can be very different and perhaps quite removed from the constraints of empiricism, but not removed from the constraints of memorized formulations or of the character of human contemplation.

This interpretive project I engage in is itself located within its own moment, aimed at developing reflexive, complex, literate praxis for our eclectic, mobile, and self-conscious time. The desire for such a self-conscious praxis of language in the production and use of knowledge seems indeed to motivate volumes such as this and the more general movement toward rhetorical studies of disciplines. The rhetorical, reflexive turn in scholarship is difficult to attribute simply to the appearance of some ideas within continental philosophy, because similar ideas have been readily available since at least the time of the sophists, if not before. More fundamentally, the social sciences have been undergoing a reorganization of knowledge based on increasing information and results, which have strained the limits of early broad-stroke generalizations in social sciences, on increasing variety and availability of approaches produced by an expansion of active research-ers, on increasing access to extensive accounts of history and other cultures, on an extension of professional status to individuals of many backgrounds, on the advent of the cheap air ticket and the sharing of global economic and political power beyond the North Atlantic, and on a thousand other things that have made us less able to maintain unreflective allegiance to exclusive stable social views. How are we to contend with such a world? What do we make of the variety of claims we come across? How do we stand back from our own words and literate transactions with sufficient skepticism and self-knowledge so as not to appear patently foolish to ourselves and others? We indeed feel compelled to work out a new attitude toward language and our statements of knowledge so that we will not be held speechless before the babble of worlds constantly before us.

It is not surprising that social science would feel this problem acutely, for in our academic society the social sciences are where we gather knowledge of human beings in all their varieties, their relations, and their attendant beliefs about who they are. Moreover, in the social sciences we formulate our own beliefs about who we are. The social sciences provide the space in which to compare humanity. Moreover, it is hardly surprising that anthropology is the first place this issue has come to a head, for anthropology has always been concerned, as Geertz (1988) has pointed out, in bringing the there over here, even now when the here and there are so intermixed. History has had a longer concern over the implications of its narratives, but the issue was largely contained to limited questions of politics and morals, so the question was only seen as one of Whig and Tory in past moments rather than of fundamentally constituting who we are as literate creatures at this moment. Literary studies long had a knowledge of power of language to shape relations and reality, but that knowledge was thought relevant only to the special class of writers who dreamed dreams within that privileged unaccountable world of the imagination and spirit. Sociology is somewhat of a latecomer to reflexivity, but its long concern with social realities and symbolic interactions gave the project a remarkable enthusiasm among its adherents. Large parts of academic psychology for many reasons have been able to keep themselves at a distance from reflexive puzzles, but cognitive and social psychologies do seem to be edging toward the brink and are starting to generate their own crops of constructivists and reflexologists.

As a teacher of writing, someone professionally concerned with enabling people to use the written language effectively for their own purposes, I find it particularly interesting that this movement towards reflexive examination of language is carried out by people who think of themselves as users of language. Some reflexologists appear to have an ideological axe to grind and to use their reflexive stance to undermine the claims of their perceived opponents, but far more often people reflecting on the language of their discipline seem to be trying to figure out where they stand and what they can say. They are trying to find a way out of the hall of mirrors they find themselves in.

I do not believe that reflexivity must end in a world of unreliable appearances. By reflection one can come to know the systems of which one is part and can act with greater self-conscious precision and flexibility to carry forward and, if appropriate, reshape the projects of one's discipline. Meaning can be contingent and local without becoming meaningless, and experience need not be universally uniform beyond an experiencing and reporting subject to be the grounds of an empirical discourse. Rhetorical self-consciousness need not end in a distrustful disengagement from all knowledge-making and a privileging of radical skepticism where one wisely savors the moment of profound disbelief, freed from attachment to the idols made of language. Rather in rhetorical self-consciousness we can find the beginnings of new skills to help us make our meanings, our useful meanings, our local meanings, as we find our way around the human world.

References

Bazerman, Charles. 1988. *Shaping Written Knowledge: The Genre and Activity of the Experimental Article in Science*. Madison: University of Wisconsin Press.

Berkenkotter, Carol, Thomas Huckin, and John Ackerman. 1988. "Conventions, Conversations and the Writer." *Research in the Teaching of English* 22:9–44.

———. 1990. "Social Contexts and Socially Constructed Texts: The Initiation of a Graduate Student into a Writing Research Community." In *Textual Dynamics of the Professions*, edited by Charles Bazerman and X. Paradis. Madison: University of Wisconsin Press.

Cozzens, Susan. 1985. "Comparing the Sciences: Citation Context Analysis of Papers from Neuropharmocology and the Sociology of Science." *Social Studies of Science* 15:127–53.

Geertz, Clifford. 1988. *Works and Lives: The Anthropologist as Author*. Stanford, CA: Stanford University Press.

Geisler, Cheryl. 1990. "Towards a Sociocognitive Model of Literacy: Constructing Mental Models in a Philosophical Conversation." In *Textual Dynamics of the Professions*, edited by Charles Bazerman and X. Paradis. Madison: University of Wisconsin Press.

Myers Greg. 1985a. "The Social Construction of Two Biologists' Proposals." *Written Communication* 2:219–45.

———. 1985b. "Texts as Knowledge Claims: The Social Construction of Two Biology Articles." *Social Studies of Science* 15:595–630.

Chapter 4

No Anthro-Apologies, or
Der(r)idaing a Discipline

Renée Denūvo[1]

> At the precise point at which sense emerges
> from non-sense . . . at this frontier . . . we
> realize that man defies his very destiny
> when he derides the signifier.
>
> —Jacques Lacan, *Ecrit: A Selection*

A Review of Books . . . without Consequence

Anthropology as Cultural Critique: An Experimental Moment in the Human Sciences.
George E. Marcus and Michael M. J. Fischer, Chicago and London: University
of Chicago Press, 1986.

Writing Culture: The Poetics and Politics of Ethnography. James Clifford and George
E. Marcus, eds., Berkeley and Los Angeles: University of California Press,
1986.

I had a bad dream *and* in slow motion, or rather SUPER SLO-MO
according to the new technologies. With the detail and magnification of an
ob-scene and obsessed pornographic representation, it was clearer than
clear, more real than real. It was hyper-real!

I remember two voices, like a dialogue. But out of phase it sounded as if
there were many. A symphony? a polyphony? no . . . a cacophony! These
were hollow-phonic sounds, precisely out of phase at their point of
divergence (pi/2) to produce a false sense of depth when recombined on a
shiny support surface. The false, seductive depth of interpretation, where
the asynchronous multiplexing of representations generates a hollow-
graphic image of culture; ethnography with an added dimension: 10% real
pulp/people.

Now, you've long since received the message but the images continue to haunt you in incessant re-play, fore-play, back-play, slo-mo, freeze-frame, the parody of the real, the uncanny familiarity of the simulacrum. And even though you are sure and assured that, at one time, all of this was meaningful, you can't help but enjoy the vertigo and exhilaration derived from free-floating signifiers: "play it again."

Is anthropology replaying an old familiar tune: modernism or post-modernism? Habermas or Lyotard?[2] Is the literary turn (*Writing Culture*), or the experimental moment (*Anthropology as Cultural Critique*), anything more than a slo-mo replay of a distinction that has long since lost its excitation energy, now involuting and centripetal? And, what is the *alternative*? What does it take itself to be? a line of escape from "positivism . . . that increasingly ill-defined slogan word" (*AC*:179)?[3] Or perhaps, what we have here is a less hegemonic and totalizing anthropological response to a (perceived) crisis in representation, which, ironically, is occurring *everywhere*? "Why should a preoccupation with genres of description, rather than with usually more prestigious and totalizing theoretical discourses, be a current vital concern?" (*AC*:5) we are asked.

I won't pretend to capture the intentions and drives behind this *moment* in intellectual history and historicizing; there are too many voices here to synthesize (at least nine for the moment). It would be impossible to orchestrate such a polyphony, in any case it would not be sincere. I propose instead to offer, not an accounting (with its illusions of balance and summation), but rather a recounting (the lure of the strategy and the summons); a kind of "so to speak" story, perhaps:[4]

The Literary Turn: A Fatal Strategy

It is said that contemporary anthropology has made a literary turn (figuratively speaking). One can wonder, of course, whether this is to the left (post-Marxism), to the right (poststructuralism), or whether this is the promised U-turn or you-turn (posthumanism). The two "texts" I have chosen to review celebrate this equivocal turning point in the "coming of age" of American anthropology. Among the various anthroapologists who celebrate this turning point, there are of course differences, for example, in their individual "commitment" to the hermeneutic enterprise and the extent to which culture is to be textualized, or again, in the significance each assigns to the "modes of textual production." Nevertheless, certain elements or motifs (if not motivations) do seem to cross-cut these various projects of "literary experimentation": (1) a focus on textualization, discursive practices, and their dialogic articulations;[5] (2) an investment in interpretive anthropology, both historical and epistemological, with some ambivalence to the Father (Geertz) and a deconstructive flair that signals this ambivalence; and (3) most centrally, in the word(s) of Steven Tyler (1987), an emphasis or focus on "RAYTING" ethnography in the hopes of decentering the author and monophonic authority.

By situating their projects in the wake of what Lyotard described as our "postmodern condition" (1984)—consequently *après la crise*: a crisis in representation for (*AC*) and a *crise de conscience* for (*WC*)—these anthro-apologists have placed "contemporary anthropology" in a clearing where metanarratives have been razed and univocity fragmented, where voices proliferate, and where incommensurability (the *différend*) is apotheosized. Although it is claimed that "these essays do not prophesy" (*WC*:24), their tone is nonetheless apocalyptic![6] Listen:

> Once cultures are no longer prefigured visually—as objects, theaters, texts—it becomes possible to think of a cultural poetics that is an interplay of voices, of positioned utterances. (*WC*:12)

> Once dialogism and polyphony are recognized as modes of textual production, monophonic authority is questioned, revealed to be characteristic of a science that has claimed to *represent* cultures. (*WC*:15)

The tone and text proclaim the end of monophonic authority, the end of culture as object, and the end of representation; but also the end of vision, at least in/as one sense: the end of the eye, of the image (the prefigured) as the privileged metaphor (and metaphysics) of (re)presentations. This is the all too familiar end of history, end of representation, end-of-man apocalypse; an intellectual climate that conditions these project(ion)s. *The end of vision (sight) but not the end of vision (insight and self-consciousness)*: "the end approaches but the apocalypse is for the long haul [*longue durée*]" (Derrida 1983:81).

The anthro-apologists of the literary turn, like the mystagogue priests whom Kant denounced, reveal and decipher the secret mysteries of Culture (and the RAYTINGs it provokes):[7]

> The[ir] *grand-seigneur* tone is sanctioned by a *salto mortale*, . . . the projection [*saut*] of concepts into the unthinkable and the unrepresentable, the obscure anticipation of a mysterious secret coming from above. This projection in the immanence of a vision without concepts, this impatience focused on the most encoded secret, liberates a poetic-metaphoric excess. (ibid.:34)

The apologists of anthropos revel in the liberated "poetic-metaphoric excess" revealed in the apocalypse: a leap (*saut*) of faith into the mysteries and mystification of "profound half-understandings." Marcus, for example, in what appears to be a celebration of the strategies of the "modernist form of the essay," writes:

> The essayist can mystify the world, leave his subject's actions open-ended as to their global implications, from the rhetorical posture of profound half-understanding, half-bewilderment with the world in which the ethnographic subject and the ethnographer live. This is thus a form well suited to a time such as the present [our postmodern condition?], when paradigms are in disarray, problems intractable, and phenomena only partly understood. (WC:191)

In the end (only partly understood even while we stand under it, as our condition), the representational (and political) economy shifts (from under us) from "laissez faire" to "anything goes." But does a crisis in representation [or a *crise de conscience*, with its *modern(ist)* solution crystallized in the term *self-consciousness*[8]] necessarily entail a freedom from totalization? As if chaos (or polyphony), as the asymptotic consequence of order (or monophonic authority), could liberate an excess that is not merely a supplement. Actually, this appeal to the existence of a limit condition or crisis, driven by the human(ist) desire to outdo/undo the conditions (and irreversibility) of the second law, simply offers (those who have made the leap) the lure and illusion of an endless ("open-ended") combinatorial play of meaning. Free-floating apologies simply (although in no simple way) offer the illusion (*leurre*) of a degree-of-freedom. But with adequate speed (ex-stasis) and enough permutations, and if elevated to a sufficient power (Truth/False)"—i.e., given the right multiplier—any formal system, whether binary or circular, can emit the signs of multiplicity without necessarily relinquishing complicity with the old fissile (structured) order. These combinatorials and permutations (heteroglossia, polyphony, arenas of diversity), still re-lie on the hermetic (closed) logic of the binary (theory/description, fact/fiction, speech/writing) and all of its privileges. The "recombinant forms," exalted as experimental, retain a fatal attraction to the old structuralist "epistemology of fission": binary distinctions and their explosive (exponential) permutations, the law of excluded middles, formal closure, and, of course, the "fetishism of form" (WC:21). Intractability, partial understanding and disarray are mere simulacra, generated by the apparent open-endedness "of a time such as the present": the mere/mirror projections of a (negentropic) culture that has lost sight (but not vision) of its own grids of intelligibility (*dispositifs*); the by-products of an inflationary culture. At the "critical" point where the sheer magnitude of a culture's symbolic matrix/array accumulates and (geometrically) expands beyond any and all manageability, at that point one can begin to witness the vaporization of meaning and listen to a polyphony of voices.

But simply being resigned to (or celebrating) the fragmentation and proliferation of narratives (and authority)—the *petits récits*—or merely denouncing totalization, closure, and the metanarrative, or rejoicing in "the carnivalesque arena of diversity" (Clifford 1983:136) guarantees no response-ability (in the extramoral sense) to our postmodern condition, dialogic or otherwise. "For when the One is pulverized," warned Lacoue-Labarthe, "and identity dislocated, when *polemos* reigns, then, contrary to what the speculative believe, there is no longer any question of doing whatever one wills, and it is urgent to be just" (1984:34). Justification, however, does not end with RAYTING the wrongs of ethnographic presentation; it requires, as the term suggests, a realignment (political and epistemological) of phrasal or discursive regimes and strategies of communication that can *respond* to the sound-byte hyper-spin new-speak, the current (electrified) idiom of advertising and politics.

The apologies (in the name of anthropos), however, in their ecstatic form, are easily absorbed and defused in the simulation of distinctions, of dialogues, and of positions; expressions without consequence articulated on the frame of a previous polemic: modernism/postmodernism.[9] Consequently, and despite themselves, these voices become caught in the scenario of a second life, a second script, where the hollow-phonic echoes of the dialogic provide the sense of depth. Witness the resurrection of certain motifs and motives that "merely disappeared from the horizon of a life whose trajectory, specifically diverted by these events, *bends* sufficiently and unconsciously to offer it a chance at a second life" (Baudrillard 1983:267).

The second coming is the fatal strategy of the literary turn in "contemporary anthropology."

Modernism/Postmodernism: The Second Coming

All of the elements are present. The stage is set: fragmentation, partiality, collage, polyphony, indeterminacy, equivocality, crisis/chaos, the death of metanarratives, and, of course, the magic trick of the vanishing referent. The signs of our time!

The images projected are so real (more real than real) that the simple "evocation" of postmodern fragments and their epistemological "partiality" has induced reactions that mimic, or parody, the old modernist anomie: vertigo or dizziness before the void. Here are some all too familiar retorts, from B. Scholte, which I offer without much commentary:[10]

I find an exclusive appeal to aesthetics and poetry politically inadequate. (1987:41)

> Spinning textual tapestries inspired by native designs does not, of course,
> guarantee a moral center. In fact, the latter threatens to disappear from
> anthropological praxis altogether. And there is the rub. (ibid.:44)
>
> Could the literary turn itself be an ethnographic illustration of "bourgeois
> chique"? (ibid.)

A heightened sense of class consciousness (bourgeois, laborer), a moral
center, and "adequate" political action are recommended in lieu of social
indistinctness (the masses, consumers), nihilism, and schizo-politics.
But is there not something uncanny here—a déjà vu? For these are the
very terms with which Habermas (1981) "framed" the poststructuralists
as neoconservatives; the terms (words and conditions) that have been
responsible for the skeletal (emaciated, and not emancipating) character
of the ensuing debate. The postmodern/modern polemic, set in motion
by Lyotard and Habermas (and mediated by Rorty), exists today (and
here in anthro-apology) merely as the emptied form of a previous life;
one that continues to haunt present "undertakings."

Distant voices, from a previous life, dub over the presence of speech
and the fullness of dialogue, producing hollow-phonic reverberations
and token (pro)positions. Here we can even hear the echo of Richard
Rorty in Rabinow's shadowing of Clifford: the critic's critic, mediating
both within and without, "responsible" for recontextualizing the *différend* in practical terms, through some acute sense of the common.[11]

Everything is complete. The tenuous triad is framed: Clifford, Scholte,
and Rabinow. Or was it Lyotard, Habermas, and Rorty? No matter, this
is without consequence. Since, in this reenactment and restaging of a
prior articulation (modern/postmodern), in the simulacral replay of this
debate, in its ecstatic form, in an escalation to extremes in order to
"outmatch and outbid," in the exaltation of the sublated form, the
setting or ground has been eliminated, sublimated.[12] There is no longer
a setting for confrontation, which is a consequence of the logic of
deterrence and of dissuasion. In the logic of dissuasion, new contexts
are de-signed where the energies of distinctions, debates, and positions
are sublimated and defused, a simulated slo-mo replay that implodes
the poles and short-circuits oppositions: this is the result of the "fetish-
izing of form" (WC:21) and the event without consequence, where
things spin on their own axis with vertiginous exhilaration/acceleration
until all excitation energy has been dissipated.[13] And even though these
texts project images (motifs, elements, propositions) that simulate and
stimulate positions, distinctions, and dialogues that are familiar, there is
something uncanny, as if all of this were lacking a dimension: depth.

"Not Yet Thoroughly 'Post-modern'!"

The anthro-apologists of the literary turn may object, as does their *porte parole* James Clifford, that "[m]ost of us at the seminar, excluding Steven Tyler, were not yet thoroughly 'post-modern'!" (*WC*:21). And yet, one can read in(to) this equivocation/hesitation some of the tensions and retentions specific to the anthro-apologetic replay.

The "approach" to the postmodern (the not yet thoroughly) is neither asymptotic, probabilistic, nor telic, it is of a quite different order. Perhaps this approach should be rephrased the "not yet thorough postmodern." For there is a lie here in excess, a secret withheld. The truth of the matter is that this anthro-apology is *not* postmodern, is *not* deconstructive, is *not* poststructural, despite and, more importantly, because of the "signs" it emits. On this point Tyler is unequivocal:

> *Writing Culture* is not post-modern; its authors [except for the exception?] neither invert the relationship between aesthetics and epistemology nor revolutionize the three-fold hierarchy of epistemology, politics, and aesthetics. . . . It preserves the myth of a privileged discourse that founds or grounds all the others. (1987:50)

And yet, neither is this anthro-apology strictly modern(ism), nor specifically an interpretive/hermeneutic enterprise. There is a play (a give and take) in these projects, an unresolved tension that can be heard in their apocalyptic and apologetic tone.

In the hollow-phonic reverberation of the dialogic we can hear, not the Nietzschean laughter of deconstruction, but a nervous laughter, which Freud perhaps would have read as an ambivalence towards the Father: Geertz. An interpretive moment underwrites and undermines the deconstructive intentions of this anthro-apology; an interpretive inertia (hysteresis) dampens the deconstructive ecstasy (hysteria) of the literary turn.

The experimental moment in contemporary anthropology, according to the historiography of Marcus and Fischer, lies in the wake ["in the trend" (*AC*:16)] of Geertz's interpretive anthropology, but not (and "there is the rub") at Geertz's wake. Although the death of the Father is simulated in the ecstatic and sublated form of this contemporary anthro-apology, a strong libidinal investment in the economy of interpretation (hermeneutics) persists.

Crapanzano's reading of Geertz's reading of a cock fight as a reading of Balinese culture (in *WC*, appropriately titled "Hermes' Dilemma . . . "), for example, attempts to deconstruct Geertz's "phenomenological-hermeneutical pretensions." He observes, that

despite these pretensions, . . . there is in fact in "Deep Play" no understanding of the native from the native's point of view. There is only the
constructed understanding of the constructed native's constructed point of
view. Geertz offers no specifiable evidence for his *attributions of intention,
his assertions of subjectivity*, his declarations of experience. (WC:74; emphasis
added)

Certain "significant" points, both epistemological (the origins of the
construction of "native-ity") and metaphysical (the attribution of inten-
tionality and the assertion [presence] of subjectivity), surface from this
reading only to be resubmerged, absorbed, and defused, in the essay's
overriding concern with the "modes of authority," and its obsession
with legitimacy that old phallogocentric complement of the quest for
paternal certainty.

So when deconstruction is summoned (beyond the grave or serious)
to perform the task of demystification (of the principle of reason,
monophonic authority, textual coherence and closure, or the culture
concept) it is often present in an arrested form: called upon merely to
finger the "modes of authority," the "genres of description," or the
forms of rhetoric and "literary artifices"; a kind of textual police. But a
simple accounting (listing) of the strategies (intended or unintended)
that create the illusion of mastery, coherence, and closure in a subjected
text is only one moment (perhaps the "experimental moment") in a
deconstructive reading. Uncovering the "modes of authority" in ethnographic texts certainly initiates a "critique of the underlying assumptions
and a review of emerging textual practices" (Clifford 1983:120) in
ethnographic presentation, but as a listing it stops short of deconstructing anthropology's metaphysical investment and economy. Arrested,
stultified, and stunted, these quasi-deconstructive readings remain at
the level of textual exegesis or *explication de texte*. But a "conflict of
interpretation" (even polyphonic) is not deconstruction.

Oddly enough, it is the insistent (and hasty) distinction between
"genres of description" and (the "more prestigious and totalizing")
"theoretical discourses" (*AC*:5) that absorbs and defuses all of the
deconstructive (potential) energies. The opposition between fact and
fiction, or between description and theory, escapes unscathed in the
mere reversal (and repetition) of the (ideological) reductive strategy.
While description (and fiction) is privileged over theory (and fact), these
marks of distinction ("the epistemology of fission") are left virtually
untouched. An idealism, Baudrillard notes, that "veils the strategic
apparatus of the sign, which rests precisely on the disparity of the two
terms and on the fundamental circularity of the dominant term"
(1981:156). Consequently, the ex-scription of fact and theory in favor of

fiction and description ineluctably and fatally replays an identical metaphysics (phallo-phono-logocentrism and onto-theology).

This is an event without consequence (Baudrillard).

Closing Remarks (in Lieu of Closure)

To suggest that these quasi-deconstructive readings are arrested because they are "not quite thorough" would only be a "partial truth" and without consequence. Perhaps what is most interesting here, in this anthro-apology, is that every deconstructive reading is also *doubled/dubbed (doublée)* by some interpretive inertia or investment (both historical and epistemological), by some hermeneutic seduction, by the desire, not only to RAYT culture, but to READ (interpret) it adequately (*adaequatio*: the reproduction of what exists). Adequation, deferred in deconstruction, is full-filled in the interpretive act. An adequate RE-DING, not quite a search for the "truth" of culture, of the thing-in-itself (*Ding an Sich*) (since the anthro-apologists have broken with realism and objectivism), is something like a search for the *value* of the performance (the performative in a speech act)—not quite truth but almost (at least for the purpose of formalization and closure). The interpretive moment in RE-DING culture reinstates the fullness, presence, and positivity of meaning and dialogue, which the deconstructive moment suspended.

The apologists of anthropos remain "partially" committed to representation, to the presence of speech (in dialogue), to the positive, saturated, centered character of meaning and symbols, to the self-conscious subject (as interlocutor and critic) or to its displaced (yet not decentered) equivalents, intersubjectivity and intertextuality. A curious commitment given their strategic attachment to Derrida's *Of Grammatology*, where from the outset it is written:

> We already have a foreboding that phonocentrism merges with the historical determination of the meaning of being in general as *presence*, with all the subdeterminations which depend on this general form and which organize within it their system and their historical sequence (presence of the thing to the sight as *eidos*, presence as substance/essence/existence [*ousia*], temporal presence as point [*stigmé*] of the now or of the moment [*nun*], the self-presence of the cogito, consciousness, subjectivity, the co-presence of the other and of the self, intersubjectivity as the intentional phenomenon of the ego, and so forth). (1974:12)

Given the "subdeterminations" that organize the sequence of events known as "the experimental moment" or "the literary turn" one can question whether "writing," in "writing culture" (as a noun phrase, rather than a verb phrase), is anything more than an exaggeration or hyperextension of "the vulgar concept of writing [which] could not have imposed itself historically except by the dissimulation of the arche-writing, by the desire of a speech displacing its other and its double and working to reduce its difference" (ibid.:56); whether giving voice to the Other in a polyphonic collage (underwritten by phono-logocentrism) is anything more than lip service to the critique of authority and representation; and, whether the anthro-apologists of the literary turn, with their "partiality" to Hermes, can ever escape "the web of significations they themselves have spun."

Finally, without an entry (without consequence) from Derrida (1984:20) this essay could not be considered complete (at least for this genre of presentation): So here it is. Where? There   "No apocalypse [nor apologies], not now, full speed ahead."

Notes

1. The text is author-ized by Jacques Mourrain (aka Renée Denŭvo). Unless otherwise noted, translations are my own if referenced in the original.

2. It is without consequence to point out, or finger, the anachronism of such a replay. Were this my only goal I would give voice to Huyssen, who remarked that "[t]o reject the validity of the question Who is writing? or Who is speaking? is simply no longer a radical position in 1984 [the year of the conference "Writing Culture"]. It merely duplicates on the level of aesthetics and theory what capitalism as a system of exchange relations produces tendentially in everyday life: the denial of subjectivity in the very process of its construction. . . . After all, it *does* matter who is speaking or writing" (1984:44–5).

For a mediated version of the Habermas/Lyotard "debate" see Richard Rorty's "Habermas and Lyotard on Postmodernity" (1985).

3. Quotations from *Anthropology as Cultural Critique* have been identified in the text as *(AC)* and those from *Writing Culture* as *(WC)*.

4. In an age where plastic grocery bags come with a warning against the possibility of suffocation, and where academic writing is accompanied (para-sited) by a host of caveats, from the requisite deference in difference (esp. Trey 1989: note 1) to the recall of constructive criticism [democratic ideal(ism) of academia], I feel compelled to follow suit and offer my own caveat emptor:

WARNING: It has been objected that I have quoted passages from these two texts without always citing the appropriate authors (or authorship in-itself), that I have strayed (*la dérive*) from the path(os) of substantive (and constructive) analysis, failing to "bracket" adequately the epoch/epic under investigation, an impropriety that I (Renée Denŭvo) cannot avoid in a "so to speak story." I could say the approach here is "experimental" (not without irony); experimental in the sense that Deleuze and Guattari assign it: "Experimentation has replaced interpretation, which it no longer needs" (1980:200). This reading is not a RE-DING (see closing remarks), not the reminder of an absence or lack in the name of an-other presence, on other grounds. "Theory could never be a mere/mirror reflection of reality, nor enter in a negative dialectic with the real. This was the pious wish of the perpetual era of Enlightenment, one which continues at present to regulate the moral statute of the intellectual" (Baudrillard 1987:83). Theory cannot be content with description and analysis, Baudrillard continues, it must accelerate/exhilarate (and not excel and exile) the logic of its own object (of inquiry). But, I am anticipating the last line.

5. Lamenting the absence of contributions to *Writing Culture* from feminists, Clifford puts the focus of this project in perspective: "Our focus was thus on textual theory as well as textual form: *a defensible, and productive focus*. Within this focus we could not draw on any developed debates generated by feminism on ethnographic textual practices" (WC:20; emphasis added). Perhaps, Baudrillard would add, this is because textualization desexualizes, "[w]hich is why interpretation is so characteristically opposed to seduction, and why every interpretive discourse is least appealing [*séduisant*]" (1979:76). I will later focus, more productively, on the internal tensions of this project: tensions between interpretation and deconstruction; the ambivalence to the Father; and the "not yet thoroughly 'post-modern'!"

6. "*Apokaluptô*, I discover, I unveil, I reveal things" (Derrida 1983:11).

7. "The mystagogue priests [*prêtres*] are also interpreters [*interprètes*]"; Derrida continues, "the hermeneutic and hermetic seduction is the essence of their agogic [*agogique*] power" (1983:33). "The mystagogues profess to withhold, as if privately, the privilege of a mysterious *secret. . . . .*They reserve the right to reveal or unveil the secret, and guard it jealously. Jealousy is a major trait here. They never transmit the secret to others in common parlance, but by initiation and inspiration. The *mystagogue* is *philosophus per initiationem* or *per inspirationem*" (ibid.:27–8).

Jane Kepp's poem, "The Hermeneut's Dilemma, or, a Jargon Poem," as a preface to *Writing Culture* (ix) illustrates well this *philosophia per initiationem*. The issue I would like to highlight with these excerpts is not the (proper) place of jargon, as Kepp perhaps (in)senses (for this is the conservative and reactionary response, all too familiar in anthropology), but rather the function of *tone*—the apocalyptic and apologetic tone in the literary turn. It is the tonality of polyphonic writing that betrays a metaphysical accord.

8.   In *The Tremulous Private Body* (1984), Francis Barker describes the emergence of self-reflection, concomitant with the formation of bourgeois mercantilism, as new mode of subjection (by way of internal monitoring and control: diaries, confessions, autorepresentation in art, etc.). Only later, in the Enlightenment, is *it* (self-reflection) consciously presented as a critical moment or faculty of thought. Ever since Nietzsche, however, it has become difficult to appeal (in good faith) to self-consciousness or introspection as a critical dimension of thought. And yet, as Marcus and Fischer (and others) note: "In this essay [AC] we will consider the degree to which contemporary ethnographies insist on a *self-consciousness* about their historical context of production, and thus discourage readings of them which would fix their descriptions as eternal social and cultural forms" (AC:21; emphasis added). Or again, Clifford in his article "On Ethnographic Authority": "Alternate strategies of ethnographic authority may be seen in recent experiments by ethnographers who *self-consciously* reject scenes of cultural representation in the style of Malinowski's frontispiece" (1983:120, emphasis added). Although self-consciousness appears frequently as a motif in these writings, it must be present as a figure of speech.

9. To observe that the dialogic space has been mapped out is not to claim that the issues articulated around this distinction are *passé*: this reminder would be without consequence (see note 2). A more interesting critique would demonstrate how the framework (the previous life) of a historically and politically infused distinction shapes (haunts) and defuses (even self-reflective) discourses that orbit its field of attraction. This is a fatal strategy, where motifs and motives are ineluctably inverted and reversed. So we can ask (again with Huyssen): "Isn't the 'death of the subject/author' position tied by mere *reversal* to the very ideology that *invariably* glorifies the artist as genius, whether for marketing purposes or out of conviction and habit?" (1984:44; emphasis added).

10. Roger Keesing offers a similar reply in an article curiously titled "Anthropology as Interpretive Quest": "Indeed most symbolic anthropologists, in the name of cultural relativism or interpretive detachment, have been strangely blind to the political consequences of cultures as ideologies. . . . Where feminists and Marxists find oppression, symbolists find meaning" (1987:166). This is a provocative ending, but the correction (the RAYTING of the wrong, as Tyler would say) in the name of socioeconomic structure, or historical context, undervalues the (locally and symbolically) mediated and ambivalent, character of oppression (which doesn't make its effect any less "significant"). Does one find oppression in the same way that one finds lost keys? Or does one see oppression as one (even the strangely blind) sees the solution to a problem?

In *The Philosophical Discourse of Modernity*, Habermas offers himself as another example of modernist anomie. See my essay (1989) "Staging a Better Argument: The Strategies of Communicative Action" for a commentary on this anomic (ab)reaction.

11. See Rabinow's article in *Writing Culture*, "Representations Are Social Facts: Modernity and Post-Modernity in Anthropology" (1986); or perhaps "Discourse and Power: On the Limits of Ethnographic Texts" (1985), reactions and responses to Clifford's (1983) essay "On Ethnographic Authority"; or again, the essay "Facts Are a Word of God" (1983). These three texts seem to echo the pragmatist (Rortian) concern for a happy (synthesized) communication: the search (and hope) for a common(sense) ground.

12. "Things have found a way to elude the dialectic of meaning, one that bored them: they did so by infinite proliferation, by potentializing themselves, by outbidding their essence, by going to extremes, and by an obscenity which henceforth has become their immanent purpose and insane justification" (Baudrillard (1983:9).

13. I am thinking, perhaps as an analogy, of the "Iran-Contra-verse" where the legislative and the executive collide/collude on summer TV to simulate a debate: an event without consequences where the setting (for confrontation) has been eliminated, deterred (unearthed).

References

Barker, Francis. 1984. *The Tremulous Private Body*. London. Methuen.
Baudrillard, Jean. 1979. *De la séduction*. Paris: Denoël. (*Seduction*. Translated by Brian Singer. New York: St. Martin's, 1990.)
——— . 1981. *For a Critique of the Political Economy of the Sign*. St. Louis: Telos Press.

————. 1983. *Les stratégies fatales*. Paris: Grasset. (*Fatal Strategies*. Translated by Philip Beitchman and W. G. J. Niesluchowski. New York: Semiotext(e), 1990.)

————. 1987. *L'autre par lui-même*. Paris: Editions Galilée. (*The Ecstasy of Communication*. Translated by Bernard and Caroline Schutze. New York: Semiotext(e), 1988.)

Clifford, James. 1983. "On Ethnographic Authority." *Representations* 2:132–43.

Clifford, James and George E. Marcus, eds. 1986. *Writing Culture: The Poetics and Politics of Ethnography*. Berkeley and Los Angeles: University of California Press.

Crapanzano, Vincent. 1986. "Hermes' Dilemma: The Masking of Subversion in Ethnographic Description." In *Writing Culture*, edited by James Clifford and George Marcus. Berkeley: University of California Press.

Deleuze, Gilles and Felix Guattari. 1980. *Milles Plateaux: Capitalisme et Schizophrénie*. Paris: Minuit/Critique. (*A Thousand Plateaux: Capitalism and Schizophrenia*. Translated by Brian Massumi. Minneapolis: University of Minnesota Press, 1987.)

Derrida, Jacques. 1974. *Of Grammatology*. Baltimore: Johns Hopkins University Press.

————. 1983. *D'un ton apocalyptique adopté naguère en philosophie*. Paris: Galilée.

————. 1984. "No Apocalypse, Not Now (Full Speed Ahead, Seven Missiles, Seven Missives). *Diacritics* 14(2/Summer):20–31.

Habermas, Jürgen. 1981. "Modernity vs. Postmodernity." *New German Critique* 22:3–14.

————. 1987. *The Philosophical Discourse of Modernity*. Cambridge, MA: MIT Press. 1984. "Mapping the Postmodern." *New German Critique* 33:5–52.

Keesing, Roger. 1987. "Anthropology as Interpretive Quest." *Current Anthropology* 28(2):161–76.

Lacan, Jacques. 1977. *Ecrit: A Selection*. New York: Norton.

Lacoue-Labarthe, Phillip. 1984. "Talks." *Diacritics* 14(3/Fall):24–37.

Lyotard, Jean François. 1984. *The Postmodern Condition: A Report on Knowledge*. Minneapolis: University of Minnesota Press.

Marcus, George E. and Michael M. J. Fischer. 1986. *Anthropology as Cultural Critique: An Experimental Moment in the Human Sciences*. Chicago and London: University of Chicago Press.

Mourrain, Jacques. 1989. "Staging a Better Argument: The Strategies of Communicative Action." *Canadian Journal of Political and Social Theory* 13(3):1–15.

Rabinow, Paul. 1983. "Facts Are a Word of God." In *Observers Observed*, edited by G. Stockings. Madison: University of Wisconsin Press.

————. 1985. "Discourse and Power: On the Limits of Ethnographic Texts." *Dialectic Anthropology* 10:1–13.

————. 1986. "Representations Are Social Facts: Modernity and Post-Modernity in Anthropology." In *Writing Culture*, edited by James Clifford and George Marcus. Berkeley: University of California Press.

Rorty, Richard. 1985. "Habermas and Lyotard on Postmodernity." In *Habermas and Modernity*, edited by Richard Bernstein, Cambridge, MA: MIT Press.

Scholte, Bob. 1987. "The Literary Turn in Contemporary Anthropology."
   Critique of Anthropology 7(1):33–47.
Trey, George. 1989. "The Philosophical Discourse of Modernity: Habermas's
   Postmodern Adventure." *Diacritics* 19(2/Summer):67–79.
Tyler, Stephen. 1987. "Still RAYTING: Response to Scholte." *Critique of
   Anthropology* 7(1):49–51.

Chapter 5

Textual Form and Social Formation in Evans-Pritchard and Lévi-Strauss

Michael Herzfeld

Discursive Form and Textual Event

I propose here to conflate two different dimensions of anthropological inquiry—the properties of the ethnographic text and the eventlike qualities of expressive performance—by addressing the form that events take in major anthropological texts. E. E. Evans-Pritchard's *The Nuer* and Claude Lévi-Strauss's *Tristes Tropiques* both claim to address the underlying form that structures events—*The Nuer* in the political model of segmentation, *Tristes Tropiques*, more indirectly, through the suggestive analogy between the experience of travel and the rite of passage. Here, I shall suggest that their own textual form structures our perception of how those events actually work. For both these works structurally embody what they purport only to describe.

The Nuer is sequentially organized in such a way as to express the segmentary view of cultural relations that underlies Evans-Pritchard's view of how the world should be governed (see also Galaty 1981; Karp and Maynard 1983; Dresch 1986). *Tristes Tropiques* does not so much describe as *become* a rite of passage, moving readers through well-marked stages in which they constantly meet themselves coming back in the opposite direction. What is more, *Tristes Tropiques* adopts the segmentary worldview of *The Nuer*—if not, perhaps, of the Nuer—and extends it beyond the finitude of a "tribe" or "nation" to encompass the entire gamut of living creatures, real and imaginable. Segmentation is constantly emergent in social practices, whether these be cultural encounters with the exotic or marauding raids against an armed enemy. The two books that we shall be examining here are inscribed in a larger

53

set of segmentary practices, and their formal structures are means of enacting or actualizing the sense of cultural relativity that, ostensibly, it is their goal to describe.

Evans-Pritchard's study of Nuer sociology acknowledges the political aspects of Nuer life in the absence of bureaucratic government. This was an undoubted improvement on the earlier incomprehension that had greeted the discovery that certain peoples lacked the organizational structures that most educated Europeans regarded as a defining feature of political life. One of the effects of his perspective, however, was to render the Nuer almost schematically dependent on the exigencies of their system. His discussion of authority figures in Nuer political relations, in particular, subordinates the latter to the system more, apparently, than his own ethnographic data warranted (see Greuel 1971; cf. Evens 1979). His later study of Cyrenaican Bedouin society (1949) is an attempt to show that authority figures who emerge in local segmentary societies do so as a result of their *removal* from the territorial interests of segments and their subdivisions, and attributes the final crystallization of power in such situations to the appearance of an external power of equal, and this time rigidly statist, proportions—the Fascist government of Italy.

In Evans-Pritchard's scheme, then, segmentation is itself one side of the largest level of complementary opposition: statist and segmentary. The model is entailed within itself. It is this important entailment that the structural-functional approach, with its own unmediated dualisms, rendered invisible. The model of segmentation stands, like an etic observation tower, outside and above the societies it was developed to describe, and therefore fails to render its own most comprehensive embodiment explicit.

An account that Evans-Pritchard once gave of colonial warfare illustrates this veiled entailment. In an article (1934) recently made famous (or notorious) by Geertz (1988:50; Evans-Pritchard 1973; see also Herzfeld 1990), he describes the cowardly behavior of the Anuak lineages who fought under Italian control against the "British Anuak." His own men were brave, skilled, and determined. This not only shows how segmentation affects moral categories (bravery, etc.) far more immediate to social experience than such generalized entities as the *kuth* [refractions of Kwoth, the Divine Spirit: Evans-Pritchard (1956:118); see Kingsbury (1984) for a very similar treatment of "talent"]; in addition, it demonstrates that even the less obvious appurtenances of segmentation—client lineages of the colonial powers, in this case—display the same relativity and organization as the Nuer system, "refracted," as Evans-Pritchard himself might have said (e.g., 1956), through the essentialist stereotypes of British national prejudice. Evans-Pritchard apparently failed to note the irony of his own characterization of the Italian leadership—a bit more cowardly, therefore a bit less civilized and "European," than the British.

The opposition between segmentation and European "pyramidal" systems depends upon a very narrow definition of the political. European nationalism depends on an Orwellian argument to the effect that "some Europeans are more European than others" (Herzfeld 1987:43). In similar fashion, segmentary distinctions operate within each nation-state as a means of ordering hierarchies of identity from the most local to the immediately subnational. Thus, as soon as the model of segmentation is shifted from a focus on *conflict* to one on *differentiation*—in other words a distinction that is cultural rather than merely organizational—the opposition between European hierarchy and "primitive" segmentation collapses. Evans-Pritchard's treatment of the Anuak role in the military skirmishes he describes derives not only from Nilotic political theory, but equally from his own political concerns and, it would seem, from the national stereotypes that Britons of those days rather freely entertained. This, for Evans-Pritchard, was where the limits of segmentation lay. They were set by the obvious parameters of colonialism: the natives versus the colonizing powers. In this, as we shall see, Evans-Pritchard was unlike Lévi-Strauss, who was prepared to pursue such matters to the outer edges of humanity itself.

Politically, Evans-Pritchard's treatment of segmentary logic extends the argument beyond the confines of a book about the Nuer or even about the Bedouin of Cyrenaica. Internally, too, his discourse is ensnared in the argument itself. The textual organization of the book, at one level, represents the combination of ecological and social data to generate a model of time/space relations. Politically, however, it follows another trajectory: the progression of the segmentary hierarchy from broadly inclusive models in which we can still see the shadowy presence of the colonial anthropologist as a marker for the outer limts, to the detailed exploration of political fission and fusion as a local, and characteristically Nuer, preoccupation.

Indeed, his use of diagrams sets these outer limits very firmly. Most discussion of *The Nuer* acknowledges the diagram in which he sets out the congruent senses of the Nuer *cieng*, or "community," as a relative and segmentary entity (1940:114), and on his elaborations of this ideology into more abstract figures (ibid.:193, 201–2). He both derives these and yet distances them from Nuer efforts to explain the difference between his own analytical perspective and theirs: "They see it primarily as actual relations between groups of kinsmen within local communities rather than as a tree of descent, for the persons after whom the lineages are called do not all proceed from a single individual" (ibid.:202). And again: "The Nuer, outside certain ritual situations, evaluate clans and lineages in terms of their local relations" (ibid.:203). In other words, they translate social time into social distance, reducing history to synchrony: a people lacking an organized sense of history.

Evans-Pritchard was unusual for his time in the extent to which he did acknowledge the derivation of his own model from indigenous exegesis, and to the extent that his insight into the shifting character of identity presupposes an at least implicit comprehension of what we now call "agency" (see Karp and Maynard 1983). At the same time, he seems reluctant to investigate what the descriptive idiom the Nuer brought to their discussions might mean for their conceptualization of the past. As the theorizing observer, he does not relinquish control of time. His introductory diagram of East African cultural relations (1940:3), in which he organizes cultural "types" at various levels of differentiation according to their distance from a common heritage, indicates this essentialistic suppression of local experience as relevant to history.

In that diagram, the lowest two levels (i.e., the least inclusive) are organized in the classic binary format of segmentary analysis: Shilluk versus "Shilluk-speaking peoples," Nuer versus Dinka and Shilluk-Luo group versus Nuer-Dinka group. At the uppermost level, however, all these are presented as subdivisions ("segments"?) of the Nilotic group, which is contrasted to "Nilo-Hamites" and the rather vaguely labeled "other cultures." It is this last that is most suggestive. For while Evans-Pritchard does acknowledge the complexity of the contrast between Dinka and Nuer, perhaps more so than later critics have credited, he says nothing about these "other cultures" and we are left to suspect that otherness, like Kwoth and talent (so to speak), may be another immanent characteristic liable to segmentation through the social refracting fluid.

In that case, the diagram tells us more about Evans-Pritchard's own segmentary vision than it (necessarily) does about African cultural history and variety. As a category, the nonbinary "other cultures"/ Nilo-Hamites/Nilotes level seals off the diagram against incursions of historical time. Evans-Pritchard seeks to explain the degree of differentiation here in terms of the essentially philological model of stemmatics, highly popular among nineteenth-century nationalist folklorists in Europe and now largely discredited in philology itself. This affinity, which might have raised embarrassing questions about the supposed rift between folklore and anthropology, is certainly never acknowledged here. Indeed, given the almost traditional hostility between philological folklore and social anthropology until very recent years, another level of opposition can be seen to be operating here: an epistemological division between two disciplines that between them divided up European and non-European cultures as fields of study but that, despite that sense of mutual differentiation or exclusion, both served the same ideology of European identity.

It will be argued (see Kuper 1985; Wilson 1989) that Evans-Pritchard was not *primarily* interested in using segmentation as a model for hiving "them" off from "us." This is not untrue: Evans-Pritchard was concerned to develop a model that would help him explain Nuer society, and it would indeed be an act of bad faith on our part to assume otherwise. But this does not mean that his argument does not also belong to another discourse, or that, in contrasting "their" way of representing the properties of their own society from our own *Urtext* model of both it and our own society, Evans-Pritchard was not also serving another agenda as well, however unintentionally. To have noted Evans-Pritchard's entailment in the dominant cultural frameworks of his day does not detract from our appreciation of his resistance to Radcliffe-Brownian "nomothetic" scientism. Indeed, the present argument is entailed in his. To acknowledge such a relationship is to recognize the power of Evans-Pritchard's model, a power that transcends the limitations—historically comprehensible—of the uses that he made of it.

Tropes of Passage, Rites of Sadness

In Lévi-Strauss's *Tristes Tropiques*, by contrast, we find an author who is more than willing to acknowledge his own cultural entailment in that whereof he speaks. Indeed, at times he seems to wallow in it. Autobiographical in its immediate idiom, *Tristes Tropiques* explicitly and deliberately extracts rich imagery from the concept of *passage* in Arnold Van Gennep's (1960) sense of ritual marking changes of status. It relates the experiences of a personal voyage to the New World and back, and within the New World from the transplanted culture of the European settlers to the Amazonian mysteries of the indigenous population and back.

These physical transitions in the tropics become tropic transformations—transformations, at one and the same time, of the anthropologist's quest for personal, cultural, and human identity—three concentric layers of the segmentary onion. Each quest entails a return, through which the subject is both restored and transformed: "to reach reality one has first to order experience, and then subsequently to reintegrate it into an objective synthesis devoid of sentimentality" (1974:58). The poetic resonance of this phrase swells from the endless acts of intellectual but also of experiential passage from one insight to another, the products of "that restless and destructive appetite" for illumination in which Lévi-

Strauss acknowledges his own hatred of finitude. It is in this resistance to closure that we may contrast Lévi-Strauss's self-indulgence with the modest mien of the scientist at work that Evans-Pritchard presents to us. Evans-Pritchard has "recorded only what is significant for the limited subject of discussion" (1940:7). Lévi-Strauss takes on the world.

Tristes Tropiques is then, even more, than a "twice-born spiritual adventure, pledged to a systematic *déracinement*" (Sontag 1970:191). Sontag's formulation implies a dual birth, from art and science—a curious symbolic binarism that smacks of the stereotypical Lévi-Strauss, rather than the segmentary infinity of negotiable complementarities that the work, and Lévi-Strauss's oeuvre generally, would seem to call for. It is a textual rite of passage, a trope for the anguish of that unrelenting search for disengagement at home. As such, it resembles Vico's perambulation of the cycles of history in that both these restless authors reject a literal reading of individual or collective experience, and both intend intellectual movement where so many of their readers have understood static oppositions: art or science, figurative or literal expression. Where Vico discovered the impossibility of ridding exact language of its poetic origins, as his treatment of historical fact acknowledges, Lévi-Strauss found in the tropic experience of the exotic that he could not discard his individual and cultural self. Where Vico saw a ceaseless alternation in human affairs, Lévi-Strauss emblematized his Amazonian journey as an exploration of the instability of cultural difference. Just as for Vico every event must have its potential *ricorso*, for Lévi-Strauss every journey evokes the possibility of return. And just as Vico iconically reproduced the progression of human understanding from image to metaphor and from metaphor to literality in the organizational structure of his book, so Lévi-Strauss leads us up the Amazon and back on a veritable and complex rite of passage. In both writers, theory and expression are indissolubly wedded. The comparison is especially germane in that Evans-Pritchard, too, may been as Vichian as he certainly was Durkeimian in his elaboration of the segmentary model (see Davis 1977:2; Herzfeld 1987:168).

Tristes Tropiques, then, plays upon the fundamental structures of passage. The very first chapter is "an end to journeying"; and all the part and chapter headings continue the punning image of a structural homology between the initiand's voyage out and the initiate's return home. "The Making of an Anthropologist" (Chapter 6) comes in the part headed "Travel Notes." From here, inexorably, the headings propel us towards and up the Amazon, and down again at the end ("The Return"). At various points along the quest, striking moments are marked as new, subsidiary negotiations of passage: "Looking Back" (Chapter 5), "The Doldrums" (Chapter 8), "Crossing the Tropic"

(Chapter 10), "Pioneer Zone" (Chapter 13), "On the Line" (Chapter 26). The entire narrative is framed by a gloomy play on the structural analogy between the departure of the anthropologist and his return— the formal dinner marking the latter "only a shade more dismal than the ceremony which had marked his departure" (1974:19). The rite of separation from his own society is reproduced, with *tristesse*, in the rite of his reincorporation into it.

If *Tristes Tropiques* had simply been an elegant construction of tropes upon a central theme, this textual exploration would have been out of place in the present study. But there is in fact a good reason to include it, whether or not its structural self-reproduction occurred *á l'insu* of the author—an irrelevant question, as Derrida (1976:102) has observed, since the work constitutes its own presence. *Tristes Tropiques* traverses and dissolves the discontinuities between several of the autocentrisms that concern us here, and in so doing it replaces a literal hierarchy of cultural entities with a pervasive sense of essential homology between all possible levels of collective identity. It signals the beginning of an attempt to sense the analogy between tribal identity, modern ethnocentrism, and anthropocentrism on a truly global scale:

> The end of one civilization, the beginning of another, and the sudden discovery by our present-day world that it is perhaps beginning to grow too small for the people inhabiting it—these truisms are brought home to me less tangibly by figures, statistics and revolutions than by the fact that when, a few weeks ago, after a lapse of fifteen years I was toying with the idea of recapturing my youth by revisiting Brazil in the same way, I was told on the telephone that I would have to book a cabin four months in advance. (1974:22)

The very voyage that he had undertaken in that *temps perdu* had contributed to the global shrinkage that now so complicated his search for it. No act of seeking knowledge fails to affect the knowledge itself—a point of which Lévi-Strauss, with his irrepressible jerry-can, is anxious to remind us again and again. It was as he originally began to close in on the Caduveo, the Bororo, and the Nambikwara that Lévi-Strauss had originally begun to apprehend "The Earth and Its Inhabitants" (Part 4)—a shrinkage of perspective (the natives' notion of the earth seems so small!) that anticipates his later feelings as his own familiar earth begins to shrink too. Here, poetically anticipated, are two of the key idiocentrisms, the tribal and the global.

But the articulation between concentric or homologous entities of this sort is provided by Lévi-Strauss's own gradual discovery of his identity as an anthropologist. The analogy is made explicit: "Anthropology affords me intellectual satisfaction: as a form of history, linking up at opposite ends with world history and my own history, it thus reveals the rationale common to both" (1974:58). Strange words, it might be thought, from the scholar who dismissed Sartrean subjectivism as "a sort of shop-girl metaphysics" (1974:58); but even here Lévi-Strauss is identifying common *structures*, those that link the idiocentrisms of local and global history with a personal quest that has been suitably objectified and reassimilated, as he insists that all experience should be, into the grand scheme.

The chapter on "The Making of an Anthropologist" is thus much more than mere autobiography. It is the nostalgic key trope of *Tristes Tropiques*. In it, the themes of the Van Gennepian triad are clearly enunciated. The author puns on these as he describes his initiation—for such it was intended to be—into the role of teacher through his studies at the Sorbonne. There, the young Lévi-Strauss began preparing for "the supreme ordeal of the *leçon d'agrégation* (the oral part [of the examinations])" (1974:51). The very term intimates Lévi-Strauss's recurring theme of a journey in reverse, of that voyage that begins with an end to journeying. *Agrégation* ("incorporation") is the final, *inclusive* phase of Van Gennep's tripartite model of rites of passage. For Lévi-Strauss, the very thought of becoming an educational bureaucrat suggested only the most stultifying closure. Thus, he used the very examination that threatened him with that living death to begin a journey in the opposite direction—a journey through which he came to appreciate the grave "danger in confusing the advancement of knowledge with the growing complexity of intellectual structures" (1974:52). Even more worrying to the young man, then happy enough in principle to become a *lycée* teacher, was the discovery that his physical relocation to a school at Laon was not accompanied by any matching intellectual displacement: he would have to teach the same course for the rest of his working life. The metaphor of an initiation ritual defied is explicit:

> Normally the *agrégation* is held to be an inhuman ordeal, at the end of which, one is entitled, if one so wishes, to be left in peace for ever. In my case, it was just the opposite. I passed the *agrégation* at the first attempt and as the youngest candidate in my year, and I had been in no way exhausted by my foray through doctrines, theories and hypotheses. My torment was to begin later: I realized that I would be physically incapable of delivering my lessons, unless I evolved a new course every year. This handicap proved to be still more embarrassing when I found myself having to act as an oral examiner. . . . It was as if the subjects were melting away before my eyes, through the mere fact that I had once applied my mind to them. (1974:53).

In this passage, the anthropologist's peculiar reversal of ordinary bourgeois experience evolves into a structured trope for the evanescence of knowledge. For ordinary mortals, the cruel rite of incorporation marks closure, relief. For Lévi-Strauss, by contrast, detachment can only be sought abroad (Sontag 1970:189–90). Herein lies the truly tropic sadness; the tropics themselves are markers for the only way in which the determinedly restless anthropologist can seek out that necessary distance. That this voyage is truly a rite of passage, Lévi-Strauss acknowledges in seeing it as emblematic of anthropology's role in European society generally. His key image has proved evocative for other travelers seeking an explanation of their own youthful wanderings (e.g., Llewellyn Smith 1960).

That search for a global self actually begins in the death of a teacher. A thinker of passionate mediocrity, Gustave Rodrigues committed suicide when the Germans entered Paris (Lévi-Strauss 1974:51). The event that triggered Lévi-Strauss's own voyage to the tropics and that served to immortalize his marginality, as an Alsatian Jew, to his own society, was simply too much (as Lévi-Strauss represents it) for the apostle of philosophical sophistry. To Lévi-Strauss, Rodrigues represented the self-satisfaction of a culturally narrow experience; his death, the beginning of enlightenment. It was this teacher who would have prepared the young student teacher for his *agrégation* into that same ethnocentric intellectual treadmill, anesthetized by the sense of a ritual successfully endured. But Lévi-Strauss's was a "neolithic kind of intelligence," a slash-and-burn mode of operation that left much to chance in the discovery of new possibilities (1974:53). The elaborately pseudo-Hegelian dialectic of Paris intellectuals could not satisfy this yearning for accidental discovery, and the "neolithic intelligence" needed to find its crops among societies that more closely resembled the vehicle of its metaphorical guise.

Lévi-Strauss's fascination with the New World extended to its anthropologists. Many of them were European-born; their transitional status in American society thus seemed to Lévi-Strauss to represent an analogy to his own marginality in France. Again, the geographical aspect of passage is exploited to suggest a kind of kinship among those who were capable of reflection upon their *déracinement*. Not so many had that capacity, as Lévi-Strauss discovered soon after his arrival in Brazil:

> I have often been criticized for showing too slavish an obedience to Anglo-American thought. . . . [But] the authors to whom I willingly proclaim my debt, Lowie, Kroeber, and Boas, seem to me to be as far removed as possible from the James or Dewey kind of American philosophy . . . or from . . . logical positivism. Since they were European by birth and had been trained in Europe or by European professors, they represent something quite different: a synthesis reflecting, on the level of knowledge, that other synthesis which Columbus had made objectively possible four centuries earlier: the synthesis of a strong scientific method with the unique experimental field offered by the New World at a time when

American anthropologists not only had the best available libraries, but could leave their universities and visit native communities as easily as we could go to the Basque country or the Riviera. (1974:59–60)

Here again are the key themes: the discomfort of a French intellectual whose cultural marginality is reinforced by his detractors' jibes about his Anglo-Saxon proclivities; possible allusions to the writer's ethnic as well as intellectual commonality with Durkheim; the need to take passage, as it were, with Columbus; the restless and ultimately insatiable quest for more and more data about the exotic; the inestimable value of juxtaposing the exotic with the practical and familiar; the conviction that it is in such a constant exploitation of experience that a true science of humankind is to be sought. But the writer's motivations remove what he has to say from the level of epistemological argument to that of a symbolic quest. This shows up in, for example, some discreet hints of narrative leveling. Lowie, for example, was not European-born; nor does American anthropology, with its reliance on the results of an immediately accessible and cruelly overexploited native population, necessarily represent a greater degree of synthesis than the European anthropologies born of an *external* but still intimate colonialism. In accordance with his rejection of dry philosophizing (1974:52), Lévi-Strauss removes the intellectual problems retrospectively posed by his calling to an altogether far more interesting plane. In the process, his irritation at being viewed as some kind of Anglo-Saxon hack transcends mere defensiveness; it becomes a further point of articulation between his personal experiences and what he thinks anthropology should be about. Above all, it emphasizes his impatience with a phenomenon that I have documented elsewhere in these pages: the reproduction of reified ethnicities and nationalisms in the university.

The sixth chapter of *Tristes Tropiques* is thus indeed "an exemplary personal history in which a whole view of the human situation, an entire sensibility, is elaborated" (Sontag 1970:187); but this description misses something still more striking about the chapter. Not only is the book as a whole an elaborate tropic exploration; but this chapter is a model, not merely for the anthropological profession (a comparative triviality, if we were to be completely frank), but for the trope of passage. It is itself a passage in this richly triune sense: ritual, textual, and personal. Its power, so many years after its composition, lies in its prophecy of the new idiocentrism, subtly veiled but irrevocably immanent. Lévi-Strauss is not, however, the prophet without honor in his own country; for at the moment in which he contemplates what he has so far regarded as truly his own country, its boundaries are transposed—like those of the geological metaphor that he evokes with such passionate wonder (1974:56)—to a more inclusive level. The quest goes on. Ultimately, the homologies are reductive. Levels of difference are less important than the maintenance of a sense of difference itself, as his experiences as a student of psychology soon taught him:

> No contact with savage Indian tribes has ever daunted me more than the morning I spent with an old lady swathed in woollies, who compared herself to a rotten herring encased in a block of ice: she appeared intact, she said, but was threatened with disintegration, if her protective envelope should happen to melt." (1974:20)

In such a world, how could *any* familiarity be taken for granted?

Tristes Tropiques is semiotically a more ethnographic study than anything else Lévi-Strauss wrote. This is the result of its insistently reflexive focus. The writer gives us a clear context for his own intellectual and physical explorations, the latter a grudgingly accepted prerequisite for the former (1974:17). As an exemplary text for the development of a semiotic consciousness, it would be hard to improve upon. Its constant grasping for a kind of scientific truth is just as constantly overwhelmed by the expansion of the idiocentric horizon. There is an almost Peircean quality to the search for abstraction in the face of fallibility and the infinity of possible knowledge. But the use of an autobiographical trope for the inquiry itself, a merging of the authorial subject with the object of the inquiry, renders it more instructive than any formal manual of semiotics. The entirely problematical relationship between text and context is not dismissed with an unhelpful formalism, and, as a result the narrative successfully resists the literalistic siren-song. In many ways the context *is*, or *becomes*, the text; the author is both "in" the text, yet stands out as the means to read it. The crossing of idiocentric boundaries takes place in both directions at once.

To understand this more fully, we would do well to observe how consistently the theme of passage, with its structural puns on reversibility and homology, is maintained throughout the entire work. (The great absence, amidst all the names that Lévi-Strauss recalls, is Van Gennep. Perhaps this is not ingratitude? Perhaps it is simply that for the moment it is Van Gennep's model that is taken as basic fact, needing no explanation and indeed threatened by explicit exegesis with a loss of its poetic force? Sontag (1970:191–92) expresses a sense of paradox that Lévi-Strauss should combine with a "literary" conception of the anthropologist's calling "the most unliterary techniques of analysis and research." But is this really the case? Certainly, Lévi-Strauss seems to crave scientific detachment. His detachment, however, is extremely conditional, and the widening/shrinkage of the knowable world makes it permanently provisional. Passage to and fro across ever widening perimeters of idiocentrism makes closure impossible. The method does not, then, lie in the immediate techniques of research alone, but in the awareness of their unstable context. The structures of passage are a powerful poetic device in the discourse of other societies, for example (and unsurprisingly) in ritual texts associating death and marriage; and it would be inconsistent with the present argument not to recognize the same property in the written products of our own intellectual tradition. The very simplicity of the passage trope satisfies Lévi-Strauss's distrust of "the growing complexity of intellectual structures" (1974:52), a distrust that we can usefully set against the resurgent tendency *within* semiotic scholarship to regard complexity of formulation as an index of sophistication. But this apparently formalist and reductive simplicity on Lévi-Strauss's part is *also*, as I have stressed, a powerful trope. Recognizing the literariness of an ethnological text constitutes a form of meta- or auto ethnography. Exploration of the passage motif in *Tristes Tropiques* can serve emblematically as a means of initiating the ethnographic investigation of semiotic thought in general.

Let us therefore, briefly if not indeed summarily, trace the trope through its text. It was in Puerto Rico that Lévi-Strauss first made contact with North American culture, and the effect was to influence his perception of the United States ever after. As he remarks:

> The accidents of travel often produce ambiguities such as these. Because I spent my first weeks on United States soil in Puerto Rico, I was in future to find America in Spain. Just as, several years later, through visiting my first English university at Dacca in Western Bengal, I now look upon Oxford as a kind of India that has succeeded in controlling the mud, the mildew, and the ever-encroaching vegetation. (1974:35)

In short, as soon as Lévi-Strauss began to feel that he was reaching the goal of his travels, he simultaneously initiated a reverse journey, a challenge through the looking glass at the ethnocentrism of all perception. In this backwards motion, he fends off the entropy that he discerns everywhere, the "contamination" (1974:30) of an atmosphere that encroaches everywhere and is everywhere becoming "equally oppressive" (1974:36). The anthropologist, in finding his goal, also finds that his goal recedes away from him, that his origins return; and so, too, he finds his ethical vocation: finding that his search for the exotic invariably confronts him with the familiar, he vows to fight against the assumptions of primacy in his own or any other culture.

The problem is, he discovers, that "[m]ankind has opted for monoculture" (1974:38), and that "actual experience is replaced by stereotypes" (1974:39). On the verge of embarking on his "Travel Notes" (Part 2), Lévi-Strauss anticipates a subsequent (1974:56) moment in his intellectual self-realization, in which he will discover the fascination of structure in geological formation:

One order has been replaced by another. Between these two cliffs, which preserve the distance between my gaze and its object, time, the destroyer, has begun to pile up rubble. Sharp edges have been blunted and whole sections have collapsed: periods and places collide, are juxtaposed or are inverted, like strata displaced by tremors on the crust of an ageing planet. (1974:44)

And so, concludes the saddened observer, "twenty years of forgetfulness were required before I could establish communion with my earlier experience, which I had sought the world over without understanding its significance or appreciating its essence" (1974:44). Every voyage of discovery is also a voyage of return. Lévi-Strauss's shock of realization that he was destined to be an anthropologist thus occurs quite appropriately under the somewhat opaque heading of "Travel Notes." The practice of anthropology is a kind of cosmic nostalgia for Lévi-Strauss: he *begins* the "Travel Notes" section with a chapter entitled "Looking Back," thereby reproducing simultaneously the grand scheme of a work that "sets out" with, of all things, "an end to journeying," and that never ceases to remind us that—in the logic of rites of passage—the ending of a phase reproduces its beginning, and the next (seventh) chapter, "Sunset," precedes "The New World" (Part 3, beginning with Chapter 8).

Again he evokes Columbus; and this time, he makes his intentions plain: "It was more or less in the area where we were now sailing that Columbus encountered mermaids. Actually he saw tham at the end of his first voyage in the Caribbean Sea, but they would not have looked out of place off the Amazon delta" (1974:76). The transformation of place is in reality a form of *identification*, a blueprint for the anthropologist's further self-identification with other voyagers to the transcendant "global entity" (1974:80) that constitutes the New World that each of them discovered. Prominent among these sympathetic voyagers is Jean de Léry, whose travelogue Lévi-Strauss was content to carry in his pocket as he explored the history and present topography of Rio (1974:81–83). De Léry anticipated Lévi-Strauss's rejection of ethnocentrism to a remarkable degree, especially given the time and circumstances of his voyage, and it is in his essentially antiliteralist attitude towards the customs of alien peoples that Schwimmer (1983) has perceptively discerned a clear prefiguration of semiotic concerns. In emulating de Léry's successful contact with the Tupi Indians moreover, Lévi-Strauss (1974:335), emphasizes the radical nature of the flight from the familiar and humdrum in which they shared at an interval of four centuries from each other.

But who were these Indians, whose discovery led to "the anthropological awareness of modern times" (1974:335), and began revolutions that were intellectual as well as political? Whoever they were, their status for our present inquiry is fixed by Lévi-Strauss's remark; they engendered a relativism that clearly anticipated the new and encompassing "semiotic consciousness" of de Léry's exposition. In *Tristes Tropiques*, we encounter the analogous discovery of our own day. There are, apparently, no new worlds to discover; all Lévi-Strauss could do was to retrace the steps of his predecessors. But the discovery that makes *Tristes Tropiques* so much an articulatory bond between the anthropological consciousness-raising of yesteryear and the semiotic awareness of today consists in something more radical: the realization that each journey is also its own reverse. Again, we encounter the structural pun of the *rite de passage*. Columbus thought he had found India, and his name for the inhabitants stuck, preserving his error for posterity. Lévi-Strauss knew that he was actually in America, but saw that the "magic carpet" of his imagination took him simultaneously to the Indian subcontinent. Goiania in Brazil becomes, upon reacquaintance, a memory of Karachi, just as Oxford too became a kind of Indian university in a temperate clime. Such is "the absurdity of the relationships which man consents to have with the world, or rather, which are increasingly forced upon him" (1974:127). Like the hero of Cavafy's poem "The City," who finds that he must always carry within him the physical scene of his humiliation however much he tries to run away from it, Lévi-Strauss finds an increasing inevitability in the mark that humankind has left upon the earth: "I rediscovered the Goiania hotel, but enlarged out of all proportion, in another *no less arbitrary town*, Karachi" (ibid; emphasis added). More alarming, perhaps, is the ethnographer's bemused characterization of the tattooed Mbaya-Guaicuru, whose culture turned out to be "undeniably reminiscent of one that European society playfully invented in a traditional pastime, and the model of which was imaginatively defined with great success by Lewis Carroll: these knightly Indians looked like the court figures in a pack of cards" (1974:178).

Looking-glass reversals intensify the structural pun; here, the *invention* of a European amusement emerges as the structural equivalent and semantic inverse of the *discovery* of an exotic people. The new comparativism that *Tristes Tropiques* ushers in can no longer rely upon finding genuinely *new* worlds. As a result, our resistance to ethnocentrism can only come from an unending series of more or less nightmarish looking-glasses. Self-knowledge entails increasing distortion—a distortion, an exaggeration, or a decomposition of stereotypes. To repeat the discoveries and insights of a Columbus or of a de Léry—and Columbus, too, was not devoid of sensitivity to the value of other cultures, once he encountered them firsthand (Hodgen 1964:17)—we increasingly, like Alice, meet ourselves coming the other way, and must derive our comparativist satisfactions from this apparently dissatisfying fact.

Lévi-Strauss himself is clearly not only dissatisfied, but profoundly distressed by it. Contamination is everywhere. "Campers, camp in Parana. But no, on second thoughts, don't. Keep your greasy papers, indestructible bottles and gaping tins for the last beauty spots of Europe" (1974:153)! Yet this horrid realization—and especially at the moment when the jerry-can shows up in the photograph—also produces the extraordinarily powerful reflexivity that Lévi-Strauss has bequeathed to anthropological inquiry; when he returns to France, he will infect the world with structuralism, and this can only prove beneficial if its underlying assumptions are constantly challenged (cf. also Mehlman 1974:223–24). Bricolage has become universal. The Mbororo of Cameroon have heard of the South American Bororo, a people central to Lévi-Strauss's ethnographic work; perhaps, we may surmise, it was his work that brought it, through francophone channels of barely imaginable complexity, to their attention. They have even used this knowledge, improbably enough as it must seem, to postulate a South American ancestry for themselves on the basis of being more lightly complected than the other tribal groups over which they hold sway (Barley 1983:151)! How can such a world *not* look as if through a looking-glass?

The anthropologist's position in this world once seemed entirely secure. As the representative of perfected mankind, a Tylor or a Frazer could afford to plan grandiose philologies of alien thought systems. No suspicion ever entered these thinkers' heads that perhaps the aboriginal peoples of other lands could also produce an anthropologist or two, or that exposure to European society could generate a kind of looking-glass sociology (Lévi-Strauss 1974:216–17). Lévi-Strauss felt that the existence of anthropologists was not necessarily a sign of greatness or of intellectual independence, but might represent a "symbol of atonement" for the damage wrought by their own culture (ibid.:389). Perhaps so; but the study of "other cultures" is also a condescension, analogous to the apotheosis of other forms of "rubbish" in industrial society (cf. Thompson 1979). The only salvation, the only defense against entropy, lies, for Lévi-Strauss, the universe, where man is *not* alone (1974:414). It may be impossible, but it is, Lévi-Strauss insists, the only worthy calling for humanity. This is no elegant intellectualizing of sadness (*pace* Sontag 1970). On the contrary, it is a challenge, a recognition of the greater comparativism against which the impossibility that Evans-Pritchard decried pales into relative triviality. It is the moment of truth that we can snatch "in the brief glance, heavy with patience, serenity and mutual forgiveness, that, through some involuntary understanding, one can sometimes exchange with a cat" (Lévi-Strauss 1974:414–15).

Thus, by the time that we have traversed the tropic rite in its entirety, the cultural differences that constitute the anthropologist's subject matter have been sublimated by a larger vision. We have crossed to a larger threshold, as befits an initiate. Viewed thus, anthropocentrism is no noble *défi*, but a desertion of responsibilities learned in the field, a failure of reflexivity. Whatever one may think of zoosemiotics, then, it is at least a response to the realization that the human animal is not, should not be, a discontinuous isolate in a laboratized universe.

Lévi-Strauss's anxious traversing of the tropic passage is iconic of the human experience in an increasingly globalized world, in which animal rights are now an issue congruent with, if more broadly focused than, ethnic and national ones. It reaches the point at which interspecies communication is at least sporadically conceivable; and this means that comparativism can no longer be confined to humankind. *Tristes Tropiques* is problematical as an anthropological study. Its importance lies, rather, in the poetic force with which it expresses the perplexities of identity— not national identity, not personal identity, not epistemological identity, not even human identity, but identity in general.

Completing the Pattern: Forms and Processes

In this regard, *Tristes Tropiques*—perversely, it may be—completes part of what *The Nuer* began. This is not as surprising as it may seem; both, after all, rest on Durkeimian foundations, even if both their architecture and their cultural and ideological burdens are significantly different.

One difference certainly stands out. However critical Evans-Pritchard may have been of Radcliffe-Brownian scientism, and he was all of that, he nevertheless clearly expected to gain some sociological models of a predictive kind from his Nilotic studies. His "modest" theorizings all look to that end. It is thus unlikely that he ever seriously considered the *form* of his text as *part* of his argument. If he recognized the relationship at all, it must have been as an accident of logic, rather than as the logic itself. In Lévi-Strauss, by contrast, we find a fairly explicit commitment to playing with form. His pun on *agrégation*, no less than the more famous botanical play on *la pensée sauvage*, shows an eager appreciation of the relationship between the journey, the ritual, and the text. It dissolves the distinction between science and poetry—indeed, it is a poetics of the human "laboratory," to use his own word—where Sontag sought to find a curious internal contradiction.

The relationship between Evans-Pritchard and Lévi-Strauss transcends their interest in "relations between relations," their shared (and under-acknowledged) debt to Vico, even their penchant for diagramming an argument into the form of their discourse. It lies in what made them explore these ideas in the first place. Despite the self-indulgence of

Tristes Tropiques, or the "modest theorizing" that bespeaks overconfidence in *The Nuer*, it is in their ability to demonstrate the practical limits of anthropology itself that the practice of anthropology takes its own contingent properties seriously at last. It is the impossibility of separating the "body" of their texts from the "thought" of their arguments that so confuses many of their followers as well as their critics, who would have us believe that the "standard" set by the one renders the writings of the other "unanthropological." But when poetics and science merge, then, too, it may not be so outrageous any more to suggest that the form of the argument is the argument itself. Contamination is indeed everywhere. Indeed, that is the message and logic, disturbing to any Cartesian scientism, of segmentation. To revert to the title of this paper: the forms that move ("forming") towards their "reification" *must* be present in the text. The trick is to resist the closure that prevents us from seeing them, or from perceiving their rhetorical force as a social poetic in our own complex ideological universe. Events respond in a specific way to segmentation (Dresch 1986). A text about segmentation is also an event, and we should expect it to respond accordingly.

References

Barley, Nigel. 1983. *The Innocent Anthropologist: Notes from a Mud Hut*. London: British Museum Publications.

Davis, J. 1977. *People of the Mediterranean: An Essay in Comparative Social Anthropology*. London: Routledge and Kegan Paul.

Derrida, Jacques. 1976. *Of Grammatology*. Translated by Gayatri Chakravorty Spivak. Baltimore: The Johns Hopkins University Press.

Dresch, Paul. 1986. "The Significance of the Course Events Take in Segmentary Systems." *American Ethnologist* 13:309–24.

Evans-Pritchard, E. E. 1940. *The Nuer: A Description of the Modes of Livelihood and Political Institutions of a Nilotic People*. Oxford: Clarendon Press.

———. 1949. *The Sanusi of Cyrenaica*. Oxford: Clarendon Press.

———. 1956. *Nuer Religion*. Oxford: Clarendon Press.

———. 1973. "Operations on the Akobo and Gila Rivers, 1940–41." *Army Quarterly* 103(4):1–10.

Evens, T. M. S. 1979. "Leopard Skins and Paper Tigers: Choice and Social Structure in *The Nuer*." *Man* 13(N.S.):100–15.

Galaty, John G. 1981. "Models and Metaphors: On the Semiotic Explanation of Segmentary Systems." Pp. 83–121 in *The Structure of Folk Models* (ASA Monographs, 20), edited by L. Holdy and M. Stuchlik New York: Academic Press.

Geertz, Clifford. 1988. *Works and Lives: The Anthropologist as Author*. Stanford: Stanford University Press.

Herzfeld, Michael. 1987. *Anthropology through the Looking-Glass*. Cambridge: Cambridge University Press.

————. 1990. "The Voice as Signature." [Review of Clifford Geertz, *Works and Lives: The Anthropologist as Author.[Semiotica*. $3:143–150.

Greuel, P. J. 1971. "The Leopard-Skin Chief: An Examination of Political Power among the Nuer." *American Anthropologist* 73:1115–21.

Hodgen, Margaret T. 1964. *Early Anthropology in the Sixteenth and Seventeenth Centuries*. Philadelphia: University of Pennsylvania Press.

Karp, Ivan and Kent Maynard. 1983. "Reading *The Nuer*." *Current Anthropology* 24:481–503.

Kingsbury, Henry O. 1984. *Music as a Cultural System: Structure and Process in an American Conservatory*. Philadelphia: Temple University Press.

Kuper, Adam. 1985. "The Historians' Revenge." *American Ethnologist* 15:523–28.

Lévi-Strauss, Claude. 1974. *Tristes Tropiques*. Translated by John and Doreen Wightman. New York: Athenaeum.

Llewellyn Smith, Michael. 1961. *The Great Island: A Study of Crete*. London: Longmans.

Mehlman, Jeffrey. 1974. *A Structural Study of Autobiography: Proust, Leiris, Sartre, Lévi-Strauss*. Ithaca NY: Cornell University Press.

Sontag, Susan. 1970. "The Anthropologist as Hero." Pp. 184–86 in *The Anthropologist as Hero*, edited by E. Nelson Hayes and Tanya Hayes Cambridge, MA: MIT Press.

Thompson, Michael. 1979. *Rubbish Theory: The Creation and Destruction of Value*. Oxford: Oxford University Press.

Vico, Giambattista. 1748. *La scienza nuova*. Naples: Muziana.

Wilson, Peter. 1989. Review of Herzfeld (1987). *Journal of the History of European Ideas* 10:249–50.

PART III

Social Science as a Political Discourse

Chapter 6

Communication, Persuasion, and The Establishment of Academic Disciplines: The Case of American Psychology

David E. Leary

> You must be satisfied if our account is as likely as any, remembering that both I and you . . . are merely human, and should not look for anything more than a likely story.
>
> Plato, *Timaeus*, ca. 355 B.C.

In this essay I will analyze some of the rhetorical ventures of the so-called New Psychologists who at the turn of our century strove to institutionalize a new science and to create a new set of professional roles.[1] My assumption is that their arguments were not fated to be successful. Had their major spokesmen not been so savvy and articulate, and their audiences so remarkably receptive, their arguments for the New Psychology, in and of themselves, would not have been so persuasive.

To illustrate this point, I shall survey the arguments put forth on behalf of the New Psychology and compare these arguments with the reality of psychology's historical situation. More particularly, I shall try to tease apart the rhetorical fabric surrounding the birth of the New Psychology by focusing, one by one, on different strands of its discourse. There is nothing absolute about these strands: historical reality cannot be decomposed without overlap or remainder into just so many strings of argumentation. But for practical purposes it seems reasonable to focus separately, so far as possible, on (I) what persuaded the first generation of American psychologists to take an interest in the New Psychology; (II) the arguments these aspiring psychologists presented to university presidents and trustees to insure that they could pursue their interest within particularly institutional settings; (III) the arguments they put forth against the rights of other persons to engage in similar, competing pursuits; (IV) the arguments they laid before various administrators, officials, interest groups, and the general public to guarantee continued and even increased support; and (V) the arguments they presented in the form of theories and practices developed between approximately 1880 and 1920. In conclusion, I will suggest (VI) that all of these rhetorical contexts and activities help to explain why Americans have so often been persuaded and assuaged by modern psychology, and why the role of communication and persuasion in the establishment of academic disciplines deserves increased attention.

By focusing on these various rhetorical contexts, I hope to construct a likely story about the establishment of the New Psychology in the United States. At the same time, by focusing this story particularly upon William James, I hope to underscore—on the centenary of his magnificent *Principles of Psychology* (1890)—the central role that James played in the establishment of modern American psychology. However, it should be understood from the start that I will be using James as a representative of a larger set of individuals who constituted the first generation of modern American psychologists.[2]

I

What could have persuaded anyone, in 1880, to pursue a career in the New Psychology? The term *New Psychology* had been around since at least 1845, but scientific psychology itself—a psychology in which measurement and experiment had an important place—was still more dream than reality. Still, it had been known for more than a decade that something distinctive was happening in Germany, and at least two Americans had already visited Germany and observed the nascent science.

The first of these was a young medical student who had been convalescing in Europe when it occurred to him—suffering as he was from a number of apparently nonsomatic illnesses—that "the border ground of physiology and psychology . . . would be as fruitful as any" for him to study. As a consequence, he decided to go to Heidelberg "because Helmholtz is there and a man named Wundt, from whom I think I may learn something of the physiology of the senses without too great bodily exertion." Soon he was writing that he planned to continue studying "in a general psychological direction." Although he was uncertain about the "practical application" to which this study might lead, he mused that it might earn him "a professorship of moral philosophy in some western academy," if such positions were open to "men of a non-spiritualistic mould" (letters from William James in Perry 1935; vol. 1:254, 274, and 276).

It was then 1868, and this "non-spiritualistic" medical student—William James—was more than a decade away from fulfilling his self-proclaimed "vocation" to become a professor of philosophy. Before reaching that goal, James served for seven years as an instructor and assistant professor of physiology, inaugurated the teaching of the new "Physiological Psychology" at Harvard University, and saw his first graduate student in psychology, G. Stanley Hall, go to Germany to do postgraduate work in the new science.

These first steps led to others, and by the mid-1890s the New Psychology was bedecked with all the trappings of an established scientific discipline. There were laboratories, journals, professorships, graduate programs, a professional organization, and at least one clear case of the application of psychology to the solution of real-world problems. And besides all of these, there was James's masterful textbook, *The Principles of Psychology*, certainly one of the major factors in the establishment of the New Psychology in America.

But to repeat our initial question, Why did James and others of his generation choose to pursue a vocation in the New Psychology? The answer for James is that the New Psychology offered an opportunity to resolve personal conflicts concerning science and religion, materialism and spiritualism, determinism and free will. In this as in so many other respects, James's situation is emblematic and worthy of review.

James's first vocation was actually that of an artist, but after a brief period as an artist's apprentice he switched his attention from art to science in the early 1860s. Soon thereafter, he came to feel oppressed by the vision of a completely determined world, and with the loss of all sense of free will and moral responsibility, he became depressed and seriously contemplated suicide. Still, he refused simply to turn his back on science. His respect for science was such, he reported, that he would feel "as if all value had departed from . . . life" if he had to forgo the possibility of becoming a scientist.

It was in this context that psychology, as a prospective science dealing with the operations of the mind (including, most notably, the human will), offered him hope of an eventual rapprochement between his scientific ideals and his personal need to overcome the feeling "that we are Nature through and through, that we are wholly conditioned, that not a wiggle of our will happens save as a result of physical laws" (letter from William James in H. James III 1920, vol. 1:152–153). With the dawning of this hope, he resolved to study the New Psychology. And indeed, in the course of this study he eventually developed a scientific purview that left a "crack" for freedom and hence for meaning in life.

Similar concerns motivated the career choices of many other first-generation New Psychologists, not to mention a significant number of later psychologists. But motivation alone was not adequate, in and of itself, to bring about the institutional changes that would make such career choices feasible and successful. In the creation of academic positions, then as now, it was rarely a question of what was good for a given individual. The concern was more typically for the good of a particular college or university: what suited its students, what appealed to its president, what was acceptable to its board of trustees. Up to the 1880s, what had been good for colleges and universities was traditional mental and moral philosophy, in the context of which the "old psychology" was still taught, often by the college president and generally as the crowning pinnacle of college education. To transform their personal concerns into academic and professional careers, the New Psychologists—including James—had to make their case for a different kind of psychology.

II

In 1869, the same year that William James completed his studies at Harvard Medical School, Charles Eliot became Harvard's twenty-first president. Consequently, it became James's task over the next decade to persuade Eliot that the new "mental science" should have a place in his plans for educational reform at Harvard, and furthermore, that he, William James, was the best person to teach this new "philosophical" course.

In this task, James faced some significant obstacles. Putting aside the abilities he later displayed, in 1869 he was an unemployed, often convalescent young doctor, whose record in Harvard's scientific and medical schools had been undistinguished, and who could claim no coursework, much less a degree, in philosophy. He hardly seemed a person from whom to expect much by the way of scientific and philosophical innovation or distinction.

Fortunately, Eliot was a former teacher of James as well as a neighbor, and he was willing to give him a chance to lecture on physiology, once James had recovered from another period of convalescence. As it turned out, James proved equal to the job, and in 1872 he was made an instructor of physiology. Within a year James had become so popular as a teacher that Eliot offered him an additional course in anatomy for the subsequent year. It was at this point, with his reputation as an open-minded, stimulating teacher firmly established, and with Eliot clearly desiring to increase his role in the college, that James made his long-term intentions known to Eliot. He turned down Eliot's invitation to teach a course in anatomy with the assertion that he "had resolved to fight it out in the line of mental science" (letter from William James in Perry 1935, vol. 1:341).

Having made this assertion, James became ill again and spent much of the next year in Europe. Then, returning to Harvard for the 1874–75 academic year, he dutifully took over the direction of both the laboratory and museum of comparative anatomy upon the death of the incumbent professor. But in the fall of 1875, having exhibited both patience and collegial responsibility, James announced his intention to offer a graduate course on what he astutely called "The Relations between Physiology and Psychology." In thus avoiding the title "New Psychology" or "Physiological Psychology" and simply proposing to examine the relations between two supposedly independent fields, James obviated any possible controversy about the new "scientific philosophy" itself, which was in fact his subject matter. And in listing the course as one of Harvard's few graduate offerings, he sidestepped the issue of the course's appropriateness for the undergraduate curriculum.

Even more astutely, James then used the course to highlight his own recently developed argument that a proper understanding of physiology did not rule out the existence of free will nor denigrate the importance of the human mind. The Board of Overseers took appreciative note. In their annual report for 1875–76 they indicated their pleasure with the new course and commented specifically upon its critique of materialistic views, even suggesting that such a course would be valuable on the undergraduate level, where philosophers had unwittingly abetted materialism by ignoring "the physical side of mental phenomena" (Stern 1965:184).

With this pronouncement, James's foot was in the door, and he took another step forward when he was allowed, with the Overseers' encouragement, to teach "Physiological Psychology" as an undergraduate course in natural history in the fall of 1876. Finally, when this course proved to be so popular that the students petitioned to have James repeat his lectures for those not in the course, Eliot saw a way to insert some nondogmatic teaching into the Department of Philosophy, to boost its lagging enrollments, and to assuage the overseers' concern about materialism. Eliot was pleased, and so was James. In helping Eliot to deal with Eliot's own problems, James had established the desired foothold for himself as well as for the New Psychology in the Department of Philosophy. By 1880 he was an assistant professor of philosophy, regularly teaching courses in the New Psychology, enjoying a solid following of students, and working on his *Principles of Psychology*.

In order to institutionalize the New Psychology as a widely recognized academic discipline, however, the securing of an individual niche within an individual institution would hardly suffice. For the newly emerging discipline to become the legitimate voice for matters psychological, it soon became apparent that its proponents would have to discredit the credentials of those competing for the same positions in the job market and in the marketplace of theory and practice. For even as the New Psychologists were learning to speak the argot of nerves and reaction times, others were continuing to speak of souls and faculties and still others were waxing eloquent about spirits and trances, alternate selves and mind cures. If the New Psychologists were to become the acknowledged authorities on mind and action, they had to make certain that theirs was the language, and theirs the voices, that would be heard.

III

New languages grow out of old ones. Though often posed as a rejection of traditional philosophical psychology, the New Psychology was an outgrowth of the rational and empirical psychologies of the past, and its new language was essentially an emergent dialect of the old philosophical language, refurbished with a generous admixture of physiological terms. Whereas the "old psychologists" talked about souls and endeavored to explain human dynamics by reference to innate faculties, the New Psychologists simply put aside the concept of souls and tried to explain the same set of faculties by reference to more basic physiological and psychological processes. Through their language sounded different, it appropriated and mapped much the same territory covered by the earlier philosophical psychology. Still, not all mental and moral philosophers stepped aside cheerfully and promptly to make room for the new scientific psychologists. Furthermore, there were a number of aspects of the role of the mental and moral philosophers that the New Psychologists were wise enough not to claim as their own. Any direct handling of religious or moral issues, for instance, was studiously avoided by the new generation of psychologists, who as a group shared the disadvantage of being "yet smoothed-faced and generally quite inexperienced" (Baldwin 1894:382).

Even so, the transition from the old philosophical psychology to the newer scientific psychology was less radical than it may have seemed and certainly less radical than it has been protrayed by later historians and psychologists. In many ways, it was more like a changing of the guard than a palace revolution. The fresh troops had new uniforms and followed a revised code of conduct, but their major duty—at least in the early days—was much the same as that of the old guard: they kept their eye on the normal faculties of the average adult white male, presumed to be the prototype of psychological functioning. Although there were some changes in the ways they fulfilled this task, far more dramatic and interesting changes were beginning to occur as a result of a different confrontation—not between old and new psychologists but between the New Psychology and Psychical Research. It was largely through this confrontation that modern scientific psychology broadened its scope and extended its language to the point where it could tell likely stories about far more than the sensory, cognitive, and motor capacities of the average adult white male (see Leary 1980).

Ironically, William James was in the vanguard of those interested in Psychical Research. As a corresponding member of the English Society for Psychical Research since its inception in 1882, he became a founding member of the American Society for Psychical Research (ASPR) in 1884, and in many ways he remained its central figure throughout the remainder of the century. James's interest in Psychical Research followed naturally from his earlier personal crisis, which had been precipitated by the specter of a completely materialistic and deterministic world. Like others in the Psychical Research movement, James had become critical of naively materialistic science, and he sought through Psychical Research to provide empirical support for "the dramatic probability" that some kind of transpersonal consciousness exists behind individual human consciousness (see James 1909). He sought this support in a variety of ways, but primarily through the study of what he called "exceptional mental states"—trances, mediumship, "veridical hallucinations" (visions), telepathy, subconscious phenomena, dual consciousness, alternate personality, automatic writing, and so on (see Taylor 1982). Right up to his death in 1910, James remained open, curious, and yet critical about these sorts of psychical phenomena, which fell outside the domain of traditional psychological research. Although he felt that there was some remarkable evidence in favor of his belief that there is more in the universe than isolated human minds and inert matter, he did not feel that the issue was definitively decided, and he granted that there was no compulsion to believe on the basis of what had been discovered to date. All he asked was that others remain open on the issue.

However, most of the New Psychologists had closed their minds, at least publicly, before the publication of his *Principles of Psychology*. Although many had been members of the ASPR in the 1880s, virtually all but James had backed away from the Society by 1890. The reasons for this are complex and include the fact that the first half-decade of Psychical Research, conducted by respected scientists from a variety of disciplines, had produced no clear-cut evidence for the society's most publicized concern, namely, the existence of a spirit world. But other factors concerning the institutionalization of the New Psychology were also at work.

For one thing, from its very beginning, Psychical Research attracted considerable public attention. At a time when the New Psychology was little known outside the world of academia, Psychical Research was being trumpeted in the daily press and in popular magazines, and it even received notice in scientific journals. This had the generally positive effect of bringing the study of psychological phenomena to public attention. (In fact, Psychical Research was the original concern of many who ended up among the first and second generation of New Psychologists.) At the same time, however, the popularity and visibility of Psychical Research made it a powerful contender in the marketplace of ideas, applications, and jobs. In fact, the ASPR was explicitly committed to "the systematic study of the laws of mental action," not simply to "an exact study of that border-land of human experience" that was overlooked by both traditional and scientific psychology (ASPR 1885). Thus, the ASPR was the first professional organization in the United States committed to the support of psychological research of a general as well as specific nature, and membership in the ASPR was recognized, very early on, as the appropriate professional affiliation for psychologists. Perhaps it was not coincidental, then, that many of the New Psychologists began to leave the ASPR when it decided to "expand its scope" by appointing a Committee on Experimental Psychology in 1887 (Anonymous 1887). Rather than being totally subsumed under the banner of Psychical Research, the New Psychologists retreated from it.

Even in their retreat, however, the New Psychologists did not hesitate to use the public interest in Psychical Research to advance their own cause. For instance, G. Stanley Hall, who had been vice-president of the ASPR in 1885, turned some financial backing he had received through the association toward the establishment of his new *American Journal of Psychology*; and James McKeen Cattell did not scruple to seek a chair at the University of Pennsylvania that had been endowed with the intention of supporting the investigation of Psychical Research.

By 1890 the task facing the New Psychologists was quite apparent. If they wanted their own version of psychology to receive greater recognition and support, they had to discredit Psychical Research, set up an alternative professional organization, and appropriate the theoretical and practical concerns that made Psychical Research so popular.

This is exactly what they did: the New Psychologists, with a few exceptions such as James, turned away from Psychical Research, began to criticize it as unscientific, publicly ridiculed belief in psychic phenomena, and presented the New Psychology as the scientific psychology of the future. But an interesting thing happened: the New Psychology *now* presented to the public was considerably different from the New Psychology that had been presented *before* the emergence of Psychical Research. In addition to its prior focus on the states of mind and action typical of the average adult white male, the New Psychology now had things to say about atypical, nonadult, and nonmale states of mind and action. (It took considerably longer for psychologists to talk about nonwhite experience.) Indeed, the new Psychology even had things to say about nonconscious states of mind, which had previously been banned from the concerns of the new science. Furthermore, the things it had to say about these topics were remarkably similar to what Phychical Researchers had already said.

What had occurred, and what continued to occur throughout the 1890s, was a process of silent appropriation by which the vision and language of the New Psychology were radically enlarged. Although acknowledgments of this appropriation were rare (for obvious rhetorical reasons), the process did not escape the notice of everyone. William James, for instance, observed and commented on the "legitimation" that had been conferred upon "occultist phenomena" by means of their introduction into psychology "under newly found scientific titles" (James 1902:501). And as noted above, it was not only the phenomena of Psychical Research, but also its theories about these phenomena that made their way into the New Psychology.

At the same time that the New Psychologists were thus engaged in publicly discrediting and privately appropriating Psychical Research, G. Stanley Hall was organizing the American Psychological Association. This new organization, founded in 1892, was to serve an important role in the institutionalization of the New Psychology in America. From the beginning, it was presented not simply as an alternative professional association, but rather as the one and only organization whose conferral of membership certified individuals as psychologists in good standing. Together with their journals and various graduate programs, this gave the New Psychologists a decided advantage over their competitors. They had not only argued and maneuvered their way to center stage, they had also gained control of the stage door. Now, having improved their speech through the incorporation of many "new" terms, they were ready to present their pitch to the public, and especially to the administrators, officials, and various interest groups who could provide continued and even increased support for the New Psychology. But to win their support, the New Psychologists had to keep in mind that actions speak louder than words—that the advantages of their new discipline and emerging profession would be presented most persuasively within the context of practical application.

IV

In 1890 William James published his classic *Principles of Psychology*, which was subsequently to play a major role in the establishment of the New Psychology as a respected scientific discipline in the United States. Two years later he noted that

> we live surrounded by an enormous body of persons who are most definitely interested in the control of states of mind, and incessantly craving for a sort of psychological science which will teach them how to *act*. What every educator, every jail-warden, every doctor, every clergyman, every asylum-superintendent, asks of psychology is practical rules. Such men care little or nothing about the ultimate philosophic grounds of mental phenomena, but they do care immensely about improving the ideas, dispositions, and conduct of the particular individuals in their charge. (James 1892:148)

As usual, his comments were prophetic. At a time when the early proponents of the Progressive Movement were beginning to call for scientific technique, professional expertise, and efficient management in education, business, and government, many of the first and second generation of New Psychologists were eager to offer a practical psychology. In this context it was not long before James's thoughtful appeal for attempts to apply psychology was drowned out by other New Psychologists making vociferous, but unsubstantiated claims of actual achievements.

The primary realm in which these assertions were made was the field of education. Indeed, in many ways the institutionalization of modern psychology depended upon developments in modern education. Between 1880 and 1920 the states not only passed and enforced compulsory attendance laws, they provided considerable financial support for an incredible expansion of the educational system in the United States. Between 1890 and 1918 alone, slightly more than one public high school was built every twenty-four hours, while enrollments increased sevenfold. This growth, reflected on the primary as well as secondary level, created a massive need for adequately trained teachers, and the New Psychologists were more than willing to offer their services in the training of teachers, even though their nascent science could presently provide to teachers, in James's words, no more than "arrant bosh and humbug, in the main" (James 1898).

However much or little the New Psychologists were actually able to offer, there was a deep and persistent belief among educators that their association with psychologists would pay dividends. This belief may best be understood in the context of the educators' own quest for professionalization, which depended upon the development of scientific and technical bases for educational expertise. In any case, as one well known psychologist described it, the situation was such that psychologists, on the one hand, were "forced to win a hearing by somewhat magnifying their own office," while teachers, on the other, looked "more or less wonderingly toward the laboratory." Not surprisingly, the "vast promises" of the New Psychologists left teachers (and others) "promise-crammed," but no wiser (Royce 1898:88–89). Meanwhile the demand for—and the promise of—assistance had a detectable effect on the institutionalization of psychology and on the efforts of many psychologists: it is not by chance that twentieth-century American psychology came to be dominated by learning theory.

Besides educators, businessmen were naturally interested in getting ahead of their competition, and some of them stimulated the development of "business psychology" by requesting (for example) that psychologists determine the qualities that make a good typesetter and that they study the habit formations involved in learning telegraphy (e.g., Bryan and Harter 1899). By the early 1900s such demands from the world of business had escalated to the extent that a thriving new field of industrial psychology had evolved to stand beside the slightly older field of educational psychology. Similarly, the beginnings of clinical psychology can be traced to specific requests by the public that psychologists deal with this or that personal problem. For instance, the first Psychological Clinic resulted from a teacher's challenge to a New Psychologist, that he prove his mettle by doing something to help a "chronic bad speller" (Witmer 1907). And further, the relationship between psychology and government can be traced to some very effective argumentation on the part of psychologists in the second decade of this century. Two illustrative instances occurred in 1917. One involved the establishement of the Iowa Child Welfare Research Station, which was to play an important role in the development of child psychology in America. The other involved the institution of psychological testing in the United States Army, which is commonly seen as a critical turning point in the development of public recognition and support for the New Psychology.[3]

In sum, much rhetorical and political savvy went into the institutionalization and professionalization of the New Psychology. Key psychologists observed what was wanted and addressed their audiences accordingly. As they did so, the prospects for psychology vastly improved. By 1920, even though psychology was still far from fully established, it was clear that psychologists had won a hearing, and they finally seemed to be on the verge of fulfilling the promises they had been making for almost four decades.

V

If the rapid growth of psychology in America was due to "conditions of the soil as well as to vitality of the germ," as one early psychologist said (Cattell 1896:135), I have tried to point out how the first generations of New Psychologists took full advantage of these conditions in their efforts to gain recognition and support for their new discipline, even to the point of sometimes exaggerating its actual accomplishments and its immediate prospects. But however fertile the soil, the pronouncements made by the New Psychologists were shaped by intellectual premises as well as by social conditions and demands. The ultimate test of these premises—and hence of the new science and budding profession—lay in the degree to which the New Psychologists were able to articulate likely stories about mind and action. Insofar as they failed to bring these stories into systematic coherence with one another and with the practical activities of research and application, to that extent they would have failed on their own terms to bring the New Psychology to its desired state of perfection.

Ironically, at the very moment when their rhetoric of applicability had opened the door to their coveted goal, a tone of disappointment began to creep into the pronouncements of psychologists regarding the state of their discipline. James McKeen Cattell captured the mood when he regretfully admitted in 1917 that "our accomplishment falls far below what it might be and should be" (Cattell 1917:280). More than a decade later, in 1929, E. G. Boring reached the same conclusion (Boring 1929:658–661), and so have many others right up to our own time (e.g., Koch 1964). As each of these commentators has known, the failure of twentieth-century psychologists to achieve even a relative unanimity regarding theory and method has entailed a corresponding failure to establish disciplinary authority in psychology. After winning so many earlier battles—over personal crises, with college presidents and boards of trustees, against philosophers and Psychical Researchers, and for public opinion and support—the New Psychologists failed to complete their mission by putting the finishing touches on the discipline they had constructed.

Had he still been around in 1920, or even in 1990, William James would not have been surprised or particularly perturbed by this state of affairs, and there is good reason to think that his own philosophy of science was much more appropriate than the dogmatic view of science typical in his age and still espoused in our own (see Leary 1990b). The goal of presenting an argument that would end all argument was foreign to James's temperament and, as he pointed out, it is foreign to the historical reality of science itself. Following in the steps of his beloved Ralph Waldo Emerson, James had come to agree that "science is nothing but the finding of analogy" and that the analogies of science—like the analogies underlying every other form of knowledge—are "fluxional" rather than "frozen" (Emerson 1983:55 and 463). A staunch empiricist, James insisted that there is always a new way to experience any reality and a new way to categorize any experience. To him, a creative genius in any field, in science as in the arts, is simply someone who has an unusual native talent for perceiving fresh analogies that have not yet occurred to others, but which when presented to others, are seen as revealing something salient about experience (James 1990; vol. 1:423–424, 529–530; vol. 2:109–110, 360–365).

Salience, James knew, is not something that is absolute or that can be judged once and for all. Even James's well-known pragmatic criterion of truth is susceptible to variable interpretation: what works for one person may not work so well for someone else, given different fundamental concerns. In the end James felt that humans, including scientists, had to humbly accept the fact that the salience of the "spontaneous" creations of individuals will ultimately be judged by the "consensus" of their social or professional group (James 1990; vol. 1:192; 1907). The achievement of scientific consensus, from this point of view, depends to a significant degree upon the rhetorical power of any particular analogy, or rather, of any particular story based upon a given analogy. This power will draw upon the experiental sensitivities of the particular scientific community, but it will not be reducible in any simple or direct fashion to "the brute facts of the matter." No analogy or likeness of reality is exactly identical with reality—or as Samuel Taylor Coleridge, another of James's admired men, put it: "no likeness goes on all fours" (Coleridge 1981). Therefore, no story developed from analogical premises can be definitive or final. As Timaeus told Socrates long ago, we should not expect more than a likely story in such matters.

Many of the analogies and metaphors that have shaped the positions and oriented the theoretical arguments and practical activities of twentieth-century American psychologists were firmly established by 1920. Some are quite well known, though not all of them are recognized as analogical or metaphorical in nature. For instance, many realize that John B. Watson, generally regarded as the founder of modern behavioristic psychology, was speaking metaphorically when he said that all organisms, including humans, are "stimulus-response machines." Organisms may be like machines, but they are surely not machines in exactly the same way that cars and typewriters are machines. But few realize that the first elements in Watson's bacic premise—the concepts of "stimulus" and "response"—are also metaphors. As he noted in 1919, these terms are used "in psychology as in physiology. Only in psychology we have to extend somewhat the usage of the term[s]" (Watson 1919:10). Despite this admission, however, it was not long before "stimulus" and "response" were taken by most psychologists as "objective" and "neutral" terms in the description and explanation of behavior.

Such subtle movement from a metaphorical to a supposedly literal conceptualization of psychological phenomena is typical of the historical development of twentieth-century psychological rhetoric. The apparently pure, neutral psychological language mandated earlier in the century by the dominant positivist philosophy of science was always, deeper down, informed by what might be called comparative thinking; and many of the theoretical arguments and developments over the past century have been the result, essentially, of analogical redescription of psychological phenomena. For example, in his presidential address before the American Psychological Association in 1915, Watson stated: "It seems to me that hysterical motor manifestations may be looked upon as conditioned reflexes." This is a reasonable analogy, and pursuing it might have enlightened our understanding of hysteria, but Watson slid without further justification from this suggestive analogy to the matter-of-fact declaration that "the conditioned reflex can be used as an explanatory principle in the psychopathology of hysteria" (Watson 1916:99).

This sort of linguistic sleight of hand, by which an analogical redescription is taken to be a new theoretical explanation, was noted in 1934 by a perceptive observer, Grace Adams, who complained that "psychology, for all its theories, has performed no miracles. It has renamed our emotions 'complexes' and our habits 'conditioned reflexes,' but it has neither changed our habits nor rid us of our emotions. We are the same blundering folk that we were twelve years ago, and far less sure of ourselves" (Adams 1934:92).

Even those who would be more generous in their assessment of modern psychology will probably sympathize with this critique. Yet it is a measure of the success of modern psychology's rhetoric that so many people feel that psychology, whatever its shortcomings, has developed knowledge and techniques by which we *could* become better. Here, one might observe, contemporary psychologists' discussions of the potential for personal growth are often reminiscent of rhetoric borrowed from the realm of religion, with its emphasis upon personal sinfulness and the possibility of redemption. In fact, upon closer inspection, it becomes clear that a great deal of twentieth-century psychological discourse and practice has incorporated religious motifs and imagery. Examples include William James's discussions of transliminal consciousness, Carl Rogers' postulation of the fundamental dignity of the individual, and B. F. Skinner's secularized contention that, in essence, "there but for the grace of the Environment go I." In this context, it is interesting to note that many Americans now turn to psychology rather than religion in times of need.

In addition to religion, psychologists have drawn their analogies and metaphors from a wide variety of cultural realms. James, for example, took many of his insightful analogies and metaphors from the domain of art, and he took his most fundamental concepts—the Darwinian metaphors of variation, selection, and function—from psychology's neighboring domain of biological science. (All psychological states, according to James, are the products of spontaneous variation and/or selection in terms of consequential functions.) Later "functionalists," including Skinner, have used the same set of metaphorical concepts, with varying but generally persuasive results—persuasive, that is, not only to the majority of American psychologists, who remain functionalistic in orientation, but also to the public that American psychology serves.

Other general features of American psychology are also reflective of the general culture from which it has arisen. This observation is particularly relevant to an understanding of the rhetorical power—and ultimately, the political significance—of contemporary psychology. For instance, when one reflects upon the high value that American society has placed on efficiency throughout this entire century, it seems more than coincidental that American psychologists have used metaphors of efficiency (e.g., regarding the leading of "integrated" and "productive" lives) at the very core of their thinking and rhetoric. Similarly, it is hardly surprising that American psychologists, situated within a capitalist society, have given metaphors of productivity and exchange a prominent place in their analyses of social behavior. And given the virtual obsession with technology in America, we could have expected American psychologists to base their cognitive and perceptual theories upon cybernetic, holographic, signal detection, and other technical analogs.

In these and in many other instances, American psychologists have drawn their inspiration from their surrounding culture, basing their disciplinary and professional work upon analogies and metaphors that are familiar to themselves and their audiences. Clearly, this has aided communication of their psychological insights, made their theories more persuasive, and helped to establish the legitimacy of psychology as a discipline and profession. Conversely, it has served to confirm—to give scientific legitimacy—to cultural values and arrangements, some of which may be more deserving of critical review than passive confirmation.[4]

VI

In the last few paragraphs, I have pointed at developments in psychology extending beyond the 1920s up to the present day. These developments have been based upon the foundation—and rhetorical practices—established by the first generation of New Psychologists. In closing, it seems appropriate to suggest that the various topics covered in this essay might help explain why so many Americans since the 1920s have been persuaded and assuaged by psychology—why, in other words, so many people have found the theories of psychology to be likely, and its practices to be reasonable. Recapitulating these topics in the order in which they were treated, section by section, in this essay, I would suggest that Americans have been persuaded and assuaged by modern psychology in large part because psychology's stories have addressed their experience and tried to resolve their personal problems; because modern academia and other social institutions have conferred their blessing upon the discipline; because people have learned—and wanted—to believe the claims of science; and because the stories themselves have been constructed around familiar cultural categories, analogies, and metaphors.

None of these factors should be taken to indicate that the claims and practices of psychology are necessarily false. They do suggest, however, that increased attention to the role of communication and persuasion in the establishment and maintenance of modern American psychology—not to mention other academic disciplines—is warranted.

Notes

1. Much of the material in this essay is drawn, adapted, and revised, with permission, from an article of mine (Leary 1987) that appeared in the *Journal of the History of the Behavioral Sciences*, and from the introductory chapter (pp. 1–78) in *Metaphors in the History of Psychology* (Leary 1990a).

2. I give considerable attention to two other founders of modern American psychology—G. Stanley Hall and James McKeen Cattell—in Leary 1987.

3. I discuss these instances in Leary 1987:324–325.

4. I discuss these matters at greater length in Leary 1990a:51–53.

References

Adams, Grace. 1934. "The Rise and Fall of Psychology." *Atlantic Monthly* 152: 82–90.

American Society for Psychical Research. 1885. [Editorial note]. *Proceedings of the American Society for Psychical Research* 1:50.

Anonymous. 1887. [Editorial note]. *Science*, 9 O.S., 51.

Baldwin, James Mark. 1894. Psychology Past and Present. *Psychological Review*, 1:363–91.

Boring, Edwin G. 1929. *A History of Experimental Psychology*. New York: Century.

Bryan, William L., and Harter, N. 1899. "Studies of the Telegraphic Language: The Acquisition of a Hierarch of Habits." *Psychological Review* 6:345–75.

Cattell, James McKeen. 1896. "Address of the President before the American Psychological Association, 1895." *Psychological Review* 3:134–48.

Cattell, James McKeen. 1917. "Our Psychological Association and Research." *Science* 45:275–84.

Coleridge, Samuel Taylor. 1981. *Logic*, edited by J. R. de J. Jackson. Princeton: Princeton University Press.

Emerson, Ralph Waldo. 1983. *Essays and Lectures*, edited by Joel Porte. New York: Literary Classics of the United States.

James, Henry III (Ed.) 1920. *The Letters of William James*, 2 vols. Boston: Atlantic Monthly Press.

James, William. 1890. *The Principles of Psychology*, 2 vols. New York: Holt.

James, William. 1892. "A Plea for Psychology as a 'Natural Science.' " *Philosophical Review* 1:146–53.

James, William. 1898. *Letter to James McKeen Cattell* (4 May 1898). In the James McKeen Cattell Papers, Manuscript Division, Library of Congress, Washington, D.C.

James, William. 1902. *The Varieties of Religious Experience: A Study in Human Nature*. New York: Longmans, Green.

James, William. 1907. *Pragmatism: A New Name for Some Old Ways of Thinking*. New York: Longmans, Green.

James, William. 1909. "The Confidences of a 'Psychical Researcher.' " *American Magazine* 68:580–89.

Koch, Sigmund. 1964. Psychology and emerging conceptions of knowledge as unitary. In *Behaviorism and Phenomenology*, edited by T. W. Wann. Chicago: University of Chicago Press.

Leary, David E. 1980. *William James, Psychical Research, and the Origins of American Psychology*. Unpublished Paper Presented at the Annual Meeting of the American Psychological Association, Montreal, September.

Leary, David E. 1987. "Telling Likely Stories: The Rhetoric of the New Psychology, 1880–1920." *Journal of the History of the Behavioral Sciences* 23:315–31.

Leary, David E. (Ed.). 1990a. *Metaphors in the History of Psychology*. Cambridge: Cambridge University Press.

Leary, David E. 1990b. The Psychologist's Dilemma: To Subject The Self to Science—or Science to The Self? *Theoretical and Philosophical Psychology* 10:66–72.

Perry, Ralph Barton (Ed.). 1935. *The Thought and Character of William James*, 2 vols. Boston: Little, Brown.

Royce, Josiah. 1988. "The New Psychology and the Consulting Psychologist." *Forum* 26:80–96.

Stern, Sheldon M. 1965. William James and the New Psychology. Pp. 175–222 in *Social Sciences at Harvard, 1860–1920*, edited by Paul Buck. Cambridge: Harvard University Press.

Taylor, Eugene. 1982. *William James on Exceptional Mental States: The 1896 Lowell Lectures.* New York: Charles Scribner's Sons.

Watson, John Broadus. 1916. "The Place of the Conditioned Reflex in Psychology." *Psychological Review* 23:89–116.

Watson, John Broadus. 1919. *Psychology from the Standpoint of a Behaviorist.* Philadelphia: Lippincott.

Witmer, Lightner. 1907. "Clinical Psychology." *Psychological Clinic* 1:1–9.

Chapter 7

Poetics and Politics in Ethnographic Texts: A View from the Colonial Ethnography of Afghanistan

Jon W. Anderson

> What wonderful men these Firingees are!
> Three months ago four of them came into
> the country; now one is at Cabool, one at
> Candahar, one here, and one at the source
> of the Oxus! Wullah! Billah! they neither eat,
> drink, nor sleep; all day long they make sly,
> and all night they write books!
>
> —Murad Beg (in Burnes 1842:180)

Recent critical attention to the textual construction of ethnographies has illuminated their production in challenging ways and eclipsed older autobiographical genre's for disciplinary self-examination. This mood and movement to deconstruct the authority and the authorship of ethnography (e.g., Marcus and Cushman 1982; Clifford 1983; Clifford and Marcus 1986) complements earlier postcolonial critique which focused on its contexts (Asad 1973; Hymes et al. 1969). Both place authority and authorship in ethnography at issue as part of broader critiques of the social sciences generally and specifically their claims of objectivity. In these terms, deconstructivist turns to issues of representation (Handler 1985; Fabian 1990) link with wider issues of cultural agency (e.g., Giddens 1979, 1982; Archer 1988), much as anticolonial critiques turned on limits of deterministic understanding raised from critical (Habermas 1975) and hermeneutic (Gadamer 1960; Ricoeur 1985) perspectives; both "bring home" elements of wider critiques of scientific practice to the texts of ethnography, particularly to exemplary texts, through critique of their production. Both also tend to stall around their points of departure in macrostructural and microprocessual perspectives on ethnographic production, thereby ignoring the middle range, intermediate phenomena between context and text. These include phenomena of social organization in which ethnographic production becomes accessible as a corpus, an intermediate phenomenon between paradigm and practice that together produce a corpus. Focusing on a corpus opens this ground between macroscopic structures and microscopic processes from which to ask After deconstruction, what? and to restore critique of ethnography to social analysis.

Ambiguously constituted as both text and context, and by fashions of reading as well as of writing, a corpus above all emerges through time as a sort of extended or, in Burke's (1957:94–97) sense, "unending conversation." One of these is the colonial ethnography that emerged on the North-West Frontier of British India over a century and a half of efforts to grasp, often literally, the society and culture of its Pakhtun people. This is very much the sort of material that more aptly than professional ethnography submits to the postcolonial critiques: nearly all of it was gathered, sifted, and gleaned for political intelligence. In direct service of imperial design, it was a genuine handmaiden of imperialism by comparison to the camp follower role of anthropological ethnography. But for that it is ambiguously authored and submits more aptly to the sorts of concerns with representation and interpretation addressed in deconstructive terms. Unlike the single authors and even single texts that are palimpsests of recent reflexivist turns (e.g., Clifford and Marcus 1986; Geertz 1988), colonial ethnography comes extended in time and space as a jumble of topics and jostling perspectives, in a multiplicity of voices that are variously self-conscious and often self-referential. Reading such a corpus is like fieldwork amid a buzz of partial and often contradictory perspectives whose multivocality and intertextualities are part of the data.

Colonial ethnography, no less than any other discourse, develops in extended conversations that are themselves socially organized and organize interests and forms for conveying those interests. The now familiar critique that such intensely interested material conveys more of the colonizers than of the people is less illuminating today than when it was fresh (Hymes et al. 1969; Asad 1973). Indeed, it now appears that such critique itself tends to flatten complex situations, underestimate capacities for impression management, collapse time and diverse settings, and seize on caricatures from the twilight of empire when they were already thin and ironic.[1] In a nexus of forms, personnel, policies, and intellectual technology that grew up for processing information on Pakhtun tribes, each element was frequently controversial, and controversy is one of the first threads of a corpus that organize interpretive activity and connect it to settings. Such features—along with redundancy, quotation, and other kinds of reprocessing down to the house styles of institutional jargon—trace a "hum and buzz of implication" (Trilling 1953:200–1) that further locate specific works within an overall corpus of material that is part of the data. I first outline some key forms of British colonial ethnography on the Frontier, then turn to their organizational settings between the incorporation of the Panjab into British India beginning in 1849 and routinizations that were in place by 1901 when the Frontier was made a separate province from the Panjab. None of this is an apology for colonial ethnography, still less a full study of the colonizers. Instead, with Beidelman (1982), I believe this sort of material can be instructive for an ethnography of knowledge that puts the problematic character of cultural understandings back into the social organization that frames their own accessibility, and in conclusion I will return to issues raised about such knowledge.

North-West Frontier Studies

For more than a century, British India had a wild west that generations of British officers endeavored to fathom and even to domesticate as a sort, but only a sort, of *cordon sanitaire* for their Indian empire and that Kipling christened the "Great Game." The endeavor became institutionalized around what Ainslie Embree (1977) characterized as separate boundaries of administration, sovereignty, and influence over the Pakhtun tribes. With Pakhtun tribes astride both the administrative borders of empire and its claimed international frontier with Afghanistan, the Great Game became a matter of limits on power to influence Afghanistan, to control ceded tribal areas, and to enforce imperial law and order in directly administered ones. Unable to conquer Afghanistan, the British settled for a monopoly on its foreign relations; unable to occupy tribal areas detached from it, they settled for indirect rule beyond the boundaries of their own imperial political-economic system.

This stratification was reflected in studies and surveys of tribal dispositions monitored by political agents, who produced detailed accounts of locations, manpower, and leaders of the border tribes (Merk 1898; King 1900; McMahon and Ramsey 1901; Howell 1931; Ahmed 1980). On Afghanistan itself, geographic data on places and groups, usually gathered during previous military incursions, (e.g., Broadfoot [1839] 1886; Rawlinson [1841] 1910; Burnes 1842; Raverty 1888), were combined with contemporary information from "native agents." Overall, this record tends to be geographical and general for Afghanistan, ethnographical and often in great detail for the tribal areas, and routinized economic surveys for the "settled areas" under direct administration. Figure 1 shows this trailing off of ethnographic information from the "tribal areas" into Afghanistan.

At the same time, the record is densely interwoven. Materials were frequently combined from sources generations old, and in time into a limited number of genres. The more accessible memoirs of Frontier service mix sweeping and often contradictory generalizations with minute recountings of events surely oft-told before they reached print. These romances of Frontier service commonly published internal and otherwise classified material, such as the ethnographic and tribal maps that every anthropologist on this region has used; certain accounts became classics and were the syllabus for generations of new officers who quoted, excerpted, and updated their material. These personalized and frequently polemical memoirs of service are linked to a larger body of reports and compilations by citation and frequent quotation of previous work and by their fixation on certain themes and interpretive problems. Across reports and surveys, accounts of tours or "traverses," lists of villages, tribal segments, and leaders, to studies of particular political (especially boundary) problems, this corpus also extends to composite handbooks for guidance and gazetteers for reference. Material in the latter can easily span several generations. The encyclopedic *Gazetteer of Afghanistan* went through four editions over thirty years and grew into five volumes, still quoting material up to a century old, until it was finally edited into a fifth edition just before World War I, when routinization of the Frontier's status was complete and its administration stabilized in a provincial form retained through independence in 1947 to the present.

The gazetteer is a characteristic document and the only other form common to all zones. There were no monographic studies of tribes in settled areas, nor in Afghanistan, and no income and production surveys such as were produced on the directly administered areas. But there were gazetteers in the India provincial series for "settled areas" integrated into the imperial economic system inside the administrative boundaries, a political series for the unadministered "tribal areas" up to the international boundary with Afghanistan, and a separate series for Afghanistan itself. These reference compendia sorted data alphabetically by place and local groups. They might contain snippets of history and reference to past events, often directly extracted from field reports, but their detemporalized abstracts or digests are the other, complementary style to the romantic narrative of the service memoir. Where the

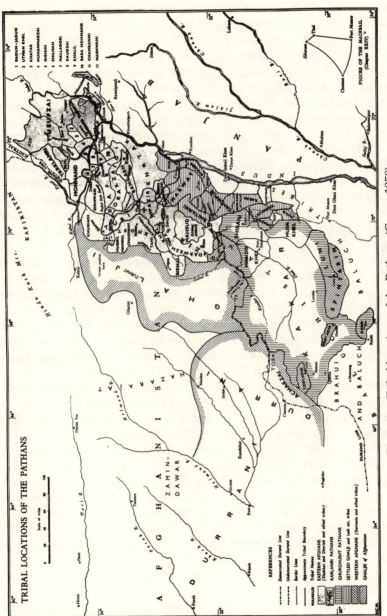

Figure 1. Tribal locations of the Pathans (Caroe, 1958).

framework of the latter is the example-minded witness, the model of the gazetteer is the card file and dictionary comprehensiveness. From this format were spun off dictionaries of biography on tribal notables, and constantly updated handbooks for military guidance combining general advice with detailed information on routes, potential sources of supplies, and previous "outrages," the grudges awaiting retribution. Together, these composed the official institutional memory.

Behind both institutional memory and personal memoirs lay a steady stream of reports that recorded local events, hearsay, administrative actions, and interpretation. While reports particularly on the tribal areas were confidential studies for internal purposes, many were published openly and written for advancement of policies and careers. Winston Churchill's memoir of a late-nineteenth-century campaign in the tribal area was first published seriatim as journalistic dispatches while he was still a junior lieutenant (Churchill 1898). It combined firsthand accounts with overt policy analysis and advocacy in the fashion of "leaks" for a public not much larger than officialdom itself. This genre was established over half a century earlier by the first generation of active interventionists who debated frontier policy as much in public as in council. The most notorious is Alexander Burnes, whose account (1834) of travels across Afghanistan brought him enthusiastic public acclaim, a knighthood, and a role in the intervention in Afghanistan he advocated that proved fatal to him as well as to that policy shortly after he dispatched his account of it (Burnes 1842). Widely followed for the same mix of career and policy advancement (e.g., Masson 1842; Ferrier 1857; Bellew 1920; see Trousdale 1985), the form was eventually absorbed into the professional service memoir written in retirement and drawing on a similar mix of personal experience, internal documents, and previously published works that also compose lineaments of this corpus.

Internal material was made indirectly public also through working local specifics into global generalities about Pakhtun. The process extended from the most original public report, Montstuart Elphinstone's *Account of the Kingdom of Caubul* (1812), which became the touchstone work of Frontier studies, down to the memoir of the last British Governor of the North-West Frontier Province on the place of the Pakhtun in history (Caroe 1958). Elphinstone's report of the first British mission to the Pakhtun kingdom of Afghanistan provided the most synoptic and in some ways most integrated account of Afghanistan and Pakhtun society, history, geography, tribal organization, government, and, more briefly, economic life. Nearly all subsequent synthesis was written in its shadow, frequently reintegrating its substance in schematics that shifted to history. While its fresh comprehensiveness was never duplicated, it established a model of generalization and a source on relations of tribe and state that were treated in far different terms when the state was the British Empire.

These documents of Frontier service are intermediate, partly processed, and value-added products that bear witness not just to its redundant mode of production but to its modes of interpretation. They weave and reweave syntheses of firsthand observation with history, direct testimony, and research into dynastic chronicles and legends, often in the original language (Dorn 1892; Ferrier 1858; Priestley 1874; Malleson 1878; Raverty 1888), together with local studies and topical surveys (e.g., Baden-Powell 1896). They include appropriated and reappropriated discourse, particularly in a stream of historical studies after midcentury, when Pakhtun territories were annexed and the 1880s after Britain came to war with Afghanistan over them. Largely focused on personalities, these histories were sifted from dynastic chronicles for facts that would inform current critical assessments and became sources for later political histories (e.g., Fraser-Tytler 1967; Caroe 1958). More specialized genres similarly mixed description and assessment in monographic studies of tribal distributions, authority, and "laws" in the Frontier agencies. The local dimensions of the Frontier involved different relations with Pakhtun tribes, with tribesmen, and with the Pakhtun of Afghanistan. Beyond geographic and topographic knowledge of Afghanistan and the tribal areas for military purposes, the British sought a similarly precise knowledge of tribal composition, and of "tribal law," where they could claim to enforce it (Berry 1966), although precision there proved to be spurious. In much the same terms, they eventually surveyed nomad trade and its carriers who came down from Afghanistan to India (Robinson 1934) and, where they were in a position to regulate it, property rights of settled agriculturalists. Census, survey, and reduction to rules only partly set a frame of reference. In this context, they are pieces of extended and overlaid conversations that are ambiguous, contradictory, and multiply determined.

Structural Settings

Major frames of reference on Frontier relations were set by the change to a viceregal system after the Indian mutiny of 1857–58. Direct political rule in place of the East India Company set up a continuing debate and a series of experiments over what came to be known as the "forward policy" and the "close border" that increasingly turned on ethnological grounds for what was known as a "scientific Frontier." This was always a muddled notion, part geographical, part ethnological, rationalized as much in strategic as in geopolitical terms. It came to focus on different kinds of Pakhtun within a larger argument over identifying and consolidating other "natural" boundaries between the Hindu Kush, which would have included them all, and the Indus, which would have excluded most of them. Actual local boundaries included Pakhtun in a wide range of capacities. Locally, a close-border policy meant closing the lowlands from the hills, both occupied by Pakhtun, a forward policy meant occupying and closing them both from Pakhtun in Afghanistan.

On the ground, this meant that knowing whom to deal with merged with knowing how, in order to collect as well as to evaluate information and influence events. Fluency in Pakhtu became essential, as early British officers complained that Pakhtun in negotiations with them would switch from Persian, which served as the lingua franca of the area, to their own language when they wished to keep their discussions secret. More important was a cultural fluency in what the British termed Pakhtun "character," which became a major topic of British interpretations. In the beginning, many were set in nuanced appreciations of social relations; but in time and with repetition, "character" was generalized and abstracted into lists of traits that only restated the problem. An extreme example is from the preface of the *Handbook of Kandahar Province*, prepared and regularly updated by the General Staff of India for guidance in the event of military operations:

> The Afghan character is a strange blend of virtue and vice. Hardy, brave, proud, simple in their mode of living, frank, prepared to die in accordance with their code of honor yet faithless and treacherous; generous to a degree yet devoured by greed for money; capable of great endurance and of feats of energy but constitutionally lazy; merry, cheerful, humorous and fond of music yet inclined to be austere. Cupidity, instability, a suspicious nature, intense jealousy, bitter vindictiveness, excitability, impatience and want of self-control, and a complete disregard for truth form the chief characteristics of the Afghan nature. They are capable of strong personal attachments but never forget a wrong. Grossly credulous, superstitious, fanatical and bigoted, yet knowing little of their religion. Tribal feuds are seldom allowed to be forgotten but on the threat of a common danger widespread fanaticism kindled by "mullahs" and other leaders would have the immediate effect of uniting all the tribes to meet the emergency. Severity and harsh justice are understood and not resented but nagging merely acts as an irritant. They appreciate justice, an open hand, firmness, patience, good humor, and the English disposition to punish and be friends again. They are great travelers and keen observers, shrewd men of business, good traders indefatigable in the pursuit of gain, intellectually wide awake, of mental ability and avaricious to a degree. The race in short is a mass of contradictions which are accentuated by the strong individuality of the people.

The frank confusion of this decontextualized formulation begins to resolve as it goes on pragmatically to judge Afghans by British standards:

Plausible and specious in their arguments, they often succeed in imposing on Europeans with their protestations of good faith and honorable intentions, but experience of a very positive nature impresses on us the fact that no Military Commander should ever rely on their good faith alone for the fulfillment of any promises they may make. It is in short useless to make any terms with them unless the observance of such terms can be enforced. The treachery and guile of the Afghans in their dealings with foreigners and enemies are but a phase of Afghan patriotism, and of an unscrupulous character, doubtless, according to our own standards, but nevertheless practical in its methods, as we know to our cost. (1933:7–8).

Sociologically, this text condenses more situated experience into an encyclopedic composite. The beginning is an unattributed quotation from Henry Bellew, a military physician seconded to the Afghan court in 1857 who eventually published his report on it (Bellew 1920) after he had turned to ethnological speculation to unravel these contradictions into multiple pedigrees for Pakhtun (1891). It had already been reused to describe "the character of the tribes" by Malleson (1878:51–52) in his historical background to the Second Anglo-Afghan War. Its own polyphony distills a century of experience into a cultural frame of interpretation that affected and was affected by strategic debate throughout the imperial period. It is deeply ambivalent, both descriptively in its list of "a mass of contradictions" and interpretively bringing that to rest on "strong individuality of the people." It abstracts actions drawn from friend and foe into a composite fact, read in a particular British fashion as "character," with its "natural" locus in tribalism.

The problems of dealing with Pakhtun came to focus on tribal groups and character before the imperial period, which this extract reflects. With Afghanistan closed to them and hostile since British intervention in one of its civil wars, British analysts had collected and merged disparate information from dynastic chronicles and firsthand material most like them, personal genealogies and those of groups, into a composite reconstruction of Pakhtun relations. Research into grounds for political loyalties and group identities was systematized in the collection of tribal genealogies. Their own significances in these respects were recast in the broad racialist notions of nineteenth-century Victorian thought, which were so magnified in postmutiny India and replaced earlier biblical notions about "lost tribes" of Israel.[2] In debate over the forward policy and the close border, efforts to delineate different types and descent lines of Pakhtun combined a reading of tribal genealogies as history and of "character" as its natural frame (esp. Bellew 1891). By the late imperial period, broad innatist readings of "character" (e.g., Fraser-Tytler 1967; Mayne 1955) were advanced un-self-consciously to rationalize existing or projected boundaries, while locally genealogies were put to the same use, both primarily in compilations and assessments.

Figure 2 shows this amalgamation of tribal genealogies through common "ancestors" of tribes, whose own ancestors are the termini in this diagram.

Compiling, sifting, and evaluating these and other data for particular uses, projects, policies, and offices grew up under the viceregal system that replaced the East India Company after 1858. Its particular selection of ideas and practices included some brought to India in the ambitions of its personnel and some developed in the services there. The most notable centered on bureaucracy as a vehicle for Whiggish and utilitarian reformers (Mill [1820] 1975; see Stokes 1959) prior to the empire and racialism during it. An early mix of gentlemen and not-so-gentleman adventurers in the East India Company on the Frontier only "briefly served with their regiments . . . [until] they had passed an interpreter's examination" for political work with the local populations (Yapp 1980:183). During this period,

> Political work, by virtue of its interest, its financial rewards, and the power and responsibility which it offered to young men, attracted some of the ablest and most ambitious men in the Company's service. In the Political Department seniority mattered less than the capacity to seize the right opportunity at the right time; hence Political Agents tended to be men of considerable initiative, or to put it more crudely, men with an eye to the main chance. (*ibid.*).

An imperial bureaucracy replaced the "corrupt" Company with civil service based on the Macauley reforms that instead recruited Oxbridge, or at least public school, men selected by examination in academic subjects for new imperial services (Kennedy 1982; Braibanti et al. 1966). While the Civil Service of India (CSI) still drew the excess sons of the English middling classes, recruitment for academic success in a general curriculum provided public careers that depended on and institutional-ized its culture of "character" (see Rosenthal 1986), a philological bias and amateur "naturalism" (not at a professional level), and a taken-for-granted racialism that marked Victorian confidence in the superiority of British institutions and its attendant paternalism. But not all at once, and not evenly.

In the beginning, a significant number of British on the Frontier had been Scots. A clear Scots' sensibility runs throughout the un-self-conscious and unproblematic application of "clan" to Pakhtun lineages by Elphinstone. Himself a Scot, Elphinstone displayed a subtle sense for the dual character of lineages as both territorial/political forms and as mystic/kinship ones, and for how these social and cultural logics could pull in different directions. From largely hearsay evidence, Elphinstone discerned differences between what he called "republican" tribes, which

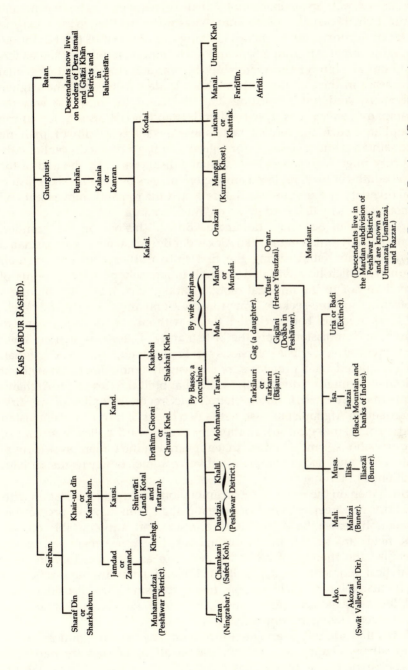

Figure 2. Composite genealogy, Imperial Gazetteer of India: North-West Frontier Province (Government of India ca.1904).

preserved patrilineal institutions that keep their leaders weak, and "monarchial" ones, in which lineage ties wither relative to more exigent ones of territory and chiefship. Coming not only out of the Edinburgh Enlightenment but from a Scotland of clearances, in which clan leaders sold out kinship for proprietorship, he was an acute analyst of similar processes in the Pakhtun tribes whose leaders allied with the Afghan monarchy and those resisting it at the court to which he was the Company's envoy. His clear-eyed understanding of how the single form could have such different characters displays the sensibility of firsthand acquaintance and a classicist formalism that has a decidedly eighteenth-century ring. Such sensibilities virtually disappeared by the end of the nineteenth-century, replaced among orientalists by emphases on historical diversity and uniqueness that reflected the romantic movement and among others by flattened views of "human nature."

A stream of Scotsmen dominate "British" history on the Frontier. Some cut a Byronian figure, like Alexander Burnes, who was assassinated by a mob in Kabul during the first British attempt to occupy their country, which he advocated through immensely popular accounts of travels. Prior to the imperial reorganization, such men were among a flotsam of fortune-seekers drawn to the Company's service after Wellington's reforms had excluded those without the private means to purchase commissions from the British army. These marginal but able, and themselves "tribal" versions of Englishmen, mimicked Afghan styles, quoted their predecessors extensively (and sometimes without acknowledgment), added to the work that built the corpus on Afghanistan. Maj. Gen. Sir Charles Metcalf McGregor, compiler of the first gazetteer on Afghanistan, also wrote two books of travels in Baluchistan and Iran, a strategical justification for the forward policy, a stream of "appreciations," and opinions that appeared in the Indian press (Trousdale 1985) and had a complete native costume, down to the turban, fashioned of tartan material.

Such men on the Frontier set an ambiguous style of identification with Pakhtun in careers at once of bureaucratic routine and unpredictable danger. Bureaucratic discipline (the office) and unpredictable danger (the field) are twin tensions throughout the service memoirs, which organize the themes of character and clan as its repository in their analytical moments (e.g., Wylly 1912) and later, in their reflective moments, themes of civilization and barbarism. They also identified subtleties of Pakhtun comportment, interpersonal relations, standards, and values when gathering information.

What they identified, and identified with, has its own significance and imperatives. Demeanor and information about lineage are part of a discourse of honor that is the most avidly "published" of Pakhtun knowledge. Lineage and posturing convey at once the claims and most solemn rationalization of identity in situations that are sociologically fluid and endlessly contestable (Barth 1959; Anderson 1983). Lineages record claims to proprietorship as a record of division of conquest that are linked with honor as aspects of the same thing (Anderson 1975). Tribal notions of honor rather than social morphology are expressed in lineages and in the demeanor the British read for "character." This most public and most contentious of knowledge is laid over the practical composition of power bases that commonly contain clients and relations that are equally mediated by marital ties (Anderson 1982; Christensen 1982; Tapper and Tapper 1982). Affines in particular almost never appear in the lineage lists compiled in increasing detail throughout the imperial period, and then only anecdotally rather than in the catalog fashion of accounts of descent lines and lineages. What was not recorded on the Pakhtun tribes is as interesting as what was. Affinal ties, economic relations, and relations of feud that compose the practical structure of Pakhtun tribes are guarded, strategically important information about them. The structural significance of relations of descent is that they are calculable in many ways, while these other relations form the practical setting of calculations (Tapper 1983); even lineage designators persist while specific components come and go, and may be completely redefined demographically (Anderson 1980). "Lineage" itself represents a wholly different frame of reference than the mobilization of groups or their histories. An even more interesting omission in this colonial ethnography is information on religious leadership and networks that cross-cut lineages and were more significant for mobilizing armed resistance to the British. Kakar (1979) interprets late-nineteenth-century internal history of Afghanistan, for instance, as a steady displacement of tribal leaders by religious ones who had been more effective in mobilizing resistance to the British in eastern Afghanistan. A similar argument has been made for resistance to the British on the Frontier at the same time (Ahmed 1976; cf. Anderson 1984).

What came to be recorded in detail and with interest about Pakhtun tribes may be a "logical" extension of the census and survey of the administered areas, and even a practical resort to available data; but projects to amalgamate and then restore a history to them rest also on a broader mix of interests and taken-for-granted assumptions. British interest in tribal classifications goes beyond census to analytical models for limning Pakhtun into different types. The early dispersion-of-peoples model was by the end of the century replaced by genus-and-species preoccupations. At a practical level, it was realized that Pakhtun tribes had many more contemporary ties than the model of a genealogical tree implied, and that their behavior was a response to

British behavior; but in isolation both from other facts as well as from the settings that elicit them, naturalist models interpreted it within the concerns to identify a scientific frontier. Under this regimen, Pakhtun were parsed into various extinct peoples and historical groups of which they were interpreted to be variously survivors or mixes. And categorical information about "character" effectively reified what Pakhtun commonly say about each other into another discourse and stereotypy of honor.

The Record as a Social Product

Some of this interpretive activity can be laid to divide-and-rule strategies; but by itself that obscures rather than reveals contexts and motives in bureaucratic practices of social classification and social distance. This is not to suggest some unconscious transference, but to point out that two major topics that came to dominate analysis of Pakhtun also dominate the intellectual and social settings of that analysis—namely, character and lineage. Both the assiduous collection of genealogies and their reification are less immediately a reflection or projection of an institutional structure than a rationalization of intuitive firsthand notions about clan and the situation of character into blunter, one-dimensional indicators of something more "basic," even natural. This setting must include the general and taken-for-granted frameworks of evolutionism running through Victorian social thought (Burrow 1966), some of which was developed in British Indian comparative studies of community (Maine 1861, 1871), and the racialism of their hand-me-down popular versions. The generalization of "character" and psychological identification with Pakhtun became tropes of this effort. "Character" became something these British officers came to recognize stereotypically in Pakhtun and taken for granted as a basis for relating to them. In time, such assessments were divorced from particular social relations that they shaped and that were shaped by them as "old boys" with families replaced buccaneers and bachelors (see Ballhatchet 1980). Generalized and categorical assessments by educated bureaucrats who limited their contacts to official business extend a recognition of common human nature that becomes explicit in British writing on Pakhtun as "worthy opponents" in the beginning, "treacherous" and changeable at the height of empire, and "after all just like us" in its twilight (when at least one was knighted). In fact, a limited range of interaction had come to define a large part of what "us" meant for the British in India.

Lindholm (1980) has argued that the high colonial ethnography of the Frontier reflects the colonizers more than the Frontier peoples. Certainly, much of what British "case officers" experienced reflected the specific interactions of hospitality extended to those who come as guests and the suspicion extended toward those who do not. But colonial ethnography is denser and more diversely set in institutional contexts that define and are defined by it. Particular nineteenth-century social institutions including the bureaucracy invented for India and its recruitment in England also developed over time in multiple contexts of the British Empire in India that included the racialism it fostered, the new men that it brought out, and the intellectual technology that it selected. All of these changed with the shift to the viceregal system. The reifications of "character" and of lineage representations were read and reread into far different sorts of evaluation and became part of another system of communication and knowledge with its own institutional setting that organized and transmitted methods and modes of knowledge.

In such terms, the colonial ethnography of the Frontier is specifically different from the other great example—the French in North Africa (Burke 1972). By comparison to the French enterprise, it retained an amateur quality and the intellectual qualification by general rather than by professional education. For the British, there was nothing comparable to the French "colonial science." Theirs was by comparison "colonial practice," specifically enshrining pragmatic inquiry using any tools at hand. There was no institute of Pakhtun or Frontier studies; and interest in Pakhtun was by ethnographic standards even of the day (which featured speculation about primitive marriage, kinship, and religion) rather narrow and like the avocational collecting that could as well have been rocks or butterflies, and frequently was. Due in part to philological biases in the education of "all-rounders," abetted by the premium on acquiring native languages, its data were also frequently words, sometimes manuscripts, less often customs. But its analysis was contemporary less with the professional anthropology of its day than with the popular strain of thought derived from professional reflections of a previous generation.

In the presentation of material, an epistemology and its institutional setting are socially organized and transmitted as part of the realities they construe. The gazetteers of Afghanistan, for instance, grew from one to six volumes between the 1880s and the first decade of the twentieth-century. The first edition combined material published over the previous half-century with systematic surveys and inquiries begun with the second Anglo-Afghan war (1878–80) that continued in ceded Tribal Areas. This period coincides with the growth of Frontier services into a regular bureaucracy that monopolized the field and was responsible for various and changing implementations of close-border and forward policies that inflected all British relations with Pakhtun during this period, effectively effacing earlier one's. The effacement of discordant voices in the gazetteer is complete in the rewritten edition (begun 1914), after the corresponding volume on the North-West Frontier Province (in the *Gazetteer of India*) had been completed in the previous decade, when the North-West Frontier Province was separated from the Panjab administration. Merging survey and place data in a thoroughly anonymous document, the North-West Frontier Province gazetteer (ca. 1904), although in the Indian provincial series, included a long historical introduction focused on Afghanistan and the border issue, making clear its context as a briefing and reference manual, for the chief commissioner of the new province continued to report to the Foreign Department of the Government of India.

British frames of reference on Pakhtun tribes were limited by what they brought intellectually to the encounter as well as by their purposes for being on the Frontier. While guided by political purposes to the dispositions and relations of the tribes, their inquiries were also guided, and divided, by taken-for-granted, literally commonsense, ideas that defined the particular worldviews brought to the Frontier and developed there over time. Elphinstone's rationalist universalism gave way to philological romanticism, the orientalism of philologians to the racialisms of high Victorian imperialists. Others were notions of "character," so central to high Victorian self-conceptions and selection for service and notions about human nature that evolved over different generations, as did concepts of "clan" brought by Scots and eventually domesticated to more contemporary English standards. What happened with the entire intellectual technology of Frontier service might perhaps be better put as involution with the development of the empire. In comparison to the adventurous and miscegenous Company that proceeded it, hallmarks of the empire were racialism, or in practical terms a policy of social distance, and bureaucratization, two forms of "rationalization" that typically try dealing with things in fewer dimensions than they have in life. Nuanced assessments of social relations by the first "case officers" for Pakhtun affairs gave way to more broadly stroked, categorical, abstracted, and decontextualized "backgrounds" for bureaucracy. In a context of social distance, these assessments came to be objects of their own analysis, driving it back to a paradoxical recognition of their source, but with the result that Pakhtun became a kind of tribal everyman at the frontier of civilization, their culture and even their language viewed as a veneer much as thoughtful imperialists came to see their own.

Similarly, appreciation of the multiply determined and ambiguous qualities of territorial lineage groupings gave way to interpretation of them as reflecting some prior historical or genetic datum that could be read from them. Research into them developed under limited agendas and, in time, even more limited models very much like that of the bureaucracy itself. This is not a simple matter of projection. Its importance is its displacement of other contexts and conditions of service in the imperial period. This can be as subtle as identification with its overall ethos, and as specific as simply following bureaucratic practices and instructions for producing specific data on specific problems, few of which ever reside wholly "in the field." So to methodology must be added an appreciation that the sources and purposes of its social organization are multiple and situational, conveying to it a liminal character that is frequently obscured by the very multiplicity of ideologies that create it. These sources and purposes are part of the same middle ground, subjective and objective, as the corpus, lying between and partaking of both microinteractional processes and macroscopic structures.

Conclusions

The features in this material pointed to here—citation, reuse, updating, narrowing of focus and topic—build the corpus that is the missing middle in critiques of ethnography. Additional features of paradigm and practice more apparent in a corpus and in its development include the transformation over time of rationalist-universalist and romantic-orientalist perspectives into naturalist and race-minded ones, and the smoothing of individual voices—both of Pakhtun and of their British interlocutors—into more corporative ones. These are socially conveyed and organized aspects of a corpus that constitute parts of its intermediate phenomenology between text and of context. Looking at their development helps us to retrieve the missing mediators between paradigm and practice, between text and context, that puts those into perspective. It also helps us to put interest in those into perspective.

After a generation of disappearing-into-the-woodwork, a reflexive revival of Malinowski's it-is-I-who-write-them reopens the balance of authority and authorship in the production of ethnography. This mood and movement is wholly consonant with situational factors of opportunity in postcolonial ethnography and with contemporary critiques of objectivity in the philosophy of social science (e.g., Kuhn 1972; Feyerabend 1978; Habermas 1975; Gadamer 1960) as well as with attention to discursive strategies (Foucault 1971; Derrida 1978; Bakhtin and Medvedev 1978) that address sociological issues concerning agency. As liberating as this deconstructive turn has been, critical attention to microprocesses replicates problems of interpretive paradigms (Mascia-Lees, Sharpe, and Cohen 1989) much as macrostructural critiques earlier pointed to their own problems of objectivity.

Focusing on texts can be insidiously misleading if, in directing attention to properties of interpretation, it diverts attention from other equally, and in some respects more, social properties. It produces a prisonhouse of reflection that Hayden White has called "the narcissism of the reader" confronted with texts (1978:265). Against this diversion, Bakhtin and Medvedev (1978) argued a model featuring not reflection but contention. For looking at texts, they articulate a vision of conversations whose extended, multivocalic, and contradictory (because partial) perspectives more accurately are social properties, and reflect more of them. The problem of how to admit these additional data can exhaust models drawn from "text." Just as models drawn from language itself cannot contain the data of speech, but only of restricted formal properties (Silverstein 1976), neither does "text" adequately model its own practical surroundings.

A better model that would proceed from those surrounding is Bourdieu's stratification of practical and discursive knowledge, which places the latter, exemplified in ideology, as a subset of the former rather than its model (Bourdieu 1977). Bourdieu's argument resolves a series of parallel impasses between analytic approaches to aggregate behavior and hermeneutic approaches to intention. It does this by treating discourse as a subset of practices rather than as their representation in other terms. Focusing more on the actor, Giddens (1979, 1982) likewise envisions a ground between the unconscious (unintended) aggregate and fully conscious intention that he calls practical consciousness (1982:9), in which both intention and unintended consequences are met. Turning to the settings of interpretive activities suggests a similar conceptualization of interpretive practices that fall between the conventionalized interpretive projects Bourdieu called "doxa" (such as, here, tribe models) and the total surround of taken-for-granted knowledge and consequences he called "habitus" (here, notions of "character," "nature," and racialism). It is in this intermediate ground that social institutions and interpretive practices (such as personnel selection, bureaucracy, and philological methods) mingle and can be seen either way (Figure 3).

Viewed as extended conversations, Frontier genres reflect and constitute the situations of their composition. These conversations extended over generations through citation and reuse of older material amalgamated with new, in the establishment of restricted codes of institutional communication, and in common themes and topics. They also emerge in multiple voices, overlapping topics, and differentiated, often contradictory perspectives brought together in time and space, which they only in part measure. Far from being akin to notes in bottles, such texts record additional and more social properties of extended conversations rather than the flatter ones of either objectivizing description or dialogue with subjects. These are features of social organization that practically organize an ambiguous middle ground between macroscopic structures and microscopic processes. It is on a middle ground between paradigm and practice that the social organization of ethnographic knowledge composes not just individual texts but the corpus(es) in which texts are most immediately related to each other as parts of an extended conversation. Between the selective abstractions of structure and the totalizing engagement of practice we find more interesting candidates for addressing issues that polarize in these terms.

Interest in texts and their deconstruction belongs with wider interests than that of ethnographic accounting. Arguments in anthropology about textual constructions of knowledge converge with arguments in the philosophy of science about hiatuses between objectivity and relativity. Ethnographies hardly need to be relativized further. In sociology, they already occupy the low status of "qualitative" inquiry, more appropriate to first steps, a mere first step to serious "quantitative" investigation. In anthropology, their status is marginally better; they are its central documents and proofs of theory (in practice), but they are also commonly characterized as "art" forms, and not the objectivity and system that ethnography continues to seek. To embrace attitudes taken from art does not make them clearer. Critical stances toward methodological objectivity in the social sciences, like Habermas's (1975), or

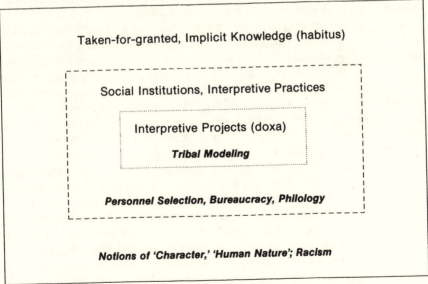

Figure 3.   The social organization of knowledge (Bourdieu 1977).

Gadamer's (1960) more hermeneutic approach, are echoed in analytic and hermeneutic critiques down to the postcolonial and deconstructive critiques that focus on individual texts or on their most distant contexts, while ignoring the more immediate settings of texts in a corpus that emerges over time as an extended conversation. The declared crisis of representation (Marcus and Fischer 1986; Fabian 1990) is a crisis of formulating the problematics of description in narrations of one's own historical situation, in ethnography no less than in more analytic approaches (Brown 1987).

Here, I look at analysts and analyze analysis, but not to judge it or them against later standards. These works are still dated and anachronistic. But outlining some of the gross features of textualizations that unfold in time and (social) space can show narrative structures not just as text but also as an organization that is problematic in its own right. As Trilling pointed out before the deconstructive turn,[3] what we miss in the past that we know intimately in the present is culture's "hum and buzz of implication." Something else fills the space where inquiry does not go. Any conversation carries and is carried by silences, which, while complementing it, are not another order of fact but part of the same ordering in different media for different messages and so data of the same sort as any particular limited range. The mistake of critiques that flatten ethnographies to texts is that they seize upon one or another clearly limited model—whether interrogation, eavesdropping, or "dialogue"—when on internal evidence alone a restricted form cannot be the source of properties of its broader setting.

Colonial ethnography is deeply paradoxical and ambiguous in its own setting. It is interested in both what it brings *and* what it finds in the world. It is constructed, but not solipsistic, even when fanciful, because it is so clearly socially organized. It is practical and self-reflective, but within limits enforced by traditions that emerge and change over time, often in response to something else, also socially organized. Neither ideology nor inscriptive practice wholly accounts for it because neither wholly encompasses its situation or that of the other. These and other properties are not, however, obscure save in the elision of their historical situation and development as interpretive practices and problems. A corpus of colonial ethnography, a genre despised for its provenances, has the characteristics of Kuhn's (1972) paradigms: a large part of it consists of additions, deletions, and amendments within (and also to) frames of problematizing what is to be understood, and in which interest is ultimately abandoned for at least partly extrinsic reasons.

None of this warrants a new particularism. The properties of a corpus that situate its texts between macrostructure and microprocess suggest a way out of the impasse between deterministic (analytic) and hermeneutic (interpretive) perspectives. What cannot be in texts, only between them, is the development of a corpus, the one truly social feature of interpretation. Arguments from macrostructure and microprocess both overlook the middle ground, where those meet as partial descriptions. This middle ground helps reunite traditional views of culture as shared, unified, and consensual with contemporary visions of heteroglossia and actors who are also listeners, without accepting everything they hear, or rejecting it.

Acknowledgments

This paper is based on research supported by grants from the National Science Foundation for fieldwork in Afghanistan (GS-30275), the National Museum of Norway for research at the India Office Library (London), the Smithsonian Institution, and the Fulbright Program for research in Pakistan. I am also grateful to Myron Aronoff, John Baines, Richard Brown, Phyllis Chock, Jean-Paul Dumont, Dale Eickelman, Johannes Fabian, Graham Fuller, and Richard Handler for helpful comments on earlier drafts.

Notes

1. The critique has been pressed for this region by Akbar Ahmed (1976, 1987, 1988), who as a political officer has also been instrumental in resurrecting for republication in Pakistan some of the substantial body of Frontier ethnography from the colonial period, among others Howell (1931), King (1900), McMahan and Ramsay (1901), and Merk (1898).
2. Curiously, the proponents of this idea were philologians from Sir William Jones, who discovered the Indo-European language family through his studies of Sanskrit, and the Pakhtu lexicographer Henry G. Raverty (1867). Pakhtu is an Indo-European, not a Semitic language.
3. I am grateful to Ruel Tyson for bringing Trilling's (1953) essay to my attention.

References

Ahmed, Akbar S. 1976. *Millennium and Charisma among Pathans: A Critical Essay in Social Anthropology*. London: Routledge and Kegan Paul.
———. 1980. *Pukhtun Economy and Society: Traditional Structure and Economic Development in a Tribal Society*. London: Routledge and Kegan Paul.
———. 1987. *Toward Islamic Anthropology: Definition, Dogma, and Directions*. Lahore: Vanguard Books.
———. 1988. *Discovering Islam: Making Sense of Muslim History and Society*. London: Routledge and Kegan Paul.

Anderson, Jon W. 1975. "Tribe and community among Ghilzai Pakhtun." *Anthropos* 70:575–601.

———. 1980. "Segmentary Lineages Are Primitive Classifications." Paper presented at the School of Oriental and African Studies, London.

———. 1982. "Cousin Marriage in Context: Constructing Social Relations in Afghanistan." *Folk* 24/25:7–28.

———. 1983. "Khan and Khel: Dialectics of Pakhtun Tribalism." In *The Conflict of Tribe and State in Iran and Afghanistan*, edited by Richard Tapper. London: Croom Helm.

———. 1984. "How Afghans Define Themselves in Relation to Islam." In *Revolutions and Rebellions in Afghanistan*, edited by M. N. Shahrani and R. L. Canfield. Berkeley, CA: Institute for International Studies.

Archer, Margaret S. 1988. *Culture and Agency: The Place of Culture in Social Theory.* Cambridge: Cambridge University Press.

Asad, Talal. 1973. *Anthropology and the Colonial Encounter.* New York: Humanities Press.

Baden-Powell, B. H. 1896. *The Indian Village Community.* London: Longmans, Green.

Bakhtin, Mikhail M. and Pavel N. Medvedev. 1978. *The Formal Method in Literary Scholarship: A Critical Introduction to Sociological Poetics.* Translated by Albert J. Wehrle. Baltimore: Johns Hopkins University Press.

Ballhatchet, Kenneth. 1980. *Race, Sex and Class under the Raj: Imperial Attitudes and Policies and their Critics, 1793–1905.* London: St. Martin's.

Barth, Fredrik. 1959. *Political Leadership among Swat Pathan.* London: Athlone.

Beidelman, T. O. 1982. *Colonial Evangelism: A Socio-Historical Study of an East African Mission at the Grassroots.* Bloomington: Indiana University Press.

Bellew, Henry W. 1891. *An Inquiry into the Ethnography of Afghanistan.* Woking: Oriental University Institute.

———. 1920. *Afghanistan, A Political Mission in 1857, with an Account of the Country and People.* (Reprinted, Lahore: Sh. Mubarak Ali, 1978.)

Berry, Willard. 1966. "Aspects of the Frontier Crimes Regulation in Pakistan." Duke University Program in Comparative Studies on Southern Asia, Durham, NC.

Bourdieu, Pierre. 1977. *Outline of a Theory of Practice.* Translated by Richard Nice. Cambridge: Cambridge University Press.

Braibanti, Ralph, et al. 1966. *Asian Bureaucratic Systems Emergent from the British Imperial Tradition.* Durham, NC: Duke University Press.

Broadfoot, James S. 1886. "Reports on Part of the Ghilzai Country, and Some Tribes in the Neighborhood of Ghazni and on the Route from Ghazni to Dera Ismail Khan by the Ghwalari Pass." *Journal of the Royal Geographical Society of Bengal, Supplementary Papers* 1:341–402 (orig. 1839).

Brown, Richard H. 1987. "Positivism, Relativism and Narrative in the Logic of the Historical Sciences: A Review Article." *American Historical Review* 92:908–20.

Burke, Edmund. 1972. "The Image of the Moroccan State in French Ethnological Literature: A New Look at the Origin of Lautey's Berber Policy." In *Arabs and Berbers: From Tribe to Nation in North Africa,* edited by Ernest Gellner and Charles Michaud. London: Duckworth.

Burke, Kenneth. 1957. *The Philosophy of Literary Form: Studies in Symbolic Action.* New York: Vintage Books.

Burnes, Sir Alexander. 1834. *Travels into Bokhara.* London: John Murray.

———. 1842. *Cabool: Being a Personal Narrative of a Journey to, and Residence in that City, in the Years 1836, 7, and 8.* London: John Murray.

Burrow, J. W. 1966. *Evolution and Society: A Study in Victorian Social Theory.* Cambridge: Cambridge University Press.

Caroe, Sir Olaf. 1958. *The Pathans, 550 BC–AD 1957.* London: Macmillan.

Christensen, Asger. 1982. "Agnates, Affines, and Allies: Patterns of Marriage among Pakhtun in Kunar, Northern Afghanistan." *Folk* 24/25:29–64.

Churchill, Winston. 1898. *The Story of the Malakand Field Force: An Episode of Frontier War.* London: Longmans, Green.

Clifford, James. 1983. "On Ethnographic Authority." *Representations* 1:118–46.

Clifford, James and George Marcus, eds. 1986. *Writing Culture: The Poetics and Politics of Ethnography.* Berkeley: University of California Press.

Derrida, Jacques. 1978. *Writing and Difference.* Translated by Alan Bates. Chicago: University of Chicago Press.

Dorn, Bernard, trans. 1892. *History of the Afghans.* London: Oriental Translation Committee.

Elphinstone, Montstuart. 1812. *Account of the Kingdom of Caubul and Its Dependencies in Persia, Tartary, and India.* London: John Murray. (Reprinted, Graz: Akademische Druck- und Verlagsanstalt, 1969.)

Embree, Ainslie T. 1977. "Pakistan's Imperial Legacy." In *Pakistan's Western Borderlands,* edited by A. T. Embree. Durham, NC: Carolina Academic Press.

Fabian, Johannes. 1990. "Presence and Representation: The Other and Anthropological Writing." *Critical Inquiry* 16:752–72.

Ferrier, James P. 1857. *Caravan Journeys and Wanderings in Persia, Afghanistan, Turkistan and Beloochistan, with Historical Notices of the Countries Lying between Russia and India.* London: John Murray. (Reprinted, Karachi: Oxford University Press, 1976.)

———. 1858. *History of the Afghans.* London: John Murray.

Feyerabend, Paul. 1972. *Against Method: Outline of an Anarchistic Theory of Knowledge.* London: Verso.

Foucault, Michael. 1971. *The Order of Things: An Archaeology of the Human Sciences.* New York: Pantheon Books.

Fraser-Tytler, Sir Kerr. 1967. *Afghanistan.* 3rd ed. (orig., 1950). London: Oxford University Press.

Gadamer, Hans Georg. 1960. *Truth and Method.* New York: Seabury Press.

Geertz, Clifford. 1988. *Works and Lives: The Anthropologist as Author.* Stanford, CA: Stanford University Press.

General Staff of India. 1933. *Handbook of Kandahar Province.* Simla: Government of India.

Giddens, Anthony. 1979. *Central Problems in Social Theory: Action, Structure and Contradiction in Social Analysis.* Berkeley: University of California Press.

———. 1982. "Hermeneutics and Social Theory." In *Profiles and Critiques in Social Theory*. Berkeley: University of California Press.

Government of India. ca.1904. *North-West Frontier Province. Imperial Gazetteer of India, Provincial Series.* (Reprinted, Lahore: Sang-e-Meel Publications, 1979.)

Habermas, Jürgen. 1975. *Legitimation Crisis.* Boston: Beacon Press.

Handler, Richard. 1985. "On Dialogue and Destructive Analysis: Problems in Narrating Nationalism and Ethnicity." *Journal of Anthropological Research* 41:171–82.

Howell, Evelyn. 1931. *Mizh: A Monograph on Government Relations with the Mahsud Tribe.* Simla: Government of India. (Reprinted, Karachi: Oxford University Press, 1979.)

Hymes, Dell, et al. 1969. *Reinventing Anthropology.* New York: Pantheon.

Kakar, Hasan Kawun. 1979. *Government and Society in Afghanistan: The Reign of Amir Abd al-Rahman Khan.* Austin: University of Texas Press.

Kennedy, Charles H. 1982. "Technocrats and the Generalist Mystique: Physicians, Engineers, and the Administrative System of Pakistan." *Journal of Asian and African Studies* 17:98–121.

King, L. White. 1900. *The Orakzai Country and Clans.* Simla: Government of India Press. (Reprinted, Lahore: Vanguard Books, 1984.)

Kuhn, Thomas. 1972. *The Structure of Scientific Revolutions.* Chicago: University of Chicago Press.

Lindholm, Charles. 1980. "Images of the Pathan: The Usefulness of Colonial Ethnography." *Archives europeennes de Sociologie* 21:350–61.

Maine, Sir Henry. 1861. *Ancient Law.* Oxford: Oxford University Press.

———. 1871. *Village Communities in the East and West.* Oxford: Oxford University Press.

Malleson, G. B. 1878. *History of Afghanistan, from the Earliest Period to the Outbreak of the War of 1878.* (Reprinted, Peshawar: Saeed Book Bank, 1984.)

Marcus, George and Dick Cushman. 1982. "Ethnographies as Text." *Annual Review of Anthropology* 11:25–69.

Marcus, George and Michael Fischer. 1986. *Anthropology as Cultural Critique.* Chicago: University of Chicago Press.

Mascia-Lees, Frances E., Patricia Sharpe, and Colleen Ballerino Cohen. 1989. "The Postmodernist Turn in Anthropology: Cautions from a Feminist Perspective." *Signs* 15:7–33.

Masson, Charles H. 1842. *Narrative of Various Journeys in Balochistan, Afghanistan and the Panjab, Including a Residence in those Countries from 1826 to 1838.* London: John Murray (Reprinted, Graz: Akademische Druck- und Verlagsanstalt, 1975).

Mayne, Peter. 1955. *The Narrow Smile.* London: Allen and Unwin.

McMahon, A. H. and Ramsay, D. G. 1901. *Report on the Tribes of Dir, Swat and Bajour Together with the Utman-Khel and Sam Ranizai.* Calcutta: Superintendent of Government Printing. (Reprinted, Peshawar: Tribal Affairs Research Cell, 1981.)

Merk, W. H. R. 1898. *The Mohmands.* Simla: Government of India. (Reprinted, Lahore: Vanguard Books, 1984.)

Mill, James. 1975. *The History of British India*. Chicago: University of Chicago Press. (Abridged from the second edition of 1820.)

Priestly, Henry, trans. 1874. *Afghanistan and Its Inhabitants, Translated from the "Hayat-i-Afghan" of Muhamad Hayat Khan, C.S.I.* Lahore: Indian Public Opinion Press. (Reprinted, Lahore: Sang-e-Meel Publications, 1981.)

Raverty, Henry G. 1867. *A Grammar of Puk'hto, or the Language of the Afghans*. 3rd edition. London: William Norgate.

——. 1888. *Notes on Afghanistan and Baluchistan, Geographical, Ethnographical, and Historical; Extracted from the Writings of Little Known Afghan and Tajik Historians, Geographers, and Genealogists; the Histories of the Ghuris, the Turk Sovereigns of the Dihli Kingdom, the Mughal Sovereigns of the House of Timur, and Other Muhammedan Chronicles; and from Personal Observations*. (Reprinted, Sang-e-Meel Publications, Lahore, 1976.)

Rawlinson, Henry. 1841. "Report on the Durrani Tribes." (Reprinted in the Gazetteer of Afghanistan, Part V: Kandahar, General Staff of India, 1910.)

Ricoeur, Paul. 1985. *Temps et récit*. Paris: Editions du Seuil.

Robinson, J. A. 1934. *Notes on the Nomad Tribes of Eastern Afghanistan*. Simla: General Staff of India. (Reprinted, Quetta: Nisa Traders, 1978.)

Rosenthal, Michael. 1986. *The Character Factory: Baden-Powell and the Origins of the Boy Scout Movement*. New York: Pantheon.

Silverstein, Michael. 1976. "Shifters, Linguistic Categories and Cultural Description." In *Meaning in Anthropology*, edited by Keith H. Basso and Henry A. Selby. Albuquerque: University of New Mexico Press.

Stokes, Eric. 1959. *The English Utilitarians in India*. Oxford: Oxford University Press.

Tapper, Richard. 1983. "Introduction." In *The Conflict of Tribe and State in Iran and Afghanistan*, edited by Richard Tapper. London: Croom Helm.

Tapper, Nancy and Richard Tapper. 1982. "Marriage Preferences and Ethnic Relations among Durrani Pashtuns of Afghan Turkestan." *Folk* 24/25:157–78.

Trilling, Lionel. 1953. *The Liberal Imagination*. Garden City, NY: Doubleday-Anchor.

Trousdale, William. 1985. "Introduction." In *The War in Afghanistan, 1879–90, the Personal Diary of Major General Sir Charles Metcalfe MacGregor*. Detroit: Wayne State University Press.

White, Hayden. 1978. *Tropics of Discourse: Essays in Cultural Criticism*. Baltimore: Johns Hopkins University Press.

Wylly, Harold C. 1912. *From the Black Mountain to Waziristan*. London: Macmillan.

Yapp, Malcolm. 1980. *Strategies of British India: Britain, Iran and Afghanistan, 1798–1850*. Oxford: Clarendon Press.

Chapter 8

Listening for the Silences:
The Rhetorics of the Research Field

Joseph R. Gusfield

Conferences and publications on rhetoric in the social sciences are no longer an exotic rarity in academic life. If they are not as common as dirt they are not as surprising as snow in Samoa. Such occasions are part of that attentiveness to language and text that is part of the intellectual movements of the past two decades. It is a movement that I like to call the "linguistics revolution" and is part of what many now are calling "postmodernism" (Lyotard 1984). It is actuated by many currents of thought, most notably by the structural influences of Lévi-Strauss and Noam Chomsky. These have turned intellectual concerns toward one or another focus on the "deep structures" of cognition and communication. They have led us to become analysts of text and discourse in realms where such methods have been absent. They portend a world in which we are all linguists in the morning, philosophers in the afternoon, and literary critics at night.

In the social sciences this emergence of interest in rhetoric is part of the way in which humanistic disciplines, especially literature and philosophy, and social sciences, especially anthropology and sociology, have been developing common meeting ground. The turn toward the study of rhetoric in philosophy, literature, and history preceded that in the social sciences (Burke 1951; Booth 1961; White 1973, Gusfield 1989). It is largely from the literary studies that the new rhetoricians of social science have borrowed their analyses and discussions (Brown 1977, 1987; Edmondson 1984; Geertz 1980; Gusfield 1976, 1981a,b; McCloskey 1985). This historical path of borrowing has been immensely productive of new ideas but has also encountered some hurdles. The hurdles are resident in the differences between humanistic studies and social science.

In recent years there has emerged what Herbert W. Simons refers to as "the rhetorical turn" (Simons 1990). That turn has involved the rhetorical and literary examination of social research as a method of inquiry. In that endeavor the research report—the written report of the social scientist in the form of articles, books, and other studies—has been the subject of analysis (Bazerman 1988; Rosaldo 1987; Gusfield 1976, 1981a,b, 1991; McCloskey 1985). This paper is, I hope, one link in a chain of studies that may develop a study of rhetoric that is sensitive to the special character of the social sciences.

The Rhetoric of the Field

Social Science and the "State of the Art"

Humanistic studies have a long tradition of studying texts and specific authors. In many ways it is the distinguishing characteristic of humanistic as distinguished from social science studies. Much of literary study has been preoccupied with the stuff of "high culture"—the "great books" of philosophers, historians, playwrights, novelists, and poets. What humanistic and social scientific academicians and intellectuals have come to share in the social sciences are the master theorists and the contemporary "stars." It is Durkheim and Marx, Goffman and Giddens, that are the common area of social science that humanistic scholars share with social scientists. Here the rhetoric of literary study, in the examination of the text, can be borrowed with little strain. Discursive and analytical work examining the literary and rhetorical styles of classical sociological theorists is another burgeoning industry (Brown 1977, 1987; Green 1988).

Much of social science, however, is of a humbler, less exalted variety. It consists of soda pop rather than of French champagne. It is here that the social sciences have had much influence both in shaping perceptions and in affecting policies and public judgments. These studies are not widely circulated nor do they generally produce the single, definitive research that goes undisputed and universally applauded. Their impact comes less from any specific text than from the total impact, the corpus of a field. In the case of studies of alcohol, on which I will dwell in this paper, they are found in specialized journals, in chapters of books (rather than entire books), in government reports, and in conference proceedings. Occasionally they are reported in book form. Very often they are not the product of a single mind but are the collaborative effort of several people. They are specialized and narrowed reports of field research, historical investigation, or, in most cases, presentation of statistical analyses of data derived from official records or survey questionnaires. It is these kinds of texts, organized into a field, a literature, that will occupy my attention in this paper.[1]

Of course we can examine such research as specific instances of text, and some of that has been done in the materials discussed above. But there is another kind of rhetoric that is perhaps more significant. It is the rhetoric of the field, of the corpus of studies in a particular area. Here the total framework of assumptions and interests persuades the audience by the way in which the object of study is delineated and described. Any single text is less significant for this kind of analysis than the framework of questions and assumptions in which the study is set and which forms the directive thrust. No one study will yield the way in which a set of assumptions constitutes a dominant paradigm for constructing phenomena. It will provide an understanding of the rhetoric of a single study but, by ignoring the total effect of a field, tells us little about what is not studied. It gives us the voices but not the silences.

Somewhere in his writings Merleau-Ponty refers to the importance of "listening to the silences" as a way of understanding the impacts of texts. What textual analysis lacks is the understanding of what is excluded from the area occupied by the corpus of studies. What is not studied is as important as what is studied. Research, even in the natural sciences, can be seen as a relationship between the researcher and a projected audience to whom it will be addressed (Latour and Woolgar 1979; Bazerman 1988). It can be examined to see what is *not* addressed and how, by excluding specific phenomena, the reader may be persuaded to believe. Such persuasion need not be a matter of the awareness of the authors but is often so embedded in the total frame of reference, the *mentalité*, that the author of any single study is often only dimly aware of it. This kind of rhetoric is part of what Gramsci referred to as cultural hegemony (Gramsci 1972; Joll 1978; Williams 1977). It restricts and channels what is thinkable and unthinkable.

A process of social construction is necessarily involved in research through the assumed objectives and directives of study. In the process of choosing what to include and what to exclude the investigator determines the character of the object being observed and analyzed. In their seminal book, *Constructing Social Problems*, Malcolm Spector and John Kitsuse use as an example of this process the diverse ways in which two sociologists might study, and thus define, a seemingly similar behavior: "If a sociologist of occupations studying prostitution would look for people earning their livings, a sociologist of social problems would look for people engaged in defining (or promoting) the prostitution problem" (1977:75).

This distinction is not devoid of rhetorical effect. By depicting the subject in one fashion rather than another it is identified in a particular manner. That manner carries with it an attitude, an evaluation that alternative conceptions might serve as contrasting identifications. In the distinction between studying prostitution as a social problem or as an occupation the analogies drawn upon differ. To be a member of the labor force normalizes and purifies; to be a problem does the opposite.

Characteristically social science studies in a field contain not a few research reports but number in the hundreds. The so-called state of the art has a high density. When I did my major study of drinking and driving, in the late 1970s, I read approximately 300 studies (Gusfield 1981a). There are now many, many more. The abstracting organization, Sociological Abstracts, draws on 1,800 journals in sociology and linguistics.

The New Rhetoric and the Old

In an older, more traditional rhetoric the lack of intention to persuade might exempt these considerations from rhetorical analysis. In what is now called "the new rhetoric," however, such considerations are appropriate (Perelman and Olbrechts-Tyteca 1969). The pejorative implications of rhetoric as a kind of deluding or propagandistic mode of argument has been superseded by rhetoric as a study of persuasion in general, including science as well as art. Any effort to persuade an audience contains a rhetoric whether or not the speaker or writer is so aware. It carries an argument, explicitly or implicitly.

The focus of the older rhetoric was deliberate design. The focus of the new rhetoric is on the production of an effect in an audience and can then include a less directed and conscious design. The older rhetoric itself contained a rhetoric of disapproval; it carried a connotation of unfair persuasion, of propaganda and commercial advertising. The new rhetoric is the study of argument and persuasion as a facet of human interaction, of reason as well as emotion.

Kenneth Burke, who has both antedated and led the return of rhetoric, views the key word of the old rhetoric as "persuasion" and the key term of the new as "identification" (Burke 1951). And that is what I am about in this paper. I shall argue that an analysis of a corpus of studies can reveal how what is and what is not identified as the objects of study acts to affect the perception the audience comes to have about the phenomena studied. That identity comes from and in turn affects what is studied in the entire field. Research reports, like literature in general, convey images that are identifications of the author, the audience, and the objects of study. What they exclude is as important as what they contain. Insofar as an entire field is dominated by a single perspective toward its subject it cannot avoid a rhetoric by silence.

Sin to Sickness: The Construction of Alcoholism

I will examine the field of "alcohol studies" over the past forty years with an eye toward the construction of the audience, the speaker, and the subject of study. The term that has come into use by the social scientist, "alcohol studies," is a self-confining term. It carries an image of the study of a chemical compound. In point of fact, much of the social study in this field is, and has been, of drunkenness and the people whose drinking is presumed to cause trouble for themselves and/or others.

While the field has studied drinking and drunkenness, it has done so from one point of reference, with one frame in use. In the field of alcohol studies, the dominant frame has been that of pathology, of drinking as a source of danger and injury. It is as a social problem that the research studies constituting the field of alcohol studies define, describe, and analyze acts of drinking in the United States. In this fashion, drinking is implicitly described as dangerous to the drinker and to others. In this process, I am arguing, the acts of drinking and drunkenness are stripped of any appreciation and the conflicts over the moral and political legitimacy of using alcohol are ignored or converted into justification of moral deviance. It is this consequence that constitutes the political significance of the rhetoric of the alcohol studies field. The construction of such consensus is a frequent characteristic of a social problems rhetoric.

The characterization of the field was stated well in 1964 by two research investigators and, I assert, has not much changed since. It is that of the pathological framework:

> A primary reason why research attention has typically been directed to the pathological aspects of alcohol is that all drinking has frequently been conceived as abnormal, and/or as only a prelude to alcoholism. From this point-of-view the distinction between drinking, drunkenness and alcoholism has often been reduced to one of degree and duration. This focus on the most visible and dramatic aspects of alcohol use has placed a decisive stamp on orientations to the study of drinking, on the formulation of research questions, and on the types of explanations of drinking behavior which have been proposed. The personal and social dysfunctions of drinking have been emphasized to the exclusion of any broader consider-ations of drinking as an acceptable form of social behavior. (Maddox and McCall 1964; quoted in Cahalan, Cisin, and Crossley 1969)

The Alcoholism Movement

The repeal of the Eighteenth Amendment was a bitter crisis for the temperance and prohibition movements. During the 1930s and the 1940s drinking disappeared from the agenda of public and even medical attention. As it again appeared in the 1950s and 1960s, it did so in a new form: as an illness that struck a particular class of people—alcoholics (Beauchamp 1980). A sharp line was drawn between the "normal" drinker, for whom drinking presented no problem, and the addicted and afflicted "abnormal" drinker-persons who posed a problem to themselves and to the community in which they lived.

The rise of the alcoholism movement was accompanied by three developments: Alcoholics Anonymous, the emergence of a profession of alcohol therapists, and the development of a science of alcohol studies. All of these contributed to the depiction of the "alcohol problem" as the problem of alcoholism (Beauchamp 1980; Gusfield 1982). The organizations that emerged, the attention of public agencies and debate, and the concerns voiced all were dominated by efforts to explain and understand and to change the status of the victim, the alcoholic, from a state of addiction to one of sobriety.

The major vehicle for this attempted change was the portrayal of the alcoholic as ill, as the victim of a disease, alcoholism. A great deal of study and discussion has gone into the analysis of the disease concept of alcoholism (Room 1983; Conrad and Schneider 1980). Certainly one result of the shift from the "habitual drunkard" or "chronic inebriate" to the "alcoholic" was to absolve the person from a moral status, as a sinner undeserving of public support, to a status of someone analogous to other patients, as sick. But another result was to make a sharp distinction between the majority of drinkers and the peculiar person of the alcoholic. In this way the alcoholic comes to wear the garb of a true "deviant." Alcoholism and alcoholics were the almost uniform objects of study in the field.

This concentration on the "pathology" of addictive drinking "said" that for most people in American society, drinking did not create a problem, for themselves or for others. If drinking was a problem of public concern it was the arena of a deviant population—the alcoholic (Beauchamp 1980). The intellectual problem, the problem of research, was to determine why some people could not drink "normally" and to restore them to sobriety.

So deeply has the alcoholism frame of attention been infused into our perceptions and conceptions that academics and laypeople most often refer to anyone studying drinking as working on the problem of "alcoholism." In the 1950s, 1960s, and well into the 1970s, the field was almost entirely devoted to studying the attributes of that deviant population. The problem of therapy—of finding a way to treat the alcoholic—was the dominant and dominating subject of social research. The key questions were those of the cause and treatment of the alcoholic. The famous Yale Summer School of Alcohol Studies was narrowly directed toward alcoholism as the single subject of study (Keller 1974).

In what guise and with what voice does the researcher address his/her audience? The voice of such research is that of the untroubled researcher doing something to help a less able subject—the alcoholic. The emergence of professionals in this field was similarly based on alcoholism as the problem of drinking. (I have referred to this professionalism as the "troubled persons industries.") Having for many years defined chronic drunkenness or habitual inebriation as a matter of moral choice, the shift from sin to sickness inherent in the disease concept made it possible to consider the treatment of alcoholics as a medical and thus a professional function. The authors appear as professionals or as academics whose findings and conclusions will be of use to the professional. As such the drinking habits and styles of the author and the audience are not part of the identity such studies create. (The one deviation from this is the writing of those identified as recovering alcoholics whose abstinence is central to their persona.)

Constructing the Deviant

One significant result of defining alcohol problems in this manner is, in benign fashion, to ignore the study of drinking and the drinker who is not an alcoholic. In keeping with the medical model of disease, a sharp line is drawn between the chronic, addictive drinker and others. It portrays the alcoholic as incapacitated and leaves the impression that chronic alcoholism is utterly incompatible with modern economic and occupational activities, that it is a uniform and identical illness wherever found. "Normal" drinking is not an intellectual or practical problem and is not an object of study. It remains a terra incognita. The sharp line between the normal and the deviant is undisturbed.

Indeed, deviance is defined by the clear outlines of the boundary between the "normal" and the "pathological." The deviance of the alcoholic population is conveyed and constructed through the absence of other populations as objects of study. The exclusion of other than alcoholics or of "ordinary" drinking as objects of study creates the boundaries between deviance and normality. "Ordinary" drinking does not pose an intellectual or a social problem. It is not worth studying.

This assumption constrained social research into drinking. For example, although it was known that some who declared themselves to be suffering from excessive drinking carried on many useful activities, either while sober or while not sober, how the alcoholic could do this was never studied. Thus Dick Van Dyke, the TV comic actor, in declaring himself an alcoholic, maintained that he was never drunk on the set. Nor were the dangers and difficulties that came from occasional or episodic drunkenness studied. Identifying the public problem as that of alcoholics persuades both the researcher and the audience that the problem is not theirs. Pogo's aphorism need have no relevance: "We has met the enemy and he is us."

The perception of the alcoholic as a particular kind of person and the major "social problem" placed the researcher in the position of the "society" as concerned with the welfare of "troubled persons." The disease paradigm, in turn, drew attention away from the study of nonpathological drinking or the nonpathological aspects of alcoholism. Was it possible that some people could drink heavily, even addictively, and not encounter "troubles"? This was unstudied. Is it possible that people who were not imagined as "addicts" could be charged with creating "trouble" through their drinking? Could some of the dangers associated with drinking be connected with "normal" drinkers? What we do not visualize or imagine as a subject of study is not as likely to be an object of thought as that to which our attention is directed.

The resulting rhetoric can be sketched as follows: The social problem of drinking is that of deviant people who are addicted to drinking. The "ordinary" drinker is not a problem to himself or to others. The study of drinking or drunkenness as a general activity does not merit study. As a social as well as an intellectual endeavor it is "unproblematic." Therefore it is not studied. The audience is presumed to have no interest in what is not a social problem. In this fashion a sharp line is drawn between the audience and the reader, on the one hand, and the object of the research—the alcoholic—on the other hand. The object of concern, of pathology, is thus clearly differentiated as unlike the "you and I" of the audience and the author.

The frame of alcoholism contributes to the first of the silences on which I comment in this paper. The intellectual and the social problems are intertwined. The object of study is confined to "deviant" drinking and pathology attributed to that group alone. By excluding other possible pathologies of alcohol use, such as driving, job performance, or personal interaction, the social problem becomes wholly that of alcoholism. By not studying drinking behavior in diverse, nonalcoholic segments of the population, presumably not pathological, all nonalcoholic drinking is legitimated. Being attentive to one part of the spectrum serves to enhance and support the rest of the spectrum by default.

The paradigm of research and the definition of what is both researchable and worthy of research has hidden an entire range of behavior. What is more, it has eliminated any research into the elements that might help us understand drinking and drunkenness where they fail to lead to alcoholism. The assumption is that the alcoholic is sick or stupid or sinful. In any definition he or she is not "ordinary," and thus is not in the audience.

The "Malevolence Assumption" and Contemporary Research

In the early 1970s, as the federal government assumed more responsibility for support of the treatment of alcoholics and of research on alcohol problems, a less homogeneous perception of alcoholics and of "troubles" began to emerge. With the conception of the "problem drinker," the rigid image of the alcoholic career gave way to a more differentiated view of alcohol problems (Cahalan, Cisin, and Crossley 1969; Cahalan and Room 1974). Not only were personal difficulties often a phase rather than commitment to a permanent life-style, but other problems, such as industrial inefficiency and drinking-driving began to emerge into public attention. The drinker as troublesome to others as well as to him- or herself returned to public concerns.

Although research has been cast as the study of alcohol use or of drinking, the implicit focus has been on instances of drunkenness and the consequences of drunkenness. The study of drinking and driving is a further illustration of how the body of research casts its objects into the category of deviants and diminishes the construction of a problem as a political division of values and interests.

The "Malevolence Assumption"

In a review and assessment of the impact of alcohol on wife beating and child abuse, Claire Hamilton and James Collins, Jr., coined a useful phrase to describe a significant element in such research. It is a phrase that can also be used to characterize a great deal of current alcohol research. It is worth quoting a passage in detail:

> On the other hand, the family violence literature, especially that which deals with intervention strategies to address the problem, often assumes that alcohol is a cause of violence between family members. This literature is not theoretically satisfying. It is not explicit about how alcohol fits the causal scheme. The characteristics and details of violent events in the family that involve alcohol are not distinguished from those where alcohol is not present. A *"malevolence assumption"* appears to operate. An offender with a drinking problem or the presence of alcohol in an incident of family violence is assumed to demonstrate that alcohol has explanatory power. . . .
>
> The moral and political debates about alcohol and its effects have not been confined to the moral and political arenas. These perspectives also

have influenced scientific analyses and interpretation. This influence has often been expressed in the following logic: alcohol is destructive and evil, and therefore one is likely to find destruction and evil where alcohol is found. We refer to this as the "malevolence assumption" and it is an implicit attitude in much of what is written on family violence." (1982:261; emphasis added)

Elsewhere I have examined the social construction of the problem of drinking-driving (Gusfield 1981a). Here I want to point to several ways in which the research on drinking-driving, through the assumption of malevolence, limits or hides the place of drinking-driving and drunkenness in the everyday lives of many drinkers. One is found in a clear use of the assumption that wherever alcohol use is found, it is the causal factor responsible for the accident. In the hundreds and hundreds of studies of drinking-driving, I have found only one that attempted to examine and assess the fault of the alcohol factor, or even the drinking motorist, in the accident (Boston University School of Law 1969). Studies assume that if alcohol was present it was the causative factor. The lack of research into the causal role of alcohol perpetuates the identification of drinking and drunkenness as causes of the damage and death. By not directly putting that assumption to the test, the possibility in any specific case that drinking was not responsible is difficult to be conceived.

The logic of this relationship needs to be stressed. I am not maintaining that use of alcohol does not increase the risks of driving. But that relationship is an aggregate one, based on statistical generalization. It does not imply that every time alcohol is in use that an accident will occur. Nor can it imply that in any single instance of accident drinking is necessarily the causal agent.

The rhetoric of the field is found in the silence on such alternative questions. That silence perpetuates the identification of the object of concern as the drunken motorist. Other elements in the complex nature of automobile use are lost to sight: the nature of the automobile, the character of the road, the existence of emergency medical facilities, and the existence of alternative modes of transportation are but a few of the alternative elements that might be given attention (Gusfield 1981a,b, 1985; Ross 1991).

The language is often even less definitive. Conclusions are often couched as "Alcohol was involved in x percent of the cases." From this, however, policy considerations are drawn as if a causal conclusion were established. Journalists and public officials are less cautious, moving easily from "involvement" to "cause" (Gusfield 1981a,b). In what is not studied, the way in which drinking was or was not "involved," the rhetoric of silence persuades us to identify the drinker as always the villain.

Making the World Safe for Drinkers

In two other ways the possible role of drinking and drinking-driving in the leisure and culture of groups is hidden. It is also evidenced less by what is studied than by what is not. In the first case, drinking-driving is studied apart from a context, as a specific activity with little placement of it in relation to purposes, interactions, or contexts of the life of the drinker. For example, in the hundreds and hundreds of drinking-driving studies there is none that seeks to understand how drinkers do manage to drive safely. Yet most of the times that motorists drive while not sober they do manage to get where they want to go. There is no research into possible ways in which drinkers might diminish risks in driving. There is a distinct repulsion toward studies that might entertain any suggestion that drinking might be less than dangerous. The deviant character of drinking and drunkenness is not examined for differences and diversities. It is not treated as a "natural" activity.

Here again the rhetoric of the field, in its bulk and persistence, identifies the social problem as that of the deviant: the person unlike you and me. Here again the intellectual problem, the subject of the research, shuts off the alternative definitions and assumptions. It does this by not examining "deviant cases," those which contradict the generalizations.

The second way in which alcohol studies of drinking-driving limit the perception of group conflicts is seen in the dominant place given to limiting drinking as the major countermeasure in drinking-driving literature. Possibilities of alternative transportation, safer autos, or technological devices, such as ignition interlocks, occupy a marginal place in the panoply of ways to curtail accidents and deaths attributed to drinking. One can also argue that the dominant attention to drinking as distinguished from such other safety measures as more one-way roads, wider use of safety belts, and vehicles designed with more safety features also helps create the dangerous and deviant character of drinking. This approach has also been labeled "making the world safe for drinkers."

Drinking *Problems and Drinking* Problems

Both of these silences create a significant rhetoric. They connect the problems attributed to drinking as drinking problems. This sounds tautological until we recognize that to focus on one part of a complex and interrelated activity is to ignore other parts of it. A simple illustration may make my point. Some years ago a university was troubled by two different fatal accidents, which had occurred to students who had driven across the nearby state border to purchase alcohol and had been killed on their return while driving under the influence. Concerned with preventing such deaths in the future, the university began to operate a bus to and from the border. What had been conceived as a problem of drinking was now conceived as a problem of transportation.

I do not tell this story to suggest policies about drinking-driving but to indicate that it is possible to study phenomena from a variety of stances. The stance chosen and the stances not chosen are both ways of describing the subject. To focus on drinking as the "cause" of a problem is to construct one way of looking at the phenomenon. Only recently have studies begun to appear that look at elements in the phenomenon of drinking-involved driving that are not drinking-related (Surgeon-General's Workshop on Drunken Driving 1988). The intensive focus on quantity consumed to the exclusion of other elements constitutes a moral choice among policies but it is bolstered and made more acceptable by silence on other ways of studying the same phenomenon.

What sustains that choice is the voice of the author as the spokesperson of the "society." It is here that I encounter another level of the rhetoric of the field.

The Politics of the Apolitical

The absence of research on the activity of drinking, pathological and nonpathological, and the contexts of the drinking activity contain another level of rhetoric. This level is subtler than that already discussed and more profound in understanding how cultural homogeneity and consensus is obtained in public spheres. Here the silence is that of inattention to the positive joys and appreciative pleasures of drinking. Ignoring these as intellectual problems accentuates the deviant character of drinking and excludes the understanding of drunkenness as many experience it. It is a rhetoric that implies that drinking is itself a social problem. To study it as a "natural" activity is to identify it as possibly valuable and acceptable within cultural values.

To study a phenomenon as a "natural" activity is to see it as neither pathological or nonpathological but as customary behavior. In the case of drinking, the absence of many studies of drinking ignores the many instances in which drunkenness and drinking are not pathological, involving harm neither to the drinker nor to others. It perpetuates an attitude of hostility to drinking per se. It leaves the impression that most drinking behavior is foolish, stupid, or sinful. It implicitly divides the world of alcohol users, for whom drunkenness is irrational and antisocial, from a world of abstainers or light drinkers.

The result of this silence is to present a field of studies as a neutral, apolitical set of activities. By not studying customary drinking behavior in many contexts other than those creating injuries, the field implies agreement about the character of drinking behavior. Where studies of drinking as a natural phenomenon might uncover conflicts within the community, exclusive framing in the language of social problems denies the existence of conflict. It thus frames an area of social behavior as one of consensus, as apolitical.

Costs without Benefits

Looked at as a corpus of advice, legislation, and public understandings, alcohol studies and policies add up to the condemnation of drunkenness. If the policies toward alcohol are discussed in terms of costs and benefits, the costs are the focus and the benefits are rendered invisible. A focus on benefits would involve study for whom and where and how drunkenness exists. It could redefine the issue as one of preserving benefits as much as is possible within policies for preventing or limiting costs.

The disposition to deny an adversarial quality to a social problem spills over into research. In the corpus of studies of alcohol I find not a one that has studied the benefits of drinking and drunkenness. The standard study of the economic costs of alcohol makes no attempt to state the value of benefits of alcohol as well as its costs (Berry and Boland 1977). Lost productivity and treatment costs, detriments of the use of alcohol, are not balanced against the taxes collected or the workers employed in alcohol industries. The cost of alcohol in causing crime is totaled but not the benefits that drunkenness can develop by making criminals unable to commit crimes and enabling them to get caught at it.

More importantly, there is no room for understanding the carnival point of view expressed by Omar Khayaam in the Rubaiyat:

> I often wonder what the vintner buys
> One-half so precious as the stuff he sells.

What then are we to make of the many people who occasionally and even frequently drink to a point of being affected? This is far from unusual. It is a common aspect of much partying behavior in the United States, for example. Are they sinful, stupid, or sick? What is the status of drinking and drunkenness? I have long been struck by the absence of research into the benefits of the use of alcoholic beverages, of being drunk, tight, high, or whatever descriptive words are used. The research speaks in the name of a society whose consensus does not admit the validity of drunkenness behavior.

Historical studies, community research, personal observation, and the literature of fiction all point to drinking as a great source of conflict between diverse cultures and classes (Burke 1978; Rosenzweig 1983; Brennan 1988). What has appeared as undue and unacceptable rowdiness occasioned by drinking has appeared to others as acceptable fun. What the historian of popular culture Peter Burke has referred to as the conflict between Carnival and Lent has pervaded Western societies and the United States perhaps especially (Burke 1978).

The Politics of Consensus Construction

The treatment of public issues is approached from several distinct stances or "voices." A phenomenon such as child abuse is characteristically addressed from a position of consensus. The speaker proceeds from the position of a "society," which is assumed to condemn the behavior. The child abuser is decidedly not accorded the role of an opposing point of view, a different set of values that constitutes a philosophical and political issue. The act of child abuse is a deviant act. Compare this with the pro- or antiabortion issue. Here the opposition may be disapproved and condemned but the speaker cannot easily lay claim to a consensus sufficient enough to enable him or her to speak for a united society. Transferred to the realm of property, the parallel of consensus about child abuse is condemnation of robbery, whereas the parallel of conflict over abortion is labor and management relations.

The consensual phenomena possess the quality of what Barbara Nelson calls a "valence issue" (Nelson 1984). Such an issue is one in which a consensus about its detriment exists. It is "above politics," above the need for discussion and argument. Political issues are not consensual or valence issues. They are matters of opposition about goals, standards, or criteria. In excluding one or another perspective toward a subject it is as if the moral standards of the community are clear and not a matter of opposition between groups. In this sense there is a rhetoric that attempts to establish the nonpolitical character of the laws the speaker supports. The persuasion to a consensus need not be a matter of awareness among the scholars in the field. It is, nevertheless, a consequence of the very frame in which the research is enclosed. It sets the boundaries and thus the perception of the field.

In an earlier work I have distinguished three forms of deviance based on the status, or meaning, that both the labelers and the labeled can confer on behavior (Gusfield 1963). I want to illustrate these by the various conceptions of the homosexual in America.

1. *The reluctant deviant*: Here the presumed deviant agrees with his or her labelers. The behavior may be seen as sinful and the deviant admits it. The homosexual who sees his or her sexuality as a deviation

from a preferred sexual life-style, who would prefer to be other, has this status.

2. *The sick deviant*: Here the behavior is seen as the result of elements beyond the control of the deviant. The metaphor of illness is the category of explanation. The deviant shares with the labeler the same view of behavior as contrary to "society." The view of homosexuality as a biological or psychiatric disorder is within this mode of characterizing homosexuality. It is analogous to a disease conception of alcoholism.

3. *The enemy deviant.* (I now prefer the term *resisting* rather than *enemy*.) Here the "deviant" does not accept the designation held out by labelers. Instead he or she insists on the "rightness" of his or her behavior. The movement for homosexual rights has turned the question of homosexual liberties into a political question. Insofar as the movement succeeds in establishing homosexuality as an ethically and politically neutral choice it will have even abolished the issue as a matter of public attention.

Contemporary research on alcohol has treated the drinker and drunkenness by silently placing them in the first two categories rather than the third. People who get drunk or drink "heavily" are sinful, stupid, or sick. Yet since drinking and drunkenness are prevalent behaviors in American society, they represent the behavior of many who are not alcoholics. Unlike the abortion issue, as a body of consumers "heavy drinkers" are unrepresented in the political arenas except by the alcohol industries, whose commercial advantages both encourage and undermine their rhetoric in defense of drinking.

To say that the aggregate of more than moderate drinking, of the occasional and episodic drunk, is not represented is not to say that it does not represent a perspective of political significance. I see the rhetoric of the research I am describing as serving an effort to minimize and offset the validity of an opposite point of view, one that would grant importance to drinking. Such a view would be directed toward the positive benefits of drinking for many and would be directed toward preserving these and avoiding the detrimental consequences. What constitute "positive benefits" and for whom and what constitute "detrimental consequences" and for whom are precisely the questions blurred by the rhetoric of the field in contemporary alcohol research. This is why I call it "the politics of the apolitical." By framing the phenomenon in the language of deviance the effort is made, not necessarily with awareness, to construct the issue as one of consensus.

In another set of perspectives, the very framing of the issues as ones of positive and negative benefits ignores and negates opposing frames.

The rational or Appolonian orientation toward life and society has by no means completely dominated modern society. A romantic and less disciplined Dionysian attitude is found not only as the possession of some groups but in the character and styles of many who also make up the vast population of disciplined members of the society. To imagine a society devoid of its carnival spirit is to create what many would see as a monstrosity. These differing orientations to life and to leisure are also at the heart of conflicts hidden by the silence of social problems research.

Both in the era of the "alcoholism movement" and its ethos of prevention, authors of research have appeared in the guise of spokespersons of the society. The subject has been identified by constructing its deviance. The impact of research in these areas has been to convince audiences that the author, the researcher, the scholar represents the "society," that the issue or phenomenon is the action of the abnormal, the deviant, the unusual. Implicitly, the phenomena are not those of differences in perspectives and policies. They are, consequently, "above politics."

It is in the denial of conflict that the rhetoric of silence serves to persuade. It is in the uncovering of conflict and alternatives that the rhetoric of the social scientist may also persuade. Too slavish a commitment to the single text and to what is written may lead us to overlook the silences and the ways in which silence makes its voice heard.

Phenomena do not exist in a pristine state as one or another kind of issue, one or another kind of deviant. They emerge from the activities of people. They are open to change and alteration. As social constructions they can be affected by the ways in which they are imagined and are perceived. This is where a rhetorical analysis of the status of "social problems" is useful to an understanding of how public phenomena are given body and how authority is created and seized in the arena of public problems.

Note

1. A major exception to this characterization is that of historical work. Here the book form is the most typical and influential form. Historical work, however, is not given much weight in the "state of the art" but treated as background information.

References

Bazerman, Charles. 1988. *The Shaping of Written Knowledge*. Madiscon: University of Wisconsin Press.

Beauchamp, Dan E. 1980. *Beyond Alcoholism*. Philadelphia: Temple University Press.

Berry, Ralph and James Boland. 1977. *The Economic Costs of Alcohol Abuse*. New York: The Free Press.

Booth, Wayne. 1961. *The Rhetoric of Fiction*. Chicago: University of Chicago Press.

Boston University School of Law. 1969. "Investigation of Thirty-one Fatal Automobile Accidents: Final Report." U.S. Department of Transportation, Bureau of Highway Safety, Washington, DC.

Brennan, Thomas. 1988. *Public Drinking and Popular Culture in Eighteenth Century France*. Princeton, NJ: Princeton University Press.

Brown, Richard Harvey. 1977. *A Poetic for Sociology*. Cambridge: Cambridge University Press.

———. 1987. *Society as Text*. Chicago: University of Chicago Press.

Burke, Kenneth. 1951. *A Rhetoric of Motives*. New York: Prentice-Hall.

Burke, Peter. 1978. *Popular Culture in Early Modern Europe*. New York: Harper and Row Torchbooks.

Cahalan, Don and Robin Room. 1974. *Problem Drinking among American Men*. New Brunswick, NJ: Rutgers Center of Alcohol Studies.

Cahalan, Don, Ira Cisin, and Helen Crossley. 1969. *American Drinking Practices*. New Brunswick, NJ: Rutgers Center of Alcohol Studies.

Conrad, Peter and Joseph Schneider. 1980. *Deviance and Medicalization*. St. Louis, MO: C. V. Mosby.

Edmondson, Ricca. 1984. *Rhetoric in Sociology*. London: MacMillan

Geertz, Clifford. 1980. "Blurred Genres." *American Scholar* (Spring).

Gramsci, Antonio. 1972. *Selections from The Prison Notebooks*. New York: International Publishers.

Green, Bryan. 1988. *Literary Methods and Sociological Theory: Case Studies of Simmel and Weber*. Chicago: University of Chicago Press.

Gusfield, Joseph. 1963. *Symbolic Crusade: Status Politics and the American Temperance Movement*. Urbana: The University of Illinois Press. (Second edition, 1986.)

———. 1976. "The Literary Rhetoric of Science: Comedy and Pathos in Drinking-Driving Research." *American Sociological Review* 41(Feb.).

———. 1981a. *The Culture of Public Problems: Drinking-Driving and the Symbolic Order*. Chicago: University of Chicago Press.

———. 1981b. "Managing Competence: An Ethnographic Study of Drinking-Driving and Barroom Behavior." In *Social Contexts of Drinking*, edited by Thomas Harford. Washington, DC: Dept. of Health and Human Services.

———. 1982. "Prevention: Rise, Decline and Renaissance." In *Alcohol, Science and Society*, edited by E. Gomberg, H. White and J. Carpenter. Ann Arbor: University of Michigan Press.

———. 1985. "Social and Cultural Contexts of the Drinking-Driving Event." *Journal of Studies on Alcohol, Supplement no. 10*, 70–77.

———. 1989. "Introduction." In *Kenneth Burke on Symbols and Society*, edited by J. Gusfield. Chicago: University of Chicago Press.

———. 1991. "Two Genres of Sociology: A Literary Analysis of the American Occupational Structure and Tally's Corner." In *The Rhetoric of Social Research*, edited by A. Hunter. New Brunswock, NJ: Rutgers University Press.

Hamilton, Claire and James Collins, Jr. 1982. "The Role of Alcohol in Wife Beating and Child Abuse." In *Drinking and Crime*, edited by J. Collins, Jr. London: Tavistock.

Joll, James. 1978. *Antonio Gramsci*. New York: Penguin.

Keller, Mark. 1974. "Problems with Alcohol: An Historical Perspective." In *Alcohol and Alcohol Problems: New Thinking and New Directions*, edited by W. Filstead, J. J. Rossi and M. Keller. Cambridge, MA: Ballinger.

Latour, Bruno and Steven Woolgar. 1979. *Laboratory Life.* Beverly Hills, CA: Sage.

Lyotard, Jean-Francois. 1984. *The Post-Modern Condition: A Report on Knowledge*. Minneapolis: University of Minnesota Press.

Maddox, George and B. C. McCall. 1964. *Drinking among Teen-agers*. New Brunswick, NJ: Rutgers Center for Alcohol Studies.

McCloskey, Donald. 1985. *The Rhetoric of Economics*. Madison: University of Wisconsin Press.

Nelson, Barbara. 1984. *Making an Issue of Child Abuse*. Chicago: University of Chicago Press

Perelman, Chaim and Lucie Olbrechts-Tyteca. 1969. *The New Rhetoric*. Notre Dame, IN: Notre Dame University Press.

Room, Robin. 1983. "Sociology and the Disease Concept of Alcoholism." In *Research Advances in Alcoholism and Alcohol Studies*, edited by R. Smart. New York and London: Plenum.

Rosaldo, Renato. 1987. "Where Objectivity Lies: The Rhetoric of Antropology." In *The Rhetoric of the Human Sciences*, edited by J. Nelson, A. Megill, and D. McCloskey. Madison: University of Wisconsin Press.

Rosenzweig, Roy. 1983. *Eight Hours for What We Will: Workers and Leisure in an Industrial City, 1870–1920*. New York: Oxford University Press.

Ross, H. Laurence. 1991. *Life Lines*. New Haven, CT: Yale University Press.

Simons, Herbert W., ed. 1990. *The Rhetorical Turn*. Chicago: University of Chicago Press.

Spector, Malcolm and John Kitsuse. 1977. *Constructing Social Problems*. Menlo Park, CA: Cummings.

Surgeon-General's Workshop on Drunk Driving. 1988. *Background Papers*. Washington, DC: U.S. Department of Health and Human Services.

White, Hayden. 1973. *Metahistory: The Historical Imagination in Nineteenth Century Europe*. Baltimore: Johns Hopkins University Press.

Williams, Raymond. 1977. *Marxism and Literature*. Oxford: Oxford University Press.

Chapter 9

The Rhetoric of Efficiency: Applied Social Science as Depoliticization

Hilkka Summa

The Logic of Demonstration as Depoliticization

The Political as a Rhetorical Situation

Hannah Arendt's distinction between *making* and *acting* as two different realms of human performance is central to the understanding of the role of argumentation in human affairs (Arendt 1958:175–88). *Acting* is what goes on between people, within a web of human relationships, and both necessitates and is necessitated by the ability to use language. Action, distinguished from the making of objects, is only possible for a human being who is at the same time a "speaker of words," that is, capable of identifying him- or herself as the actor and accounting for what he or she does, has done and intends to do. In acting and speaking, people show *who* they are, revealing actively their unique personal identities and thus making their appearance in the human world. Action in Hannah Arendt's sense transcends mere productive activity, which has no more meaning than is revealed in the finished product.

Making, or fabrication, goes on between humans and nature, and whether the planned result is a physical object or not, it proceeds according to a predetermined model or image, which the fabricator has in mind before the product-to-be exists. The results of fabrication will be judged by comparison to this preexisting model. In contradistinction to making, the results of action are never predetermined. Action, no matter what its specific content, always establishes relationships between people, and therefore has an inherent tendency to cut across all

135

boundaries. There is a *specific productivity of action* because it may release endless chains of reaction, which can never reliably be confined to predefined partners. Unpredictability and irreversibility of outcome are outstanding characters of action. Because of the inherent unpredictability and boundlessness of the consequences of action and reaction within the web of human relationships, we can never *make* something in the realm of human affairs. According to Hannah Arendt, it is a delusion that institutions or laws, for instance, could be made as we make material objects—or that we could *make* society better or worse (ibid.).

The political realm arises directly out of acting together, from the "sharing of words and deeds." Action in Arendt's sense of the word is the one activity that constitutes the public world, or *the political* (ibid.:198–202). A peculiarity of the public realm is that it resides in action and speech; wherever people gather together it is potentially there. This view makes speaking or, more specifically, some kind of persuasive use of language a precondition of all forms of political organization—political organization contrasted to tyranny or the use of force in the coordination of action. The crucial role of the persuasive use of language in the public realm is also pointed out in Perelman and Olbrechts-Tyteca's distinction between *acting on things* with the help of tools and *acting on people* with argumentation (1971:9).

In a world of making there is no need for acting and speaking together in this sense, even if organized cooperation in order to produce complex products always necessitates communication of messages. Yet, the communication needed in processes of fabrication is different from that of action; the communication of unambiguous messages about the model of the product-to-be and about the means to achieve it is enough. To accomplish this, speech could as well be replaced by sign language. From the viewpoint of utility, speech is, as a matter of fact, "a most awkward vehicle for communicating messages" (Arendt 1958:179) in order to organize means to achieve an end. In the realm of making there is no need for argumentation.

Because of the inherent qualities of action—the unpredictability of its outcomes and the irreversibility of its processes—there is a frustration connected to it. Various ways of seeking shelter from the calamities of action can be traced in the course of history. According to Hannah Arendt, the history of political thought presents various ways of trying to *replace acting with making*. The wish to substitute making for acting seems to be the core idea of most political philosophy, and can be found already in Plato's thought. The Platonic separation of knowing and doing, with the identification of knowledge with command and rulership, and action with obedience and execution, has become authoritative for the whole tradition of political thought. This way of thought puts acting in the category of means towards an allegedly higher end, and presents it as a way of making a predetermined product. The resulting substitution of making for action degrades politics into a technique and makes it natural to speak about human affairs in terms of instrumentality. According to Hannah Arendt, the greater part of political philosophy since Plato could easily be interpreted as a series of attempts to find theoretical foundations and practical ways for an escape from politics altogether (ibid.:222).

Within modern political thought, this tendency could be called "the dream of an automatic society," which some political scientists have traced in the history of political and economic science (Lowi 1979:40; Petersson 1987:165). The theory of the perfect market, theories of pluralism, and systems theory approaches to political science are examples of political theorizing based on some version of the ideal of a self-regulating harmony. Theodore Lowi has shown how the myth of an automatic society granted us by an all-encompassing, ideally self-correcting, providentially automatic political process was a part of both nineteenth-century liberalism and twentieth-century pluralism. Besides political thought, the ideal of an automatic society can also be traced in certain lines of methodology of the social sciences and in pragmatic attempts at institution building and innovations of politico-economic techniques aiming at guaranteeing the rationality and predictability of decision-making in the public realm.

The core idea in the "philosophy of the automatic society" is a quest for techniques or structures that would guarantee the choice of demonstrably best alternatives of policy. This implies a will to depoliticize the confrontation of people and their interests, and to turn political argumentation to forms of calculation. It means that the "good" of the society should be defined by scientific methods and certified with calculations instead of leaving room for unpredictable processes of argumentation on alternative ways of action. This line of thought, characteristic of various subdisciplines of policy sciences, wants to substitute a logic of demonstration for unreasonable argumentation, and turn politics into policy*making*. The distinction between the *logic of demonstration* and *argumentation* refers to Perelman and Olbrechts-Tyteca's way of contrasting argumentation to Cartesian logic, which only trusts in demonstration as a way of proving what is rational (1971:13).

The view of politics as policymaking leaves no room for rhetoric in the realm of public affairs: if logic is the art of thinking correctly and grammar is the art of speaking correctly, then what could rhetoric have to add (Kozy 1970:251)? Yet, the fact that it does add something is part of the tacit knowledge of all language users. The point in this reasoning is that an *argument* is more than a *syllogism*: the logician's way of arriving at

adherence to truth is demonstration of the necessity of certain conclusions, while the rhetorist understands logical demonstration just as one
type of argument, interpretation and acceptance of the message conveyed being equally important parts of the process.

Bitzer (1968:1) has defined as *rhetorical* any situation in which a
complex of persons, events, objects, and relations presents an actual or
potential *exigence*, which can be completely or partly removed if *discourse*,
introduced into the situation, can so constrain human decision or action
as to bring about the significant modification of the exigence. In a
rhetorical situation, expectations and possibilities of efficient verbal
communication exist. *Rhetoricity* is thus a property of any text or speech
persuading to action or to a particular inclination to action. This kind of a
definition of rhetoric points to the power of words to change the world,
giving rhetoric both philosophical and political importance by demonstrating its connections with forces that shape reality. It also points to
the distinction between the realms of acting and making, emphasizing
that questions of *inter*action differ profoundly from questions of technical
efficiency.

In the light of this action-oriented definition of rhetoric, political and
administrative writing and speaking are a realm of rhetoric par excel-
lence. More generally, situations concerning the coordination of action
inevitably call for rhetorical communication. The activities of public
administration as well as political activities more generally can thus be
characterized as rhetorical situations. Rhetoricity will thus be an inevitable character of the activities of the public administration, even though
applications of the logic and methods adopted from the social sciences
have largely succeeded in neutralizing administrative processes from
any open persuasiveness.

Social Science Knowledge and Public Administration

Foucault (1972, e.g.) has shown how the emergence of new bodies of
knowledge is linked to the simultaneous emergence of practices that
govern the production and use of this knowledge, for instance, with a
growth of institutions and authorized professions. What are understood
as possible objects of knowledge and what is understood to be true in a
culture as well as the accepted ways to find the truth are delimited by a
shared discursive practice that constitutes a framework for knowledge.
One such conjuncture of discourse and practice can be traced in the
recent history of political and administrative practices: the emergence of
the particular field of knowledge specifying how to produce and apply

scientific knowledge to the good management of society is linked to the emergence of a concept of societal order and power practices called the welfare state. The growth of new ways of utilizing social science knowledge as well as the whole problem of how to produce "useful knowledge" are inseparable from the emergence of practices striving to organize political-administrative processes in a way that imitates the scientific methodology for truth-seeking. The institutionalization of political-administrative steering mechanisms characteristic of the welfare state, such as the planning systems, can be interpreted as an intrusion of the logic of social sciences knowledge and its applications to the public realm.

With the emergence of the welfare state there was a rapid growth of the central government administrative apparatus. A great part of this growth resulted from the creation of new public research organizations, which more or less directly participate in the planning and decision-making processes on public policies. The growth of the public sector was not only a growth of public services and income redistribution systems but also a growth of a web of intergovernmental steering mechanisms. The understanding of how these steering mechanisms should be constructed was based on applications of the knowledge and methods of social science to public administration.

During the course of the life cycle of the welfare state, the leading position of authorized knowledge production on the good management of public administration has fluctuated between different fields of social science. National economics and sociology were the dominating fields of knowledge during the period of emergence of the welfare state, whereas since about the mid 1970s management science, accounting, and business economics have taken an increasingly dominating role in the production of authorized knowledge on how to govern well. Linked to this development there has been a growth and a withering away of a whole range of subdisciplines of a body of knowledge called *policy sciences*, as well as practices related to them, such as planning theory, operations research, systems analysis, and evaluation studies. Planning theory and planning practice will be examined more closely in a later section of this paper.

The application of the new techniques and concepts adopted from the social sciences to the work of administrators caused profound changes in the ways of reasoning on public policies. A new logic and rhetoric adopted from economics, sociology, and management science intruded into an area where the logic and rhetoric of legal discourse had traditionally been dominating. The possibility to plan and control and the knowledge of what and how to plan and control were both constituted through social inquiry. The supply of new social science knowledge and methods, the need to apply it in the policy processes, and the growth of the professional core of appliers were mutually constitutive.

Two underlying tendencies connected to the emergence of this particular conjuncture of knowledge and practice can be traced: the formation and institutionalization of new professional groups specialized in the application of this kind of knowledge and the growing degree of abstraction and technicality of its concepts and arguments. Together these tendencies result in the creation of new forums for deliberation and debate as well as for the extension and development of social science knowledge. Besides new forms of occupational specialization, the conjuncture between a body of knowledge and the institutional setting coupled with its emergence is often expressed in the formation of particular argumentative strategies. A particular framework and schemes of argumentation then become the essence of professionalism of the authorized producers and appliers of the body of knowledge in question. Often this professionalism is expressed in the guardianship of a linguistic discipline, resulting in a purification and institutionalization of their particular argumentative strategy.

The authorized professional core of appliers and producers of social science knowledge within the political-administrative realm has varied during the past decades. The arising of a professional core of planners was a central feature of the development of the administrative apparatus in the 1960s and 1970s. Practices of developing planning systems as well as the growth of a remarkable body of international literature on planning theory were another side of this development. The end of the planning mission could be read in the literature on policy sciences and related disciplines in the mid-1970s. A growing skepticism towards planning was reflected in aphorisms like Wildavsky's (1973): "If planning is everything, maybe it's nothing." Yet, in many countries, the administrative *practices* had already turned towards different solutions before that. It seems that at present the rising profession within public administration is accountants and managers of accounting. Accounting as a managerial practice has gained a growing significance both in private and public organizations. Even if this is a crude generalization, the trend seems, however, to be widespread in the OECD countries (Burchell et al. 1980). There has also been a shift in the disciplines referred to when legitimization and authorization of knowledge is needed, and this shift is also reflected in the strategies of argumentation. At present a particular *vocabulary of enterprise* seems to have replaced the politico-economic language based on notions of welfare and social solidarity (Miller and Rose 1990:181).

In most OECD countries the efficiency of public-sector performance has been a major issue since the beginning of the 1980s in popular discussions, in official administrative development work, and in political and administrative studies. The crusade against bureaucracy has taken various forms, from privatization of public services to vast modernization programs of the public sector. What is common to all these efforts is that their grounds are always given in terms of some more or less specified concepts of efficiency and productivity. The introduction of what could be called "efficiency reforms" into the public administration, aimed at enhancing accountability, efficiency, and good management, has been accompanied by a gradual change in the ways of argumentation concerning government policies and public activities. A rhetoric of managerial efficiency has become dominant in the discussions on policies. This change is reflected, among other things, in the vocabulary applied to describing the public realm: citizens have been turned into clients, policies into strategies, and the conceptual apparatus of managerial accounting and corporate strategies has become a part of the natural language for discussing public affairs. The conceptual apparatus with which the public revolution is grounded is derived from business economics and from management theory and not, for instance, from a theory of democracy or any other field of political theory (Olsen 1988:296). The "goodness" of the working of the administrative apparatus is judged by standards of management, not by standards of democracy or justice.

The Planning Mission

The large-scale adoption of new planning methods and techniques alongside more traditional procedures of decision-making was a central feature in the development of the central administration in most OECD countries during the 1960s and 1970s. The amount of personnel working with the planning of welfare policies grew rapidly and information systems for these purposes were developed. The manifest aim of constructing the planning apparatus was to enhance rationality and the technical efficiency of the policy process. The ideal was a complete ends-means hierarchy covering all of the welfare questions and guaranteeing the rational coordination of policies. The problem of policymaking was understood as a technical problem of coordination and adequate data, not a political problem of creating a common will. It was another expression of the dream of an automatic society, with a harmony of wills produced by technical means of organizing and data processing. The aim was not the resolution of inevitable conflicts through open argumentation but their disappearance brought about through a calculative demonstration of the optimal alternatives for action. Orthodox planning was *anti*political, as noted by van Gunsteren (1976:12).

A body of planning literature and an international discourse on planning theory emerged during the 1960s and the early 1970s. Planning theory was essentially a collection of guidelines for the construction of rational decision-making procedures. Early formualtions like Friedman's (1969) describing planning as the application of scientific-technical intelligence to the solution of practical problems were later completed with considerations on constraints on rationality and information-handling capacity as well as participation and human growth (for instance, Faludi 1973; Dror 1973; Etzioni 1968). Within the discourse that followed, the more critical, academic discussants presented concerns with democracy and participation, whereas the more inside-administration discussants presented questions on the efficiency of strategy formulation and the usefulness of planning. In spite of the extensive theorization on planning there was relatively little interest in planning as it is actually practiced in different organizations. What was largely neglected in most of the planning literature is the view that public-policy planning is a process based on *language use*, and that language as such as well as strategies of argumentation come into play in planning processes.

The construction of administrative planning systems can be seen as one expression of "the Cartesian dream of logic," which wished to put outside the realm of reason everything that could not be included in the logico-deductive framework. This view conceives all progress in knowledge as an extension of logically proved facts and a progressively diminishing need to resort to argumentation up to the moment when it becomes entirely superfluous (Perelman and Olbrechts-Tyteca 1971:511). The logic of the planning systems neglects the fact that planning for welfare policies necessarily implies a conflict that cannot be solved by logical deduction from some generally accepted "good." Constructing the planning apparatus into public administration can be interpreted as depoliticization politics, as one of the attempts to escape from the calamities of action. How well this has succeeded is another question; in the light of the following case study it will be argued that the quest for logical reasoning in policymaking has in fact been perverted by the seemingly rational systems constructed for this purpose.

Attitudes towards planning have changed since the late 1960s and the 1970s, and enhancing rational planning as an overall solution to improving policies is no longer an issue in academic nor in more practically oriented discussions on administration. Yet, formally, the planning systems are working in the way they were planned in the 1970s, and the work done within these systems is an essential part of the daily practices in central government agencies. Even though self-criticism within theoretical and academic social sciences has long since abandoned straightforward modernist epistemology, the practices grounded and legitimized through these lines of thought still exist. The development of administrative practices is grounded on a cultural orientation described as the *managerial metamyth* (Ingersoll and Adams 1986:362), which is expressed in a promulgation of a rational-technical orientation towards tasks and relationships.

The planning mission was not only a response to perceived decision-making problems of the growing public sector. It also shaped the reality to be planned. It provided a new group of professionals and a new vocabulary for their use. Professionalism of a practicing planner is expressed in the ability to use the particular argumentative system, which, in a process of trial and error, has turned out to be successful and acceptable in the microcontext of the daily work of planners and administrators. The rhetorical conventions characteristic of this particular frame of argumentation have an influence on what is understood as possible and not possible in the planning of the contents of policies, and thus they also delimit the horizon of civic and political discussion. The planning bureaucracy often has a monopoly position in defining the tone or argumentation, the vocabulary, and the relevant pros and cons that are to be discussed. The fixing of such an argumentative strategy may distort the rationality (understood as reasonableness) of a policy discussion even if it proceeds according to a formally rational procedure. Rational techniques may thus in fact result in a subversion of rationality.

A Case of the Rhetoric of Efficiency: Argumentation in the Planning of Housing Policy

Policy Planning as Argumentation

The following part of this chapter presents results of an analysis of the argumentative strategy in a policy-planning process in the Finnish central government. The rhetoric in the yearly planning documents preparing policy and budgetary decisions on housing policy has been examined (Summa 1989, 1990). Housing policy planning is presented as a case of a policy process that follows an allegedly rational procedure constructed with reference to planning theoretical views of efficient policymaking.

From the point of view of concrete everyday practices, the process can be characterized as production and exchange of texts carrying arguments on the scope and contents of policies. The government agency in charge of a certain policy sector regularly gathers its statements and suggestions on measures to be taken in planning documents, which will be passed over to the ministry, which in turn will pass some of the suggestions over to the Ministry of Finance. The Ministry of Finance coordinates the plans of different policy sectors, giving each spending ministry feedback where the realism and the state financial effects of the suggested policies are evaluated. The role of the annual state budget in this process can be seen as a final stage, confirming the implementation of a certain policy.

The process of formulating the texts included in the planning documents at the various stages of the process is at the same time a process of negotiating and compromising in which the content of the public policy for a given sector is fixed. The form and the content of what is included in the planning texts cannot really be distinguished, as *how* something is said will necessarily be reflected in *what* will be done.

What is characteristic of this exchange of planning statements is that some successful statements will be able to survive through the whole process up to the state budget, which means the ultimate implementation of the piece of policy described in the statement. The budget can thus be understood as a document that has the power to turn words into deeds. The less successful statements will be filtered out from the process on their way "upwards" in the administrative apparatus. Some seem to receive an eternal life on some lower level, circulating year after year in the planning documents.

Planning texts are written in a technical language, void of any personal style or expressions of values. They are supposed to communicate facts in order to improve the information on the basis of which decisions on policy are made. Rhetorical figures or persuasive elements are not supposed to be present in planning texts. The technical language of planning documents is aimed at hiding all persuasive aspects or aspects having to do with the interests of the author of the text. Yet, a special planning rhetoric has developed within the central government.

The argumentative character of the planning process is part of the backstage knowledge of the civil servants participating in the process. An essential part of the planners' theory-in-use consists of knowledge about the rhetorical conventions usable in the daily planning practices. On the other hand, the official prescriptions and attitudes emphasize the neutrality and pure calculativeness of the planning texts, which blurs the argumentative character of the process. The explicit and implicit attitudes toward the planning discourse seem to differ widely.

Examining an Argumentative Strategy

In their theory on argumentation, Perelman and Olbrechts-Tyteca (1971) distinguish between the framework of argumentation, the starting points of argumentation, and the argumentative techniques. The most important factor defining the *framework of argumentation* is the relationship to the audience that is to be influenced by the argumentation. A real or a hypothetical construction of an audience always has a major role in determining the quality and procedure of argumentation (ibid.:17–23). Explicating the concept of audience inherent to a particular piece of oratory will thus tell something about the power relations and implicit cultural taken-for-granteds present in the situation. What is important in the *starting points of argumentation* is the kind of prior agreements that exist between the speaker (or writer) and his or her audience. On a very abstract level, the objects of these prior agreements are concerned with what is to be considered as real and what is to be considered as preferable (ibid.:65–66). The unquestioned agreements that the speaker supposes to exist between him- or herself and the audience will show in the kind of justifications aiming at agreements in the realm of the preferable. A fundamental dimension for describing various types of justifications is the distinction between a tendency to draw either on a quantitative or on a qualitative basis for arguments concerning values. The *argumentative techniques* or schemes of argumentation vary in different argumentative situations, Perelman and Olbrechts-Tyteca's main distinction being that between the associative and dissociative schemes.

Quasi-logical arguments and arguments based on "the very nature of things" as well as arguments by analogy are examples of associative schemes of argumentation. Quasi-logical arguments derive their persuasive strength from their similarity to the formal reasoning of logic, taking advantage of the prestige of rigorous thought. Perelman and Olbrechts-Tyteca point out that the charge of having committed a logical error is often itself a quasi-logical argument. Exposing the presence of a contradiction in a prevailing state of affairs is an example of giving quasi-logical grounds for a claim for action. Justification given in the form of elaborate calculations, the results of which may not have direct relevance to the content of the argument, are perhaps the most characteristic type of quasi-logical argument. The prevalence of a tendency to draw on quantitative justifications is naturally coupled with argumentative schemes with a quasi-logical structure.

Arguments drawing on the very nature of things lay claim to validity through establishing some kind of a dependence between already accepted judgments and others that the rhetor wishes to promote. The relationship established can be one of succession, uniting a phenomenon to its causes or consequences, or one of coexistence, uniting a person to his or her acts, a group to the individuals who form it, or more generally an essence to its manifestations. The *pragmatic* argument, which permits the evaluation of an act or an event in terms of its favorable or on-favorable consequences, is an important scheme in the logic of value judgments. Establishing a fact-consequence relationship is one of the most powerful validations of an argument, and thus arguing in terms of the usefulness of an action is characteristic of claims for decision-making. But, as Perelman and Olbrechts-Tyteca remark (ibid.:268), the pragmatic argument can be developed only in terms of agreement on the value of the consequences. Argumentation based on other techniques will be called to the rescue if the value of the alleged consequence seems disputable.

The Argumentative Scheme of Planning Rhetoric: Quasi-logical Arguments and Quantitative Justifications

The planning texts are very condensed and stripped of openly rhetorical ornamentation. The characteristic ways of giving grounds to arguments will be quite easily distinguished, as the procedures of argumentation avoid complicated elaborations. There seem to be a few main types of justifications, which are repeatedly given to the suggested courses of policy. The most prominent ones are calculations pointing out the great numbers of those concerned by the issue in question and statements assuring the efficiency of the measures suggested. *Efficiency* figures in the texts as a general notion describing a state to be preferred, and the mere statement that something will become more efficient is frequently given as grounds for suggesting a certain course of action. Another characteristic way of giving grounds to a suggested measure is a statement pointing out the possibility to cope with the whole of an issue instead of only a part of it; it is taken for granted that the comprehensiveness of a policy is a state to be preferred.

The general aims of housing policy are presented in a framework where numbers of people are related to numbers of housing units, elaborated with considerations on the sizes of households and square meters of floor space. The great number of households not reaching some of the minimum standards is the most frequently given raison d'être of housing policy. Toward the latter part of the period examined (1975–88), remarks on the need to pay attention to the quality of housing and living environment are more and more often added to this framework. Yet, when the argument is elaborated, also the policy suggestions concerning the quality of housing will draw on the great numbers of dwellings or housing areas in need of repair. Another characteristic feature of the housing policy-planning texts is that statements presenting facts about the present housing situation or about the past or coming changes in it often use concepts adopted from economics. Claims for public activity in housing questions are placed in the framework of housing demand and supply and the equilibrium of the housing market.

It seems that Perelman and Olbrechts-Tyteca's notion of the *locus of quantity* (ibid.:83–85), meaning a tendency to draw on quantitative justifications, describes one of the most important prior agreements of the planning dialogue between the housing professionals and the Ministry of Finance. More often than not, a locus of quantity constitutes a major implied premise without which the planning statement would have no basis. For example, the principle of efficiency, which is frequently and in various ways referred to as a preferred state, is as such a quantitative expression; it reflects the principle that *more is better than less, whatever the issue.* Another example is the frequent reference to policy measures or planning procedures that will cover the *whole* of an issue instead of coping only with a *part* of it. Perelman and Olbrechts-Tyteca show (ibid.:86) how the preference given to the *whole* over the *part* can be translated to the axiom "the whole is greater than a part," and thus understood as a locus of quantity. Also the concepts adopted from economics are based on quantitative reasoning.

What they call an associative technique seems to be the course of arguing most characteristic to policy-planning texts. This means that the claims for action are justified by connecting them to other statements in a way that makes the suggested element seem natural or inevitable. The most usual connections are made to prior authoritative decisions, either by claiming that the suggestion in question is parallel to one presented by an authority or by presenting it as a means to an end that is considered either self-evident or already agreed upon. Both techniques are cases of placing the argument in a fact-consequence framework, where the need to justify the suggestion is reduced because it appears in the secondary position of a consequence (or means). For example, with the exception of a few years, the statements concerning the general aims of housing policy for the coming period are presented as a direct repetition or an elaboration of a committee report or a government decision. This kind of an argumentative scheme results also in devaluing the planning document itself and thus increasing the self-evidence of the claims that it presents.

During the period examined, there has been a gradual change in the ways of argumentation in the planning documents, a change that can be interpreted as a shift in the conception of audience implicit in the planning text. The technical character of the texts becomes more prominent during the course of the period examined and also the expressions of quantitative reasoning seem to become more and more frequent. The planning texts seem to reflect an increasing need to overwhelm the addressee of the texts with irrefutable quantitative "findings." The suggestions concerning specific policy measures and appro-priations needed to finance them are, particularly in the more recent plans, presented as a result of a calculation. This is the case even when no actual premises exist for the calculation and the material content of the argument is nothing but a request for a certain appropriation in the following budgetary years. Presented in the form of a *quasi-logical* argument the suggestion will have the merit of rigorous thought and at the same time the claim itself will become less prominent because it is accompanied by uncontradictory numbers. The hypothetical audi-ence of the planning texts is the Ministry of Finance, the relative influence of which has increased during the past decade. The change in the argumentative strategies of the spending ministries may be interpreted as reflecting a change of power positions inside the bureau-cracy. As the gatekeeper position of the Ministry of Finance with regard to the scope and contents of policies, special forms of self-presentation adapted to this particular audience have been developed.

Efficiency: A Dormant Metaphor

The *metaphor* is one of the argumentative techniques drawing on analogy. It is probably the most commonly used and also the most analyzed rhetorical figure. Perelman and Olbrechts-Tyteca put the metaphor in the framework of a wider theory of argument by analogy and call it a condensed analogy (ibid.:399). As with other analogies, the metaphor is a fusion, bringing together terms taken from differ-ent spheres. However, the special powerfulness of the metaphor is not due to this visible fusion but to its ability to be detached from its ori-gin. Perelman and Olbrechts-Tyteca describe as *dormant* (ibid.:405) a metaphor that has lost contact with the initial idea of fusion and that is no longer recognized as a metaphor. A dormant metaphor is an extremely powerful tool because it will be interpreted in a single, fixed way, and thus it will be able to give a reason, unlike the "active" metaphor, which is merely suggestive. The strength is due to the fact that it draws on a stock of already accepted analogical material that is not merely known but that is integrated by language into the cultural tradition.

In view of the condensed and formalized style of the planning texts one would expect a complete lack of the usual rhetorical figures. Yet, metaphorical expressions are quite common in them. For example, the notion of *efficiency* is used in a metaphorical way as it is not connected to any specified input/output relation. When changes to the scope or the structure of current housing policy measures are suggested, an increase in the efficiency of the measure in question is usually referred to. Also suggestions concerning the resources or the organization of the housing administration are usually justified by pointing out an increase in the efficiency of the workings of the administrative apparatus, yet without giving any explicit input/output relation that would specify the change in question. The efficiency gains are often attributed to reaching a more complete way of dealing with the issue in question. For example, housing policy planning will become more efficient when a new planning system covering the whole sphere of housing questions (also those now handled by other ministries) is introduced, or housing policy measures should cover the whole of the housing stock in order to make its use more efficient. The metaphorical use of the notion of efficiency is a prominent feature of planning rhetoric, and is characteristic of administrative writing more generally.

Flexibility is another metaphorically used expression: the flexibility of administrative systems and decision-making procedures is a state to be preferred and aimed at through the suggested measures. A third example is the frequent use of the metaphorical concepts of economics, like the level of demand or the equilibrium of the market. As these expressions are often presented as justifications for suggested action, and not only as descriptions, it seems that Perelman and Olbrechts-Tyteca's notion of *dormant metaphor* fits the way they are used in the planning texts. Notions such as efficiency and equilibrium belong to the stock of mechanical metaphors that are very common in administrative writing; accumulation of a stock of such metaphors seems to be one of the most important results of the contacts between bureaucracy and the social sciences. The tendency of modern thought to borrow its metaphors from Newtonian mechanics seems to be characteristic of planning rhetoric too (Petersson 1987:165–68).

Why and How to Study Administrative Rhetoric?

The question of whether administrative rhetoric has any civic importance depends on how we understand the connection between language and politics. The claim put forward in this paper is that strategies of argumentation used in the policy process do affect who gets what and the achievement of values such as justice and equality in society. The strategies of argumentation used within the bureaucracy create a presence for a certain totality of social facts and thus have a role in defining the range of possibilities and preferable states that will be visible to those participating in the policy process. The administrative rhetoric also influences the civic discussion and the ways in which citizens' demands will be channeled to the political apparatus, because it defines and limits the vocabulary with which social phenomena are discussed. Through its own dominant argumentative strategies the bureaucracy also influences what arguments for and against certain policies will be available for civic discussion.

An antirhetorical, objectivating way of using language is one of the taken-for-granteds of administrative writing. The reliance on applying and imitating scientific methodology as a source for the right formula for the good management of society has contributed to the institutionaliza-tion of argumentative strategies that tend to mask their character as persuasive language use. This is inevitable as long as the view of language as a simple vehicle for communicating thoughts and messages is dominant in politics and science. Barthes (1970:411–16) has shown in his essay comparing science and literature how the establishment of science denies the sovereignty of language and thus enhances an un-self-conscious use of language. Yet, recent writings (Edmondson 1984; McCloskey 1986) have shown that rhetoricity is an inherent quality of any social inquiry. Even the fields of research that are explicitly committed to logical reasoning, quantitative methods, and a use of language in which "facts speak for themselves" are in fact metaphorical, suasive, and flattering some audience. This has also been noted by sociologists of knowledge (Yearly 1986:132). Economics in particular has been described as a field of knowledge that is exceptionally un-self-conscious of its rhetoric (McCloskey 1986:179).

In recent studies rhetoric is sometimes placed in the position of a metatheory or a source of methodological devices for analyzing a discipline, a discourse, or any linguistic object. Placing rhetoric in the position of a metatheory will put it into a close relationship with some other established ways of studying textual products. Concern with the underlying systems of distinctions and conventions implicit to human actions and products that make them *meaningful* is a common field of interest for a poststructuralist, a semiotician, and a rhetorician. The rhetoricity of a particular text (or speech) can be understood as a structure implicit to it, but as the particular aspect of structure that has to do with its *effectiveness* in producing adherence to the arguments it carries. Thus the poststructuralist and the rhetorist have a common interest in trying to make explicit the ways in which language lends itself to, and is itself, a means of power.

The term *rhetoric* is used in many different ways. Rhetoric may be used to indicate the argumentative structure of a text, or the particular properties through which this structure receives its efficiency as well as the faculty of producing such an efficiency; in contemporary writings it has often been used also to indicate investigation aiming at revealing this structure. Perelman and Olbrechts-Tyteca's *New Rhetoric*, for instance, can be read as a grammatical guide to constructing a persuasive discourse, but it can be also be read as an analysis of actual argumentation. Reading the theory on argumentation in the latter way will establish the structure of discourse as the object of study for a rhetorist. This is what McGuire (1982:149–51) suggests as an object of study for a modern rhetorist. Studying rhetoric, or argumentation, will thus become a kind of archeology of knowledge, the aim of which is to analyze a discourse in order to determine the rules that govern it. There is, however, an important difference in orientation compared to poststructuralist approaches. It is characteristic of rhetoric, and studies using rhetoric as a methodological device, to understand the examined textual product as a piece of purposeful *action*, that is, as conscious deliberation of a knowledgeable agent. At first sight this seems incompatible with the starting points of the poststructuralist and semiotic orientations, which want to understand the world without reference to intentions or other psychological primitives of a centered subject. Rhetoric is concerned with choice (Brockriede 1975:181). Because there is always more than one way of saying anything, and because some of these alternative ways are both grammatical and logical, criteria other than those of grammar and logic are necessary to determine the choice of which to use (Kozy 1970:251). That rhetoric has to do with the choices of a knowledgeable agent also means that it can be put into a framework of ethical and moral questions. Brummet sees this as the consequence of accepting a creative power for language: "Because it is ambiguous and because it creates reality it is the responsibility of the user of language to choose between the reality that his/her language will advocate. This choice is ethical, and it is also rhetorical" (1976:39). Thus, accepting rhetorical intersubjectivity as a basis for one's worldview implies a break with both *idealist* and *semantic ethics*. The former assumes that rhetoric is merely a servant or a channel for truth, while the latter has no place at all for rhetoric, because it insists that language be used so that the facts speak for themselves.

This view is exactly opposite to the way language is used and the way language use is understood in present political-administrative practices. As my analysis of planning rhetoric attempted to show, this has resulted in the institutionalization of linguistic practices where the veil of quasi-logical argumentative schemes and quasi-rational procedures releases the arguing partners from any responsibility for the presences they create through their argumentative strategies. An openly argumentative approach would instead emphasize this responsibility.

References

Arendt, Hannah. 1958. *The Human Condition.* Chicago: University of Chicago Press.

Barthes, Roland. 1970. "Science versus Literature." In *Structuralism, A Reader,* edited by Michael Lane. London: Cape.

Bitzer, Lloyd. 1968. "The Rhetorical Situation." *Philosophy and Rhetoric* 1(1):1–14.

Brockriede, Wayne. 1975. "Where Is Argument?" *Journal of the American Forensic Association* 11 (Spring):179–82.

Brummet, Barry. 1976. "Some Implications of 'Process' or 'Intersubjectivity': Postmodern Rhetoric." *Philosophy and Rhetoric* 9(1):21–51.

Burchell, Stuart, Colin Clubb, Anthony Hopwood, John Hughes, and Janine Nahapiet. 1980. "The Roles of Accounting in Organizations and Society. *Accounting, Organizations and Society* 5(1):5–27.

Dror, Yehetzkiel. 1973. *Public Policymaking Re-examined.* London: Scranton.

Edmondson, Ricca. 1984. *Rhetoric in Sociology.* London and Basingstoke: Macmillan.

Etzioni, Amitai. 1968. *The Active Society. A Theory of Societal and Political Processes.* London: Free Press.

Faludi, Andreas. 1973. *Planning Theory.* Oxford: Pergamon.

Foucault, Michel. 1972. *The Archeology of Knowledge.* London and Frome: Tavistock.

Friedman, John. 1969. "Notes on Societal Action." *Journal of the American Institute of Planners* 35:311–18.

Gunsteren, Herman van. 1976. *The Quest for Control.* Bath: Wiley.

Ingersoll, Virginia Hill and Guy B. Adams. 1986. "Beyond Organizational Boundaries. Exploring the Managerial Myth." *Administration and Society* 18(3):360–81.

Kozy, John Jr. 1970. "A Review of Perelman's New Rhetoric." *Philosophy and Rhetoric* 3(4):249–54.

Lowi, Theodore J. 1979. *The End of Liberalism.* New York: Norton.

McCloskey, Donald. 1986. *The Rhetoric of Economics.* Brighton: Harvester.

McGuire, Michael. 1982. "The Structure of Rhetoric." *Philosophy and Rhetoric* 15(3):149–69.

Miller, Peter and Rose, Nikolas. 1990. "Political Rationalities and Technologies of Government." In: *Texts, Contexts, Concepts. Studies in Politics and Power in Language,* edited by Sakari Hänninen and Kari Palonen. Jyväskylä: The Finnish Political Science Association.

Olsen, Johan P. 1988. "Statsvetenskap, organisationsteori och nyinstitutionalism" ("Political Science, Organization Theory and the New Institutionalism," with an English summary). *Politiikka* 30(4):295–305.

Perelman, Chaim and Olbrechts-Tyteca, Lucie. 1971. *The New Rhetoric. A Treatise on Argumentation.* Notre Dame, IN: University of Notre Dame Press.

Petersson, Olaf. 1987. *Metaforernas makt. (The Power of Metaphor.)* Helsingborg: Carlssons.

Summa, Hilkka. 1989. *Hyvinvointipolitiikka ja suunnitteluretoriikka (Welfare Policy and Planning Rhetoric.)* Espoo: Helsinki University of Technology Press.

————. 1990. "Ethos, Pathos and Logos in Central Government Planning Texts." In: *Texts, Contexts, Concepts. Studies in Politics and Power in Language,* edited by Sakari Hänninen and Kari Palonen. Jyväskylä: The Finnish Political Science Association.

Wildavsky, Aaron. 1973. "If Planning Is Everything, Maybe It's Nothing." *Policy Sciences* 4:127–53.

Yearly, Steven. 1986. "Interactive-Orientation and Argumentation in Scientific Texts." In: *Power, Action and Belief. A New Sociology of Knowledge?,* edited by John Law. London: Routledge and Kegan Paul.

Chapter 10

Fact, Fiction, and Factions: Scandal, Controversy, and "Filemaking" as Social Theory

Carl Milofsky

In contemporary social science, theories tend to be viewed as coherent, abstract depictions of the world with a tight logical structure. Theory gives direction to data collection and a critical edge to political interpretation. In more quantitative research, the theory is a formal model or a set of hypotheses that are tested against data. In more interpretive social commentary, theory often is a summary of intellectual history that provides structured criteria for analyzing political events or problems in social structure.

This conception of theory allows for great diversity in the kinds of theorizing people do and this variety is often recognized by those who talk about the nature of theory (Levine n.d.; Martindale 1988; Richards 1987; Ritzer 1988; Stinchcombe 1968). All reserve, however, a central role for the theorist. Theory is a specialty in most social science disciplines and there are journals devoted to the subject. Most academic programs require that students take courses in theory. All of this fosters a situation where theory is the province of theorists. Without them, theory would not exist. Theories are models of the world created by individuals because, in this tradition, high-quality theories have a tight logical structure and they provide a coherent rendition of how particular research efforts are positioned in relationship to tradition and within the intellectual structure of a discipline.

This chapter explores a different conception of theory, one that sees it as a product of interactive processes rather than of the creative efforts of a single author. Here, theories are symbolic constructs that actors share within the scholarly community and that animate their professional activities. I use *theory* here in essentially the same way that the sociology of knowledge uses the term *ideology* (Mannheim 1936) or that some in the philosophy of science use the term *paradigm* (Kuhn 1970).

This partly implies that theories provide a definition of reality, a way of defining truth, and rules about the proper nature of evidence. "Paradigm" or "frame of reference" implies that ideology is static, however. One might equate these concepts to a personality construct like "bias," which is something that becomes a permanent feature of individuals. Ideology in the sociology of knowledge is more active because it is a means for engaging the world and it is a product of the way people interact. To Marx, for example, ideology is an inextricable part of economic relations and class structure. Ideology is not so much "in" actors as a product of their efforts to control each other and advance their fates. Similarly, to Goffman and other symbolic interactionists, one's view of the world is not static and permanent. It is shaped as one relates to and obtains feedback from significant others.

Theory, in this chapter, refers to the symbolic universe that structures the way that a group of scholars interacts. While this formulation is vague and abstract, this is not the way I will present my ideas in the following pages. Instead, this chapter is an effort to come to terms with a phenomenon in the academic world called *filemaking*. That term arises from the activities of a specific person, a Yale mathematician named Serge Lang, who has bedeviled several prominent sociologists and political scientists in the last decade.

This chapter represents my personal effort to figure out why Lang appeals to me so much—why I have used his material to teach my course in social theory for several years. While Lang is dramatic and self-conscious about his filemaking work, I will suggest that the upheavals he has precipitated are neither isolated events nor particularly unusual. In fact, it is easy to find instances where sharp conflicts provoked fusillades of correspondence and paper writing among academics. These interchanges have, in some areas, been important sources of theoretical elaboration. Some time after the battle is over and the bodies have been cleared away, professional theorists have come along and tidied up the mess, making coherent theory.

These observations suggest to me that we conceive of theory improperly when we think of it as a collection of artifacts—the carefully crafted efforts of individual specialists. We ought to ask how theory works as a feature of the living professional activity of scholars. In other words, we should study theory ethnographically. We might discover that there are many uses for theory and many ways theories are made that those who study theory do not recognize or accept as valid. The primary use of formal theory, for example, might be to teach students how to think about a discipline. This is what the books I cited earlier are most used for in sociology and it is how Kuhn, as he explains the nature of scientific paradigms, describes scientific orthodoxy.

Filemaking shows us that theorizing is a product of conflict and argument. It is a form of rhetoric generated in response to political agendas. It is shaped by the norms of science, norms that cause scholars to submit to the discipline of making ideas and facts closely fit. Thus, in the context of filemaking, theory directs research because it gives particular information strategic value in an ongoing struggle. It becomes an essential part of how we make arguments clear and convincing when it really counts to win others over to our point of view. In this way, theory is a living intellectual process and not a summary or recapitulation of past events.

Serge Lang and Filemaking

Over the past fifteen years a mathematician at Yale, Serge Lang, has on several occasions launched pointed and widely publicized attacks on particular social scientists and their work. Recently when Harvard political scientist Samuel Huntington was proposed for membership in the National Academy of Sciences, Lang led the group that questioned the intellectual integrity of Huntington's work. Ten years ago Lang launched an attack on a study conducted by Everett C. Ladd, Jr., and Seymour Martin Lipset that they called, "The 1977 Survey of the American Professoriate."

Lang's persistent questions and frank challenges to the authority of sponsoring scientific organizations in each case have led to press coverage and extensive correspondence, which Lang faithfully assembles in a form he calls a *file* (Lang 1977). As new items are added to a file, Lang makes copies and sends them to a "cc list" composed of principal actors in the drama at hand and interested bystanders. Members of the cc list often respond to new items. A critical editorial or letter published in a national magazine or newspaper might stimulate letters to the publication, to the author of the critical piece, to Lang, or to the subjects of his criticism. As Lang becomes aware of this material he sends it along to the cc list.

Since there quite regularly are critical things written in the mass media about Lang's efforts, his communications with the cc list provide him with a means for answering criticisms and for being sure that the interested audience has access to complete information and not just to the rhetorical summaries published in the media. Files also are a variety of discourse for Lang. He manages the file in a way calculated to keep his issues alive and to force critics to confront the whole record surrounding his growing debates.

When he was accused of "McCarthyism" in a letter to the *Chronicle of Higher Education* during his struggle over the Ladd-Lipset survey, for example, Lang responded tactically (Lang 1977:179–94). Angry that the *Chronicle* printed what he judged an incomplete and defamatory account of his struggle with Lipset and Ladd, Lang concluded, when a negative letter to the editor later was published, that responding himself with a letter to the editor would only put him on the defensive. He sent the file, as it was assembled to date, to the author of the letter, who then apologized to Lang. Lang dutifully sent the apology along to the cc list. In a later conversation with me, he spoke at length about the trap posed by letters to the editor and the tactical advantage he gained by convincing the original author to retract his attack against Lang, blaming instead the incomplete reportage of the *Chronicle*.[2]

Lang and Teaching Social Theory

I became interested in Lang and his penchant for filemaking because I teach a course in social theory that seeks to help students read and respond critically to the material they encounter when reading in sociological journals. I think that major problems for students are being able to disassemble and decode the argument contained in a sociological article and then finding a tenable foothold from which to launch a confident and independent response. Students are disadvantaged because they lack the fund of knowledge and the technical skills professionals bring to bear when they read and interpret professional scholarship.

While professionals have an advantage when it comes to interpreting scholarship, most complex ideas ought to be explicable to an interested, determined audience if we professional scholars are prepared to help translate technical language into plain speech. This idealistic belief is something I acquired in an undergraduate biophysics course for non-science majors in which we read and criticized original research articles with the help of a teacher committed to demystifying scientific language. If it can be done with biophysics it ought to be doable in sociology. Armed with this conviction, off I went to accomplish this feat with my undergraduate theory students.

The problem is to provide students with ways of engaging scholarly authors as colleagues without continual input from me or another expert. Students are used to writing papers where they take for granted that the authors they cite are "experts." Their term papers are agglomerations of references to these experts in which the students usually give short book reports on each citation and add up the arguments on an issue pro and con. Modeling their writing on the style used in academic articles students try to make general claims, they use excessively formal language, and produce term papers that are ponderous and not authentic (Becker 1986). My task is to convince students to write what they think in direct, active language, and to avoid putting on the rhetorical garb of scholarly authority (Milofsky 1987, 1991).

Whatever else they might be, the articles published in the *American Sociological Review* or the *American Journal of Sociology* have to be written as though they are authoritative and as though they leave no loose ends. This never is the case but we have a variety of rhetorical strategies that help to convey an impression of command and closure in our writing. My teaching job is to undo this authoritative wrapping so that students can see the intellectual work that goes into writing an article as a matter of active debate and controversy. One might call this process, to coin a term, deconstruction.

When I first ran across Lang's published book, *The File*, in a Yale bookstore, I liked it because it seemed so useful for my class. The survey Lang attacks looks very much like surveys we routinely encounter, being citizens in a mass democracy. This is positivist social science at work, and we are used to accepting summary statistics as social facts. At first glance the survey and the articles that came out of the resulting data collection seem objective, reasonable, and uncriticizable. My hope is that students will first be fooled and that then they will see how assumptions that they may question and challenge are hidden in texts of this sort. I want students to think that what Lang undertakes in *The File* is about like what I want them to do as they read social science for themselves.

Unfortunately, students are not so easily taken in. Confronted with a book the size of a telephone directory, they know something is up. Lang's opening salvo does not help since it gently prepares them for the controversy to follow. Lang writes to Lipset:

To the Surveyors of the American Professoriate (Lipset and Co.):

I just received a second notice asking me to complete and return your questionnaire on faculty opinion.

The questionnaire made it direct to the waste paper basket. I never thought much of Seymour Martin Lipset and his "scholarship." If you want to see the latest evidence of the gross incompetence, bias, and cover up abilities of Lipset, just read the review of his "Education and Politics at Harvard" by Sigmund Diamond in the current *New York Review*.

You guys want us to take you seriously, answer your questionnaire, and cooperate, thereby transferring to you our academic responsibility. No way! Did it occur to you that many of those who did not return the questionnaire think that Seymour Martin Lipset is a (characterization deleted)? Is there any place in your questionnaire giving us a chance to express this opinion? To express the opinion that the idea of the questionnaire is stupid? To express the opinion that Seymour Martin Lipset is not qualified to send out questionnaires and does not deserve being answered by the academic community? To express the opinion that the whole manner in which the questionnaire is put together already prejudices the issues to the point where one does not want to deal with them on your terms? To express the opinion that we have better things to do than answer questionnaires, especially those sent out by Seymour Martin Lipset?

You are parasites on the academic community. Lay off!

Serge Lang

Students pick up that Lang's response is a bit intemperate. But they also soon see that Lang has a point. The survey is full of veiled claims about what are correct political and social values. Furthermore, the questionnaire coerces people to give responses that inexactly represent their personal views. Some of these deficiencies (to use a word Lang favors) might be described as failures of questionnaire design. Most, however, have to do with the nature of a survey and with the peculiar questions social scientists ask as they seek to build a scale that measures some latent personality quality of respondents. Many of the questions Lang and his associates most object to are an effort by Lipset and Ladd to measure political orientation along a left-right continuum—standard social science practice.

I struggle to convince students that the Lipset-Ladd questionnaire is competent social science, given the limitations of what social science does. The kind of thing these researchers undertake is the sort of research task social scientists are trained to do, and that even qualitative types like myself sometimes undertake. My hope is that the students will see that social research is inherently political, controversial, and subject to attack and criticism. Given a rhetoric of social science that always casts research as value-neutral and authoritative, students can nearly always find a basis for criticism and engagement with an article if they try to figure out the ways in which the article is partisan. Usually the political implications of sociological writing will be indirectly and implicitly stated. The exercise of research is inherently cooptive since it seeks to use a presentation of facts to gain readers' compliance with a value position. Lang helps students recognize the inherent politics and the unavoidable value choices that go along with research. Because this dimension is generally ignored in scholarly presentations, students are given a tool for independently, personally, and creatively engaging the author.

A Second Case

I began using Lang's material dramatically, to show students one way that they might criticize social research. The book and the man are amusing and infuriating and intemperate. Yet I find myself drawn in. I admire Lang's commitment to purist academic values of accuracy and precision in thought, and accountability in action. I feel guilty when I do not help attack his dragons as forcefully as I might. This is only a personal discomfort though. More importantly I have begun to see files being built wherever I look. Most of the filebuilders I know are not as self-conscious about the art as Lang, nor are most as persistent and outspoken. Yet their efforts at criticism fused with social action produce sharp controversies about truth claims, create solidarity among scholarly allies, and offer visible alternatives to scholarly orthodoxy. These conflicts generate and crystallize new theoretical traditions.

Here is an example. For some years I have been part of a community of scholars doing research on nonprofit organizations. Although non-profits account for about 10 percent of the employment in the United States and annually generate income in excess of $125 billion, they were mostly ignored by the scholarly community until the late 1970s. Interest grew in part because several foundations sponsored academic research centers at Yale, at the Urban Institute, and at an organization called The Independent Sector. As research grew, new teaching programs were launched, providing credentials in nonprofit management or policy analysis. Policy discussions among government and nonprofit funding agencies also began drawing on the academic literature. Despite federal funding cutbacks, assets have grown in the nonprofit sector as it more and more takes its place as an important player in the policy world.

Several years ago, a historian named Peter Hall began arguing that the nonprofit sector is an invention of the industry—of foundations and major service providers like hospitals and universities (Hall 1988, 1989, 1991; Milofsky and Hall 1990).[3] Seeking to expand their services and protect tax benefits that give nonprofits advantages in competing for resources with proprietary firms, the inner circles of the nonprofit world sought to foster academic production that would legitimate their endeavors and provide the sector with a rational basis.

Hall argues that, historically, nonprofits have grown in an ad hoc fashion, emerging as a result of local cultural traditions, from efforts by elites to disguise activities that exploited others, and because of the way sponsorship—usually religious sponsorship—led to new service industries. Because of these random origins it is hard to find tidy ways to define "nonprofit organization," to explain why they have come about, or to argue in a principled way why they should enjoy government protection or public support (cf. Milofsky and Elworth 1985; Milofsky and Blades 1990).

Hall went on to argue that the sponsorship for nonprofit research was distorting the truth in important ways. Research places undue emphasis on those parts of the nonprofit world that traditionally have interacted with government and with the academic world—foundations, hospitals, universities, social work agencies, and the like. It ignores the largest part of the nonprofit world, religious organizations, which account for 60 percent of the income among nonprofits.

Research also has been responsible for changing the world to fit the abstract models scholars generate to explain the phenomenon. Early in the nonprofits research game, several economists proposed theories to explain how organizations neither devoted to making a profit nor engaged in government could possibly exist and even prosper. Economic theory does not allow for such initiatives. Market failure, contract failure, and free-rider problems helped economists to make sense of nonprofits (Hansman 1987).

These theoretical interpretations suggest systematic causes of non-profit enterprise. Critics of the economists object that the emergence of nonprofit industries followed no such systematic pattern (Salamon 1987; DiMaggio 1987). Yet, Hall notes, in considering whether the IRS deduction for contributions to nonprofits should be altered, government policymakers have taken the economists' models as though they were descriptions of reality. They have suggested eliminating tax deductibility for those nonprofits competing directly with proprietary organizations—nonprofit hospitals, nursing homes, day care centers, and public media all do this. By following academic research, policymakers may change reality, wiping out organizations whose existence is due to factors quite different from the things economists were willing to consider.

Hall's arguments have produced a storm of angry attacks in the form of letters and bitter comments in behind-the-scenes conversations. The leading journal on the study of voluntary organizations, the *Nonprofit and Voluntary Action Quarterly* (1990), ran a series of commentaries on the issue partially in response to Hall. People prominent in the academic research community and leaders of important philanthropic organizations are particularly incensed by Hall's "intemperate" comments. Hall for his part has been rounding up support by circulating his papers and sending out photocopies of the nasty letters he has received. It never occurred to him that he was following an old practice pioneered by his colleague across Hillhouse Avenue until I alerted him to Lang's file-making.

Filemaking as Social Theory

The filemaking of Lang and Hall is a process that creates social theory. Since their efforts produce conflict, angry denunciations, and nonscholarly alliances that include newspapers, foundations, professional organizations, and laypeople, many academics would say that their activities do the opposite. Rather than produce social theory, some would argue, they degrade the academy and lampoon the sober efforts of people attempting careful measurement and the formulation of lawful theory. Lang and Hall undermine efforts of those who try to work within the established social science paradigms and, one might argue, this is hardly a procedure for strengthening and deepening our stock of knowledge.

Such complaints ignore that an enormous amount of important science serves particular ideological interests and is the product of conflict (Lewontin 1990; Richards 1987). It is easy to find theoretical traditions within sociology whose origins and membership are structured by partisan controversies. Think of the fight in community research between elitists and pluralists during the fifties and sixties (Hunter 1953; Dahl 1961; Banfield 1961; Domhoff 1978; Polsby 1980). Quantitative Marxist research on the class structure has been sharply critical of liberal theories of social stratification based on labor market theory and the study of occupations (Blau and Duncan 1967; Wright and Perrone 1977). To forestall political retaliation, economists working in the Marxist tradition routinely prepare two curriculum vitae when they go on the job market, one for departments dominated by traditional economists and another for their allies in the Union of Radical Political Economists (URPE). Network research in the 1970s was split by a conflict between more empirically oriented Chicago sociologists like Laumann (Laumann and Pappi 1976) and Galaskiewicz (1979), whose work is rooted in the sociometric traditions of structural functionalism, and the math-modeling group made up of Harrison White and his students Scott Boorman and Ron Breiger (White, Boorman, and Breiger 1976; Boorman and White 1976). The latter derided the Chicago group as "mere statisticians."[4]

Theoretical elaboration in these cases is closely tied to partisan battles, ones often rooted in political and economic affiliations that transcend the academy. Orthodoxy is a favorite target and, when those holding positions of intellectual and institutional leadership are challenged, they not infrequently respond with anger and disdain for their critics. Enjoying strategic advantages in terms of access to funding and publication outlets (Keller 1963), benefiting from the legitimacy that accompanies holding an important professorship, and with ties to other leaders of the discipline, academic elites have powerful weapons available to protect themselves from attack. At the same time, they are visible targets easily challenged by up-welling discontent among outsiders and young scholars.

One might argue that Lang and Hall are more extreme in their methods than are the partisans in most academic battles. Reviewing the record of feuds surrounding other intellectual controversies, however, this argument is hard to maintain. The controversy over whether Dr. Robert C. Gallo actually discovered the HIV virus, for example, has been played out in the halls of congress and in the popular press. The perception that Gallo imperialistically controls scientific publication has led at least one researcher to withhold dissemination of his research results (Altman 1989; Crewdson 1989; Shilts 1987).[5] Followers of political theorist Leo Strauss have been pariahs in political science, so much so that Allan Bloom did not expect his book, *The Closing of the American Mind* (1987), to be read at all. Within sociology, consider the attacks James Coleman has had to weather in recent years in the wake of his research that supports private schooling (Coleman and Hoffer 1987: xxiv–xviii).

Conflict is everywhere. One reason filemaking is so much a part of social research is that the motivations for doing the scholarship and the sponsors that pay for research often have explicit political or economic goals (Richards 1987). Sometimes scientific arguments represent lightly veiled battles between interest groups external to science. This has bedeviled research on the heritability of intelligence for nearly a century as liberals and conservatives use studies of IQ similarity in identical twins as a battleground over racial superiority (Jensen 1969; Kamin 1974). Partisan conflict is thus a common visitor to the halls of science.

Science, meanwhile, is often an important contributor to political debate. As Lindblom (1980; Lindblom and Cohen 1979) argues, appealing to the facts is one, but only one, means for making political decisions and advancing polemical arguments. Science is useful to politics partly because it is a source of legitimacy and authority. This comes from a right scientists claim to state a societal consensus about what are the facts (Stinchcombe 1990). Their broad knowledge and mastery of esoteric techniques give scientists the power to define the terms of debate. Since having the power to define reality also may control the outcome of a dispute, invoking their institutional authority can be a powerful political weapon.

Scientists are powerful because their authority is rooted in claims about truth. The postures of positivism and value-neutrality many social scientists adopt are appeals to this authority (Merton 1972). They also represent a rhetorical device aimed at enhancing their power. They do this by imposing a consensus on the audience about what are facts, how we know what is real, and what constitutes reasonable evidence in support of an argument. These are the axioms that control arguments. By using the stance of scientific objectivity to limit debate about the ambiguities of social facts, positivists hide the partisan elements of their research programs. In so doing, objectivity becomes an instrument of rhetoric.

This makes difficult the separation of truth claims based on partisan interests and "real" claims about truth. The selection of facts to promote a partisan interest do not necessarily reduce the facticity of the information involved. Does the knowledge that made atomic bombs possible become less objectively true because that knowledge was used to make weapons? We might want to say that "bad" science is corrupted by politics but that truth will eventually be established and recognized independently of politics (Richards 1987).

Maybe some scientific truth survives politics to be enshrined in the museum of absolute truth. This does not seem to apply to the arenas of discourse in which Lang and Hall have put their filemaking abilities to work. Here, truth cannot be clearly separated from partisanship. This is partly because the research involved makes sense only in reference to specific institutional contexts. Saying this means that inquiry is inherently dependent on its context and historical setting. The research becomes meaningless if the institutions change and the demand for investigation would evaporate if the political agenda were different. It is for this reason that Lang objects to the very term, social *science*. He prefers to call this work social *studies*, since in his mind "science" can apply only to inanimate, nonthinking, nonparticipating objects of research.

This is not to demean the work of professional social inquiry (PSI—Lindblom's term for this kind of work). We must, however, proceed without the crutch of believing that an absolute, universal truth exists to provide social analysts with a basis of legitimacy. Authority in science comes to the extent there is consensus about the nature of reality with scientists as the people empowered to explain and interpret that reality. Cultural resources controlled by academics (journals, famous universities, professional organizations), styles of discourse that foster the impression of objectivity, and dramatic demonstrations of technical efficacy all help practitioners of PSI to make the claim that their words define reality. However, even under the most auspicious conditions, their claims are fragile. As times change, consensus shifts, and old "truths" come to sound hollow.

This suggests that established social theory tends to be dead social theory. Filemaking is a crucible of new ideas. If the struggle in scientific conflict is over whether any party is able to impose a consensus, independence and originality exist to the extent that dissident fragments of the academic enterprise are free (and inclined) to challenge orthodoxy. Agreement about the nature of reality is not the ideal towards which social science should strive.

My argument is like those that Harrison White (White and White 1965) and Howard Becker (1978) have offered to explain what makes new art exciting. Change in artistic taste depends on reaction against an orthodoxy. Revolutionary work effectively challenges and perhaps overturns established artistic values. We do not usually think that the work of orthodox masters is "bad" work. However, we do often describe the work of their followers as "derivative," and thus it is usually less exciting than the efforts of the *avant garde* leaders. Change in artistic taste happens as the result of critical social movements.

So it is in social science. Most social research is inseparable from partisanship. This is partly because often the work is inspired by political or economic motives. More importantly, it is easier to gain insights when we criticize or react against an established intellectual position. Perhaps this is because established knowledge becomes enshrined in institutional protections, both symbolic and material. As a perspective gains followers who turn out derivative research, and as the original clarion calls of a great thinker become installed in the hall of fame of classic scholarship, it becomes harder to see why that point of view illuminates. Rather than challenging reality and providing insight through contrast, these masterworks *become* reality, and they blind us. We need critique to strip off the rhetorical crust that disables our creativity.

This is why filemaking is attractive. By cracking the facade of orthodoxy, it allows us to see the world freshly. Presumably most filemakers fail to overthrow the powerful, and so they often will seem like troublemakers and useless gadflies. They are effective when they bring to bear broader values—sometimes these are old ones that have been discarded or ignored—on new issues and conflicts. They reawaken old controversies and they provide new meaning to old metaphors. This is the way of renewal in social theory.

Ethnography for Social Theory

If theory is built through critique, we can see why the study of social theories as artifacts is limited. If we talk about them as individual products that ought to be analyzed and appreciated independently of the context in which they were written, we lose much of the meaning of good theory. If it matters, theory ought to be argument. It ought to advance a point of view and there ought to be opposition. That opposition might come from many directions. It might arise out of arguments about measurement and about technical procedure within disciplines. It might arise from the clash of metatheoretical paradigms within a scholarly community. It might reflect the participation of academics in economic and political struggles that transcend the university.

Theory is argument that seeks to impose a consensus upon debate. It achieves this by making an appeal to empirical reality following rules of form and procedure that are accepted within a given discipline. In social science, those rules of form are so complex and malleable that making effective arguments—arguments that limit opposition by achieving a consensus about the nature of reality—is a matter of high art. Making theory convincing is extremely difficult and doubly so when we embed it in the process of data collection and analysis. Consequently, we engage in a simplification. We allow effective theoretical statements to frame the mission of narrow data collection efforts. This is normal science in Kuhn's (1970) language.

A consequence is that theories become the boundaries that define and buffer research communities. As Gouldner (1970:167–78) observed (when he asked why Talcott Parsons could not write), turgid and opaque theory is functional because critics become obliged to read the canon before they object to empirical investigations. Since few people but students or true believers will struggle through writing as difficult as that of Parsons [or that of Chomsky (1965, 1970; Chomsky and Halle 1968; Derwing 1973; Grimshaw 1973), to cite another example], orthodoxy smothers criticism.

Filemaking generates theory because the arguments that compose files typically focus on the nature of reality, on the rules of academic discourse, and on the need for a new consensus about the proper focus for empirical research. Attacks are moralistic and intense because critics tend to be those outside the academic establishment. Their claims gain force because they use empirical cases to show that people who have received large grants, who hold prestigious university posts, who have easy access to publication, or who are listened to by important politicians use their prestige to impose theoretical consensus on their less powerful scholarly colleagues. Bystanders are drawn in by the drama of these David and Goliath confrontations. Here we see Serge Lang, standing by his photocopy machine, confronting Seymour Martin Lipset, the National Science Foundation, the American Association of University Professors, and the *Chronicle of Higher Education*.

Of course, neither Serge Lang (with his membership in the National Academy of Sciences and the ability to mobilize phalanxes of Nobel laureates) nor Peter Hall (shooting away from his bunker at Yale) is without resources of prestige and legitimacy. They are insiders enough that they demand attention. However, both stand naked before the judges of morality. They provide interested bystanders with documentation collected from both sides of the dispute. Meanwhile, their opponents seem to avoid direct confrontations, they capitalize upon old-boy networks, they gain inside access to prestigious outlets for publication, and they receive lush grants to support their work. Showing that their opponents use the instruments of privilege to advance their case and avoid argument is a central strategy in the moral campaign of the filemaker. The objects of their attention complain that they are being tarred by righteousness, not undone by reason.

Whether or not filemakers are right is not so important as that they are focusing attention on the empirical bases of consensus among scholars. Fights focus on the frame of reference, and arguments sharpen explanations about why specific axiomatic assumptions are necessary or about why alternative formulations fail. Since the norms of science emphasize logical consistency and value-neutrality (Merton 1972), these intense battles force combatants to make their reasoning tighter and more carefully consistent with critical cases.

All of this might seem to idealize conflict and nastiness. This is not the object of my analysis. Rather, this is an effort to view theory as a social form, used in and by communities, within and outside the academy. Instead of talking about theory as a topic in which people might specialize, filemaking causes us to think about how the symbolic world of science is linked to the creation of intellectual social movements, and then to the institutionalization of ideas. In academic life, we live in a world where norms and values tend to be downplayed. Yet at bottom, filemaking is an activity centered on basic values. It arises because trying to achieve consensus about truth is widely accepted among academics as a professional obligation. Arguing about what standards should guide the evaluation of truth claims and trying to establish specific pieces of information as truths are deeply moral issues.

Saying that theory-making is a value-laden, moralistic, and communal activity is a sharp departure from the way sociologists are used to talking about the nature of theory. We are used to talking about theories as artifacts or as tools. In either case, we would be talking about objects that exist in the world. Filemaking suggests we need to think about theories as social process. Theories do refer to analytic devices that help us to frame the world—they *are* tools—but theories also represent an uncertain social process no individual can control. Many individuals contribute to the social streams that make theories real. Some contribute by being audience members; others contribute by orchestrating complex disputes, the role of filemaker played by Lang and Hall; others are marginal actors whose efforts precipitate new phases in a dispute or who make a limited contribution that moves a conflict forward.

This chapter has not said very much about how files evolve or what differences there are between systematic scholarship that grows out of conflict and that which does not. We do not know much about the natural history of theories in social science nor about how theory-laden intellectual movements evolve. These subjects are beyond the scope of this chapter, which is primarily devoted to arguing that filemaking is a serious and important scholarly activity. The activity needs defending because the conception we have of how serious discourse proceeds makes filemaking seem nonserious, casual, and unscientific.

The problem is not with filemaking. The problem is with the way we conceive of and study social theory. We talk about theory as it ought to be. We tend not to observe it happening. We do not bring an ethnographic orientation to the study of how we do our work. Because of that, it is easy to present theory as a detached, formalized activity that is separate from politics, economics, and the rest of life.

Social theory is a technical specialty that walls itself off (as do most technical specialties) from other segments of the social science enterprise. Theorists tend to relate their work to a lineage of other theorists. They also have developed a specialized language that those outside the specialty may find impenetrable. The inaccessibility of theory is due to more than these boundary-constructing activities. Theory is difficult to create and to understand because often it talks about concepts that are abstractions of abstractions. The objects of discussion are unobservable and removed from concrete experience, and thus it is hard to find a language that is direct, accessible, and not repetitive. The technical language of theorists is partly a matter of necessity, a style of discourse that allows complex discussions to proceed.

Specialization makes theory seem important in and of itself, however. A peculiarity of social science is that our norms and the operating conditions in which we work do not allow us to see clearly what impact our theories have, or to judge whether or not we are happy with the way they work. Other professions tend to be focused on end-products and to value intellectual effort as productive work—doctors, lawyers, architects, economists. Because it is hard to gain a sense of efficacy in teaching and research, we tend to value the process of our work and the provision of services for their own sakes.

As the scientific enterprise grows, teaching and research come to rely on the truth of particular renditions of theory. Eventually, however, the context that motivated the original formulation so changes that the theory no longer makes sense. It becomes extremely difficult to recapture the original line of thought so that we can create a better theory, one more in tune with current knowledge and contemporary social concerns.

By this time, theory is so embedded in the rituals of research and the institutional interdependencies of the academy that change becomes extremely threatening and we resist it. This situation causes us to reify theory and attack those who irreverently challenge basic truths.

We can understand, thus, while filemakers cause trouble. They are iconoclasts and they challenge the institutional status that successful but intellectually conservative scholars have achieved. We need institutional stability and access to resources to function in university life. Filemakers force us to acknowledge, however, that we have a deeper obligation to support norms of accuracy and intellectual accountability. By emphasizing these values they also force the university to be open to forces of renewal and social change.

Theory is dynamic when it contributes to and draws from research. It also is important to the extent that it emerges from and interacts with other political and cultural dialogues. It can do both of these explosively—the Rushdie affair is an example of this from the world of fiction (Marzorati 1990). However, theory also can become a variety of domination or a cultlike form of self-congratulation. Good theory is attentive to the concrete world and to political discourse. Theory is not valuable for its own sake. It should guide and be guided by our empirical experiences.

Both theory and ethnography can be weapons. They are not the only weapons used to advance political and economic programs in contemporary society—guns, money, political influence, cultural domination, and the passive resistance some people can achieve with routines also are weapons. Theory and ethnography happen to be *our* weapons.

Social theory makes its impacts by advancing the fortunes of social movements. This confuses us, however, because at the same time that ideas generate and enliven movements, those who manufacture ideas can assume any of many different relationships to the application of ideas to social processes. Theorists may be authors; they may be contributors; they may be critics; they may be bystanders; they may defend the status quo or rationalize obnoxious political movements; they may be so socially distant from their impacts that they are unaware of any effect; and, sadly, they may have no effect on anything at all.

Theory, in other words, is pluralistic and this is one reason that it is hard to interpret. This is why filemaking is important, and why those of us who are bystanders need to be appreciative audiences. The conflicts that surround file creation make us uncomfortable and sometimes give us a guilty feeling. However, conflict over ideas and commitments is one of the few devices we have for laying bare the presuppositions that inform the normal science we do as professional scholars. Filemakers encourage us to examine the price we pay for our institutional commitments, and the benefits we enjoy. Filemaking also is a source of intellectual renewal, forcing us to consider whether the assumptions underlying our work continue to be valid. Good empirical work draws its energy and direction from solid theory. Since collective understandings about reality continually shift, good research cannot rely on static theory.

Notes

1. This chapter was first presented as a paper at "Writing the Social Text. An Interdisciplinary Conference," held at the University of Maryland, College Park, November 18 and 19, 1989.
2. Personal communication. Serge Lang visited Bucknell in 1988 and I videotaped much of his visit. The comments quoted here come from a videotaped interview he directed to my social theory class in which he instructed them on how to read *The File*. In his lecture to the class he talked at length about the strategy involved in dealing with letters to the editor.
3. Hall has sent me a variety of papers and letters that make up his "file" of conflict with the nonprofits research establishment. Most of the papers are in draft form so they may not be cited. He may be contacted at the Program on Nonprofit Organizations, Yale University.
4. In personal conversations in the later 1970s and early 1980s I heard this insult from both sides. Laumann once talked about how White and his students object to his approach to network analysis as mere statistics. Boorman in later conversation reiterated the point.
5. The scientific ethics of Gallo and David Baltimore, incidentally, are the object of Lang's latest filemaking efforts.

References

Altman, Lawrence K. 1989. "AIDS Finding Piques Curiosity, But Scientists Are Wary." *New York Times*, April 11, Sect. C, p. 3.

Banfield, Edward C. 1961. *Political Influence*. Glencoe, IL: Free Press.

Becker, Howard S. 1978. "Arts and Crafts." *American Journal of Sociology* 83(4): 862–889.

———. 1986. *Writing for Social Scientists*. Chicago: University of Chicago Press.

Blau, Peter and Otis Dudley Duncan. 1967. *The American Occupational Structure*. New York: Wiley.

Bloom, Allan David. 1987. *The Closing of the American Mind*. New York: Simon and Schuster.

Boorman, Scott and Harrison C. White. 1976. "Social Structure from Multiple Networks. II. Role Structures." *American Journal of Sociology* 81(6):1384–1446.

Chomsky, Noam. 1965. *Aspects of the Theory of Syntax*. Cambridge, MA: MIT Press.

———. 1970. *Current Issues in Linguistic Theory*. The Hague: Mouton.

Chomsky, Noam and Morris Halle. 1968. *The Sound Pattern of English*. New York: Harper and Row.

Coleman, James S. and Thomas Hoffer. 1987. *Public and Private High Schools*. New York: Basic Books.

Crewdson, John. 1989. "The Great AIDS Quest. Science under the Microscope." *Chicago Tribune*, November 19, Section 5, pp. 1–16.

Dahl, Robert. 1961. *Who Governs? Democracy and Power in an American City*. New Haven, CT: Yale University Press.

Derwing, Bruce. 1973. *Transformational Grammar as a Theory of Language Acquisition: A Study in the Empirical, Conceptual, and Methodological Foundations of Contemporary Linguistic Theory*. Cambridge: Cambridge University Press.

DiMaggio, Paul. 1987. "Nonprofit Organizations in the Production and Distribution of Culture." Pp. 195–220 in *The Nonprofit Sector: A Research Handbook*, edited by Walter W. Powell. New Haven, CT: Yale University Press.

Domhoff, G. William. 1978. *Who Really Rules? New Haven and Community Power Reexamined*. New Brunswick, NJ: Transaction Books.

Galaskiewicz, Joseph. 1979. *Exchange Networks and Community Politics*. Beverly Hills, CA: Sage.

Gouldner, Alvin W. 1970. *The Coming Crisis of Western Sociology*. New York: Basic Books.

Grimshaw, Allen D. 1973. "On Language and Society: Part I." *Contemporary Sociology* 2(6, (November):)575–85.

Hall, Peter. 1988. "Regulating Competition: A Reflection on History and Policy." Paper presented at New York University Conference on Nonprofit Organizations, November.

———. 1989. "A Bridge Founded upon Justice and Built of Human Hearts: Reflections on Religion, Science, and the Development of American Philanthropy." Paper presented at the Spring Research Forum, Independent Sector, Chicago, IL, March 10–11.

———. 1991. *Inventing the Nonprofit Sector, 1789–1989*. New York: Basic Books.

Hansman, Henry. 1987. "Economic Theories of Nonprofit Organization." Pp 27–42 in *The Nonprofit Sector. A Research Handbook*, edited by Walter W. Powell. New Haven, CT: Yale University Press.

Hunter, Floyd. 1953. *Community Power Structure: A Study of Decision Makers*. Chapel Hill: University of North Carolina Press.

Jensen, Arthur R. 1969. "How Much Can We Boost IQ and Scholastic Achievement?" *Harvard Educational Review* 38 (Reprint Series #2):1–123.

Kamin, Leon J. 1974. *The Science and Politics of I.Q.* Potomac, MD: Lawrence Erlbaum.

Keller, Suzanne. 1963. *Beyond the Ruling Class: Strategic Elites in Modern Society*. New York: Random House.

Kuhn, Thomas. 1970. *The Structure of Scientific Revolutions*. 2nd edition. Chicago: University of Chicago Press.

Lang, Serge. 1977. *The File*. New York: Springer Verlag.

Laumann, Edward O. and Franz U. Pappi. 1976. *Networks of Collective Action: A Perspective on Community Influence Systems*. New York: Academic.

Levine, Donald N. n.d. "On the Heritage of Sociology." Department of Sociology, University of Chicago.

Lewontin, R. C. 1990. "Fallen Angels. Review of *Wonderful Life: The Burgess Shale and the Nature of History* by Stephen Jay Gould." *New York Review of Books*, June 14, pp. 3–7.

Lindblom, Charles E. 1980. *The Policy-Making Process*. Engelwood Cliffs, NJ: Prentice-Hall.

Lindblom, Charles E. and David Cohen. 1979. *Usable Knowledge: Social Science and Social Problem Solving*. New Haven, CT: Yale University Press.

Mannheim, Karl. 1936. *Ideology and Utopia. An Introduction to the Sociology of Knowledge*. Translated by Louis Wirth and Edward Shils. New York: Harcourt, Brace, and World, Harvest Books.

Martindale, Don. 1988. *The Nature and Types of Sociological Theory*. 2nd edition. Prospect Heights, IL: Waveland Press.

Marzorati, Gerald. 1990. "Rushdie in Hiding. An Interview." *New York Times Magazine*, 4 November:31–33, 68, 78, 84–85.

Merton, Robert K. 1972. "The Institutional Imperatives of Science." Pp 65–79 in *The Sociology of Science*. edited by B. Barnes. London: Penguin.

Milofsky, Carl. 1987. "De-Mystifying Academic Rhetoric and Empowering Students: Threshold Requirements for Analytic Thinking." Paper presented at the Penn State Conference on Rhetoric and Composition, University Park, Pennsylvania, July 7–10.

———. 1991. "Writing and Seeing. Is There Any Sociology Here?" Pp 35–49 in *The Rhetoric of Social Research*, edited by Albert Hunter. New Brunswick, NJ: Rutgers University Press.

Milofsky, Carl and Steve Blades. 1990. "The Accountability Problem in Health Charities." Pp 1–14 in *Towards the 21st Century. Challenges for the Voluntary Sector*, Volume 2. Proceedings of the Conference of the Association of Voluntary Action Scholars, July 16–18, London.

Milofsky, Carl and Julie Elworth. 1985. "Charitable Associations." Pp 790–810 in *Issues in the Care of Children with Chronic Illness*, edited by Nicholas Hobbs and James M. Perrin. San Francisco: Jossey-Bass.

Milofsky, Carl and Peter Hall. 1990. "Commentary on Van Til's 'Independence of Research': Another View." *Nonprofit and Voluntary Sector Quarterly* 19(1):79–83.

Nonprofit and Voluntary Action Quarterly. 1990. Volume 19(1, Spring).

Polsby, Nelson. 1980. *Community Power and Political Theory: A Further Look at Problems of Evidence and Inference*. New Haven, CT: Yale University Press.

Richards, Stewart. 1987. *Philosophy and Sociology of Science: An Introduction*. Oxford: Basil Blackwell.

Ritzer, George. 1988. *Contemporary Sociological Theory*. 2nd edition. New York: Alfred A. Knopf.

Salamon, Lester M. 1987. "Partners in Public Service: The Scope and Theory of Government-Nonprofit Relations." Pp 99–117 in *The Nonprofit Sector: A Research Handbook*, edited by Walter W. Powell. New Haven, CT: Yale University Press.

Shilts, Randy. 1987. *And the Band Played On: Politics, People, and the AIDS Epidemic*. New York: St. Martin's.

Stinchcombe, Arthur L. 1968. *Constructing Social Theories*. Chicago: University of Chicago Press.

————. 1990. "Work Institutions and the Sociology of Everyday Life." Pp 99–116 in *The Nature of Work*, edited by Kai Erickson and Steven P. Vallas. New Haven, CT: Yale University Press.

White, Harrison C. and Cynthia A. White. 1965. *Canvases and Careers: Institutional Change in the French Painting World*. New York: Wiley.

White, Harrison C., Scott A. Boorman, and Ronald L. Breiger. 1976. "Social Structure from Multiple Networks. I. Blockmodels of Roles and Positions." *American Journal of Sociology* 81(4):730–80.

Wright, Eric O. and Luca Perrone. 1977. "Marxist Class Categories and Income Inequality." *American Sociology Review* 42(1):32–55.

PART IV

Challenges for the Rhetoric of the Human Sciences

Chapter 11

Human Needs and Control: A Foundation for Human Science and Critique

Paul Sites

The goal of scholarship has always been the production of new truth, but this is not the case for those scholars embracing the linguistic turn, who argue that "It is language all the way down" (Rorty 1989). Their stock in trade is not the pursuit of truth but the use of method to deconstruct what has been accepted as truth. Their truth is the truth of no truth since, for them, there is no foundation upon which truth can be constructed. For them, there is no basis for judgment, no criteria that can be used to establish truth; there is only regularity (Lyotard 1984). They also discount reason as a final court of appeal since it has been reason, at least since the Enlightenment, that has provided the "foundation" for what has passed for truth.

I have little quarrel with much of what is being said; all texts, including culture, which have been constructed by rhetoric can obviously be deconstructed by rhetoric. Furthermore, pure reason cannot arrive at truth since reason, like truth, must have a basis for judgment outside itself. This is why, at least since the Enlightenment and the destruction of other essence and epistemologies used as foundations, truth has used reason for its grounding and reason has used *assumed* truth as a foundation upon which to build. The folly of reason's appeal to truth and truth's appeal to reason has now been exposed.

But, some scholars embracing the linguistic turn have also deconstructed/decentered the subject in their hurry to show that for homo sapiens everything including the nature of the human subject is produced by language. We have been down a similar road before with Durkheim's collective conscience, which exists exterior to individuals and constrains them, along with his social facts, which produce other social facts, leaving little place for the subject. Parsons, following the same road, claimed he wanted to bring the subject/actor back in but his system would not permit this. For him, along with many others, culture, based on an ultimate reality of symbolism, constructs both the society and the individual, thereby producing an equilibrated harmony. Thus, this road has been well traveled for nearly a century even though there have always been one or more loyal oppositions (Mullins 1973).

The opposition most typically has taken the position, as I will be doing here, that the individual, referred to as subject, actor, or agent, must count for something in all this. It is after all people who created language in the first place and people who use language to formulate narratives that serve them in some manner. Once narratives are created, they, of course, may come back to haunt their creators but this provides no ground for the conclusion that the subject is only that which is created by language even though language is important in its creation. Nietzsche knew this and the fact that he did is evident in nearly everything he wrote, best summed up in the familiar line, "Reason in language!—oh what a deceptive old witch it has been! I fear we shall never be rid of God, so long as we believe in grammar." In short, Nietzsche's agony was that he, as a subject, wanted to be free from the morality of narratives created with language but to be free from narratives is to face the terror of chaos since it is narratives, framed in terms of nomos and even cosmos, to use Berger's (1967) terms, that make the human condition bearable. But once established, narratives produce their own terror, as Lyotard (1984) and others have pointed out.

Now, if people must use narratives and if at the same time narratives produce terror, there must be a reason. I will argue that this reason can be found in the nature of the human species giving the subject or agency causal power. That is, if it can be demonstrated that individuals have causal power grounded in the very nature of the species, the type of realism or naturalism supported by scholars such as Bashkar (1979) and Harre (1979) can be realized. By the same token it can counter the suggestion of scholars such as Rosenberg (1980) that all human sciences will be reduced to biology. More specifically, I argue that human needs, conceptualized as analogs of primary emotions, and a control orientation used by individuals attempting to gratify these needs provide the basic "flesh" of *agency* giving causal power to individuals. This takes the typical realist argument back one step and gives it a biological rather than a social basis. The typical realist argument deals with reasons such as wants, beliefs, and desires as causal. But these are constructed by language, making them spatially and temporally relative and thus not firmly grounded in the ontology of the human species being.

There have been a host of attempts to isolate basic human needs but most have been inadequate. Marx was perhaps the first modern theorist to deal with human needs and his dichotomy of true versus false needs triggered considerable scholarly debate. He was greatly concerned with the nature of the human species and saw this nature alienated under various modes of production short of communism. Indeed, this was the motive force for his theorizing. It was Marx's (1964) position that the type of society in which people live produces consequences because of the human species being.

By way of contrast, Parsons's position, and that of many others, was the direct opposite of Marx. At base, it was Parsons's position that it makes little or no difference in what type of society people live. He (Parsons and Shills 1959) took the position, at least in his general theory, that biogenetic needs are transformed in the "successful" socialization process into need dispositions. Since the latter match the values of a society, as noted earlier, people come to want to do what they have to do (and like it) to make society function smoothly. Thus, for Parsons and like-minded theorists, all explanation can be reduced to the social or cultural order under the assumption that humans are infinitely malleable. In this view, humans have no inherent nature that can be violated and thus suffer no adverse consequences (see Galtung 1988) so long as the socialization process functions properly in terms of any socially produced means-ends schema.

Merton (1968) follows Parsons's lead in his famous essay, "Social Structure and Anomie." People would always be willing to conform to socially produced means and goals if social structure permitted. Since this is not always possible because of structural strains, some people engage in deviant behavior, which leads the society toward anomie *rather than restructuring*, short of his category of rebellion. Merton's inference reflects Parsons's prejudice that a society may take any form in terms of a means-ends schema so long as everyone is permitted to "live" accordingly. If society delivers what it promises, no matter what that might be, everyone is satisfied. It is societies' "needs" that are paramount, as opposed to those of individuals, because the latter are not functionally important for system maintenance.

Agency as Needs

Since Marx, a host of scholars have attempted to isolate a basic human nature by positing various human needs. Among these were Malinowski, Ward, Thomas, Maslow, Fromm, and Marcuse. (For an excellent review see Springborg 1981.) The problems with most of these attempts were that some confused needs with socially produced interests, wants, and desires (see Fitzgerald 1977); others confused needs with conditions necessary for their gratification (e.g., Bay 1958), while others listed human needs consistent with their own ideologies (e.g., Marcuse 1969). In an earlier work (Sites 1973), I arrived at a classification of human needs based on the consequences of conditioning during the primary socialization process, which proved unsatisfactory for a number of reasons.

More recently Giddens (1984), following Laing (1967), posits a need for ontological security as an important component of agency. It was Laing's view that there are consequences if the need for security is violated. The most typical consequence is mental illness, which Laing saw as a rational solution arrived at by the individual. If interaction within the framework of "normal" social life is too threatening, people step "outside" social life and create a "reality" of their own that they can control.

Even more recently Turner (1987, 1988) proposed a classification of needs that serves as a motivational beginning point in his theory of social interaction. Turner begins his list of needs with what he calls "needs for group inclusion," "needs for sense of trust," and "needs for a sense of ontological security." If the gratification of these needs is frustrated in interaction, anxiety occurs, producing a need for its abatement, which leads to still other needs: "needs for symbolic/material gratification," "needs to sustain self-conception," and "needs for a sense of facticity" (Turner 1988:38, Fig.5.1). Turner frames his work on interaction in the same manner as did Parsons (1937) in *The Structure of Social Action* by drawing on the work of other theorists in order to deduce his categories. I agree with the thrust of his work when he stipulates that theoretical credibility must be founded on the assumption of individual needs and will later emulate his method of proof for the existence of needs conceptualized as analogs of emotions. Turner repeats the mistakes of others by confusing some of his needs with the necessary conditions for their gratification. For example, his need for a sense of group inclusion is a necessary condition for the gratification of other needs and thus not a real need, just as his need for trust is a necessary condition for security rather than a need in itself. Although his formulation is unnecessarily cumbersome, Turner makes a contribution by moving toward a basic ontology of the individual in the same sense I attempted in an earlier work noted above and continue to do here.

Touraine (1984:110) also calls for a theory of "deep, fundamental, and natural needs." This is posited in terms of his concern for formulating a sociology capable of understanding social life in a postmodern-programmed society. If agency is increasingly important in terms of choosing the future, a basic understanding of the nature of agency becomes critical. Even though the self and its needs have always been important, the long-recognized needs of the physiological organism have taken precedence over these until recently. So long as humans are hungry, have bodies racked with pain, and fear for their physical security, these physiological needs will probably take precedence over the needs of the self. Thus, Foucault (1979) sees the celebration of the self, along with technologies of the self, beginning to appear in the nineteenth century marking an important transition toward the post-modern age and its "play of differences."

In an earlier paper (Sites 1988) I made the case that needs relating to the self are best conceptualized as analogs of primary emotions using Kemper's (1987) classification of primary emotions as a point of departure. Kemper takes the position that there are four primary emotions: fear, anger, depression, and satisfaction (happiness). Many other scholars [see Kemper (1987) for a listing] agree that there are primary emotions even though some add one to six others and/or give different names to the same ones. Kemper bases his evidence for primary emotions on evolutionary survival value, ontogenetic primacy, cross-cultural universality, and autonomic structure. These emotions evolved because of their survival value vis-á-vis the physiological organism. I make the case that as a self develops in the socialization process, these primary emotions become attached to it and are important in facilitating its survival. In all this, it is interesting to note that the limbic system, the seat of emotions, differs little between homo sapiens and other higher primates (MacLean 1973; Restak 1988).

I argue that in terms of the self, a need for security is the analog of fear, the need for meaning the analog of anger, and the need for self-esteem the analog of depression. Satisfaction (happiness), the one positive emotion in Kemper's classification, becomes fully possible only as the needs seen as analogs of the negative emotions—fear, anger, and depression—are gratified. The meaning of the security need is obvious; people experience fear when survival of the self is in some manner threatened. The need for meaning is explained in terms of consistency of response over time. When people do not get what they have been led to expect based on past experience, they express the emotion of anger. In addition, they become angry if what has been accepted as truth, cultural or other, is threatened. Approval from others is the basis of self-esteem as Kemper (1978) shows (he calls it status). When approval of people's behavior, values, beliefs, etc. is not forthcoming, they become depressed. Depression can also be expected when a source of approval is removed, as in the death of a loved one or loss of a friend. It should be obvious in everyday interaction processes that one or all of the negative primary emotions may be triggered in response to the same situation. *Conceptualizing needs as analogs of primary emotions gives needs a firm ontology in the nature of the human species* and answers the criticisms of scholars who reject the idea that people have needs that are more basic than socially produced interests, wants, and desires.

Perhaps the best way to understand emotions and their need analogs is to see emotions, following Solomon (1983), as judgments. Or, as Jacobson says, *"in many respects the most important function of emotions is evaluation of reality"* (1967:125; his emphasis). Therefore, in terms of the human needs with which this paper is concerned, when a person experiences fear, a judgment is being made that the need for security is not being gratified; something in the interaction situation is threatening. When anger is experienced, a judgment is being made that the need for meaning is not being gratified; the person is not receiving expected response from others and/or what has come to be accepted as truth is being challenged. When depression is experienced, a judgment is being made that the need for self-esteem is not being gratified; the person's behavior is not being approved. If satisfaction is experienced, a judgment is being made that the need analogs of the negative emotions are being sufficiently gratified. Thus, primary emotions may be conceptualized as built-in monitoring devices that constantly evaluate interaction processes.

Much of the above is consistent with Gazzaniga's (1985, 1988) modular (social) model of the mind. The cognitive and emotional modules always interact and both are evaluative/judgmental modules. But, if there were no emotions in the very early socialization process, there would be no judgments; one type of response on the part of the socialization agent would be as "good" as any other and the infant could not be socialized to take her/his place in an organized society. As the self develops, emotions continue to be important as judgments. This is one reason it is difficult to change people's minds in spite of overwhelming evidence; the emotional module, in Gazzaniga's terms, will not permit the evidence to "pass." All this does not negate the importance of the cognitive module in his work. Once the cognitive structure develops, it has the capacity to evaluate the judgments produced by emotions as well as make judgments that produce emotions. Whether anything can be done once such cognitive evaluation occurs remains a problem in some cases. Let me give a brief example from Gazzaniga's work.

A person is in a crowded room when for some reason the emotion of fear is triggered. The cognitive structure of the mind associates this fear with "something" about the crowded condition and the person subsequently develops a phobia about being in a crowded place. It is well-known that such phobias are very difficult to "think away" using the cognitive module of the mind. The cognitive module cannot "convince" the emotional module that the phobia is "irrational." This demonstrates the power of emotion in human life and consequently why needs as analogs of emotions are important. I turn now to a brief discussion of the process by which emotions come to be attached to the self during socialization.

Needs and Socialization

It is obvious that the biological conditions necessary for the possibility of the self are present at birth. Among these are emotions (see Oster and Ekman 1977; Trevarthen 1984). As we shall see, the social conditions necessary to produce the self "reflect" the biological conditions that make possible not only the self but also social order in the first instance. This is why Mead is correct in saying self and society are opposite sides of the same coin even though part of my interpretation differs from his.

The new infant comes equipped with characteristics that enhance the chances of survival. Among these are the ability to cry when hungry, certain reflexes, and, for our concern, the primary emotions. At birth, these are useful only as survival mechanisms for the biological organism since no self is present. Attachment theorists (e.g., Ainsworth 1978; Bowlby 1982) take the position, as opposed to others (e.g., Kagan 1984), that if a self is to develop normally, certain conditions must be present in the social environment as these relate to the physiological organism. From their work I take these conditions to include a relatively high degree of security, consistency of response toward the infant, and a rate of approval response greater than the rate of disapproval response. If the environment is not relatively secure, the infant will withdraw and/or develop pathological tendencies. If responses toward the new infant's behavior are not relatively consistent, the infant cannot and will not develop a normal self. And if approval responses are not greater than disapproval responses, the infant may withdraw.

These conditions are necessary given the characteristics of the physiological organism upon which the self is constructed. This is to say, the infant comes equipped with emotions that respond negatively to threatening situations (fear), inconsistency (anger), and disapproval (depression). [Fox and Davidson (1988) call this sadness.] In short, emotions are (making) judgments in terms of the "quality" of the new infant's environment. Early on, these judgments (evaluations) are automatic, unencumbered by language-based cognition. It should be emphasized that this is not a "chicken or egg" situation; the primary emotions as evaluative mechanisms must be considered as prior. *Were this not the case, the socialization agent could treat the infant in any manner, even with random responses, without consequences* for the infant even though there would be consequences for social order.

A self begins to develop as the infant "recognizes" the *effects* it produces on the environment, including others. If the biological organism and the nascent self did not produce effects and respond accordingly, no self could emerge. As these effects are produced, "judgments" are made, and because language is minimal at this point, these judgments (evaluations) are emotions. As the child learns language, cognitive evaluations become possible as he or she develops an ability to take the attitude and role of the other as Mead shows. But even here, inasmuch as social values have not been learned, judgments continue to be (made by) emotions. These emotions become integral to the self in this process and thereafter remain in its service. Under normal circumstances, the self is processual as it continues to take new directions vis-à-vis the responses of others.

The important point here is that the primary emotions produced by the evolutionary process to enhance physiological survival are the same emotions that make the *self* and *social order* possible and necessary in the first instance. The same emotions that produce mutual dependence if needs are to be gratified are the same emotions that make the self possible. I will shortly discuss control as an important component of agency. Here, control is seen as the *production of effects* on the environment including others, which is necessary if the self is to develop. This control orientation on the part of the individual is used for the gratification of both the needs of the body and the needs of the self. This is to say that people attempt to control others in an attempt to reduce threat, maintain consistency, and gain approval. At the same time people attempt to control others, they are dependent on them for the gratification of their needs and thereby are open to their control. *In short, the self and control are twin born in that needs attached to the self can be gratified only through social interaction. Thus agents attempt control to gratify their respective needs.* This shows the genius of Emerson's (1962) early work on power-dependency relations, Kemper's (1978) work on status-power relations and Mead's (1934, 1938) contribution in combining behaviorism and pragmatism in his work on the self.

The socialization agent names emotional signs as these are variously exhibited by the infant, and the infant learns these along with what Hochschild (1983) calls emotion norms. It is obvious that the names given, along with emotions norms, are social in nature. But, it is also the case that unlearned signs for primary emotions are universal. Ekman and his associates have demonstrated this repeatedly with very sophisticated measurements (Ekman and Friesen 1978). Of course, the public display of emotions can be controlled once what Ekman calls display rules (similar to emotion norms) have been learned. Individuals in isolation, however, continue to display the unlearned universal signs. Ekman, in referring to his research conducted with his associate, Robert Levenson, among members of the Minangkabau society in Western Sumatra, Indonesia, says "Our assumption is these [physiological reactions] are biologically based and hard-wired. Culture may magnify or diminish emotional reactions, but will neither eliminate nor replace them. . . . We have found that it isn't just the look on the face, but the feelings inside that people share. *It is the first evidence of the universality of autonomic nervous system pattern.* (Ekman 1989a:59; my emphasis).

As noted earlier, Ekman and his associates, along with others, have listed primary emotions in addition to those listed by Kemper. This should not be taken as evidence against the existence of primary emotions; rather, it should be seen as confusion in terms of the number and characteristics of the primaries. Several scholars, for example, list "interest" as a primary emotion. In terms of this, there is evidence that animals as well as humans, including very young infants, explore their environments. Thus, there is something inherent in animals that causes this type of behavior. It would seem, however, that this type of emotion might better be characterized as boredom with a corresponding need for new experience or stimulation. This is the one emotion and need analog I would add, if pressed, because of the overwhelming evidence. But the emotions and their need analogs with which this paper is concerned appear to be the most important in terms of self and social order and thus I am restricting the discussion to these. Some of the others, of course, may be linked to primaries rather then being primaries. I will say a word about what are called secondary emotions for readers unfamiliar with work on emotions.

Over 400 different emotions have been named, but Kemper (1987) and others argue that most of these are linked to one or more of the primary emotions. As Kemper says, "I have argued that there is an autonomic ground—among others—for judging which emotions are primary and that secondary emotions are socially constructed but attain their emotional tone by virtue of their linkage, in the course of socialization, with the primary emotions" (1987:282). For example, he sees guilt linked with fear and shame linked with anger. These two secondary emotions are extremely useful from the point of view of the socialization agent and others who wish to gain and/or maintain control over others. If children can be taught to experience fear as guilt, along with its interpretation, they can be taught to blame self rather than conditions that threaten it. Or, if people in the working class can be taught to feel shame rather than anger as needs are violated, they can be more easily controlled as Sennet and Cobb (1978) demonstrate. Scheff (1988) sees shame producing rigid conformity, which I would argue is often the best control strategy under certain conditions.

Many who take a rigid social-constructionist view (see Harre 1986) of emotions label Kemper a positivist and consequently reject his work. It is obvious from any point of view, sociological or otherwise, that social constructionists have a point. They are correct in terms of the construction of the secondary emotions but, if Kemper is correct, these secondary emotions could not be constructed if there were no primary emotions to which they can be linked. Social constructionists would have to agree that the human has the *potential* for experiencing emotional states and that this potential is grounded in physiology. In addition, I assume social constructionists would agree that just any emotion cannot be triggered by just any contingency; that there must be some patterning to emotions if they have anything at all to do with individual survival. If social constructionists disagree that emotions have something to do with survival, the burden of proof is on them to come up with a reason as to why emotions were selected in the evolutionary process. It stretches the imagination to believe, for example, that the emotion of fear would not be experienced under threatening conditions or that the emotion of satisfaction (happiness) would be experienced if a person *did not* get what was expected in a situation. If the latter were the case and all people sought happiness because it is more pleasant, social order would be impossible since people would constantly seek chaos rather than order.

Collins's (1975) idea concerning the importance of power in controlling the means of emotional production can be fleshed out in more specific terms within this formulation. *The control of need gratification allows the relative control of populations short of coercion.* This is the "genius" inherent in capitalism. So long as the needs for self-esteem and meaning are gratified primarily by material goods and their display (see Veblen 1899), capitalism may be secure. In Marx's terms, under capitalism, people fetishize commodities and in Ernest Becker's (1968) terms a fetish gives a false sense of control. Or, if we look at Nietzsche's idea of resentment in interpreting religion, the idea comes through as well. If "weak" religious leaders are to increase their power they must invert prevailing values upon which the distribution of power rests. Jesus attempted this with his teachings, "Blessed are the poor for theirs is the kingdom of God" and "Blessed are the meek for they shall inherit the earth." People come to value and thus can be controlled by beliefs and practices that they see as gratifying their needs. As Howard Becker (1955) has argued, *people value what they need.*

Agency as Control

In addition to having needs, I (Sites 1973) have argued that individuals take a control orientation toward others attempting to gratify these needs. In this, it is often the case that individuals control their own behavior in order to control the behavior of others. This can be seen as working in the various processes Turner (1988) outlines such as frame-making, account-making, and ritual-making. As indicated in the brief discussion of socialization, the infant attempts control by producing effects, making the self possible. This control orientation is reinforced through conditioning in the socialization process and later through cognitive learning. The socialization agent attempts to control the behavior of the child using a variety of strategies. From this, the child learns that attempted control of others is a basic dynamic of social life. If it is doubted that even very young children use a variety of control strategies, all one need do is spend a day observing them (see Wood, Weinstein and Parker 1967). The idea of control is evident in Mead's concept of taking the role of the other and in Goffman's dramaturgical sociology.

By definition, people take the role of others before acting in order to anticipate possible responses so their actions (strategies) can be tailored to produce desired responses from others. Mead emphasized control in his attention to the prehensile hand; people attempt to "mold" objects and they attempt to control responses of others in a manner that will best gratify their needs. As Mead says:

> The individual organism determines in some sense its own environment by its sensitivity. The only environment to which the organism can react is one that its sensitivity reveals. . . . If in the development of the form there is an increase in the diversity of sensitivity there will be an increase in the responses of the organism to its environment. There is a direct reaction of the organism upon the environment which leads to some measure of control. (1934:245)

In Goffman's (e.g., 1959, 1969) work, agents attempt to present self strategically in order to gain gratification, most typically self-esteem.

Even Alexander, who has been so insistent that order can be understood only from a collective viewpoint, increasingly recognizes the importance of strategic action in its production. He (Alexander 1987) sees two components of action, interpretation and strategization. Once an interpretation of a situation is made by the individual so that the world is "understood," he or she then engages in strategic action based upon cost-reward calculations and this action may produce transformations. In this, Alexander is aware, as Collins (1981, 1988) emphasizes, "that knowledge is too sketchy" to encompass all possible contingencies so that strategic action can only take a "best bet" orientation. Collins bases strategy on emotional energy. Thus, these theorists and a number of others (see, e.g., Bourdieu 1986; Gibbs 1989) in diverse theoretical traditions appear to be coming to an agreement that people do take a control orientation (use strategies) in interaction. I am arguing that, at base, judgments concerning the effectiveness of such strategies are emotions. People engage in interaction to gratify needs, and emotions are judgments concerning the effectiveness of the strategies used. This is not to say that cognition is unimportant. Unlike other animals, humans have the capacity cognitively to evaluate such judgments, take the role of the other, seek out different groups (Thibaut and Kelly 1959), and negotiate (see Strauss 1977).

In addition, individuals may also use defense mechanisms. If the social world cannot be controlled through what I have called social control strategies used for the purpose of gratifying needs, they can be expected to turn to the use of defense mechanisms (psychological control strategies) in an attempt to minimize damage to the self (Sites 1973). If these strategies fail to work, they may engage in deviant acts against others and/or become what we call mentally ill (see Burton 1984). Those who doubt the importance of control or at least a sense of control are referred to Seligman's (1975) work on helplessness and Langer's (1983) work on the importance of a sense of control. Both authors show, on the basis of considerable evidence, that there are profound *consequences* if there is no control or at least a sense of control.

Primacy of Needs Versus Primacy of Culture (Text)

As Wippler and Lindenberg point out in dealing with the problem of what is stable and what is contingent: "Sociological boundary conditions are institutions and social structural conditions. They differ widely and change considerably over time, which is exactly why there is a task for sociologists and why sociological propositions are bounded by historical periods and places" (1987, p 138). They then argue that the sociological program must be expanded in order to get a handle on these changing conditions. Concerning this, they say, "In the philosophy of science there exists a formal way of dealing with this problem of boundary conditions, the inclusion of a theoretical level for which boundary conditions are more stable and more uniform" (ibid.). They then point out that in the preclassical period the answer was an invariant human nature and argue, following Homans, that the individual should be given theoretical (or explanatory) primacy. They give this primacy to the invariant rational orientation of the individual; I give it to invariant human needs but the logic of the argument is similarly oriented to the primacy of the agent/subject.

If both individuals and institutions constantly change over time there is no starting point, no foundation or fixed place in the universe from which to begin, as Newton would have said (see Hanson 1965). If everything is in constant flux, the human sciences cannot arrive at propositions that are valid over time and space. If we can agree that the individual has basic needs and that these are invariant over time and space, we have a foundation for the creation of universal propositions. This comes close to the same idea upon which modern economic theory is based when the stability of preferences is assumed. As Gary Becker has said, "The assumption of stable preferences provides a stable foundation for generating predictions about the responses to various changes, and prevents the analyst from succumbing to the temptation of simply postulating the required shift in preferences to " 'explain' all apparent contradictions to his predictions" (1976:5).

Many scholars continue to give theoretical primacy to culture or social structure, often ignoring individuals; social or cultural facts, following Durkheim, are seen as causing other social or cultural facts. In this, any move toward a consideration of individuals as causally important is labeled as reductionism or methodological individualism, both of which are seen as wrongheaded.

Much of the former orientation seems to assume that culture has a "life of its own" and ignores the obvious fact that *culture is created, used, and transformed* by people. It is only people that act and by doing so produce and reproduce the processes of social ordering. How then is culture to be conceptualized? In an earlier work (Sites 1973) I argued that culture should be conceptualized as a variety of tools and the "agreed"-upon rules for their use. Agreed is placed in quotes here since it is the case that what passes for agreement in terms of behavior is often the result of coercion or the lack of viable alternatives. The individual feigns agreement in that the *use* of a norm is often the best strategy. But norms may not be used under many conditions. For example, children often lie to their parents (Ekman 1989b), clerks make fun of customers behind their backs, workers ridicule bosses in their absence, and TV preachers commit adultery. Thus, there is not a common consensus in terms of real behavior unless such consensus is seen as useful; people are not "cultural dopes" (Garfinkel 1967). Thus, the concept of legitimacy as it relates to culture and power must be questioned. The use of power is obviously not needed if people agree (see sites 1977; Abercrombie, Hill, and Turner 1980). More recently Swidler conceptualizes "culture as a 'tool kit' of symbols, stories, rituals, and world-views, which people may use in varying configurations to solve different problems" (1986:273). Gerstein says, "A cultural system considered as a whole is like a membership library, containing stored, partially ordered, symbolisms that is in discontinuous circulation in a variety of contexts and purposes" (1987:100). Giddens (1984) conceptualizes culture as a resource and Archer (1988) emphasizes the importance of agency in her work on culture. These types of definition and concerns take us away from an "over-socialized conception of [people]" (Wrong 1961) and from the view that people are cultural or linguistic dopes.

In addition, this conceptualization permits a consistency of usage in theorizing about culture. Sociologists tend to talk about people *using* language or ritual but at the same time talk about *following* norms or values, all of which are seen as part of culture. Or, they talk about nonmaterial culture *molding* people on the one hand and about people *using* material culture on the other. If all components of culture are conceptualized as tools, a tool kit, a library, or as resources, we can get away from this type of inconsistent usage. We can say that people *use* norms or roles in the same sense that people use language and they *use* these in the first instance in an attempt to gratify their needs. Bourdieu's (1987) concept of cultural capital, increasingly utilized in theorizing, can be placed within this type of conceptualization. Again, this gives individuals theoretical or explanatory primacy and puts culture in its rightful place.

Human needs as conceptualized here work in terms of reciprocities in social interaction and this is what makes social order both possible and necessary. People come to know during the primary socialization process that if reciprocal trust is violated, their need for security cannot be gratified and the same is true for the other needs specified. If *all* "agreements" upon which interactions are based are violated, the need for meaning cannot be gratified; the world becomes chaotic in Hobbsian terms. If the need for self-esteem is to be gratified, people must approve the behavior of at least some others in order to have their own behavior approved in turn. In short, people are forced to interact with others in relatively specific ways if needs are to be gratified, thereby making social order possible and necessary. The precontractual agreement that makes society possible that Durkheim (also see Collins 1982) discussed neither is a mystery nor is it cultural; it is continuously re-created out of necessity during the socialization process. This provides a sounder solution to the problem of order than reliance on the concept of culture since the latter varies over time and place and even between parent and child, depending upon its usability for both. These same dynamics are present in secondary socialization. This type of socialization merely tells the newcomer the "rules" that must be followed, with "if you want security, meaning, and approval" being implied. The *logic* of Hechter's rational choice solution to the problem of order is similar to the one presented here when he argues that "solidarity is due to the interaction of dependence and control mechanisms" (1989:65).

The characteristics of agency have now been outlined in as much depth as possible given considerations of space, so I shall briefly summarize before concluding. I have said that agency can be understood best in terms of four basic human needs: security, meaning, self-esteem, and satisfaction (happiness), which are to be understood as analogs of human primary emotions. In addition, agency is to be seen as attempting control over the environment, including others, for the purpose of gratifying these needs. Following Giddens (1984) agency has transformative power. Giddens calls it the dialectic of control, I have called it the reciprocity of control. The degree of success in terms of attempted control obviously depends upon a variety of contingencies not the least of which is the distribution of power based upon resources in groups and larger societies. Here it should be understood that just as people use language games for some reason they also use power for some reason, and the reason is the gratification of basic needs. Those with greater power obviously have greater possibilities of gratifying their basic needs. The emperor with great power can at least shield himself from disapproval and thus maintain his self-esteem since only the small child dares tell him he has no clothes. Or, in Collins's (1975) terms, he can control the emotional means of production. In developing their realist position, Harre and Madden say, "we claim that what we have thus identified is a conceptual relation which is a reflection of a real relation of necessitation between a particular thing endowed with the power to produce an effect in virtue of its nature, in the absence of constraints and when properly stimulated" (1975:16). Even though my case for needs realism (a term suggested by Richard Brown) differs from their view of realism, this quotation can be applied correctly to what has been said above.

In addition, as will be shown in a later paper, there is considerable evidence from various theoretical formulations and what can be observed in societies across time and space that the needs specified here are both real and universal. Making needs explicit provides an invariant basis for propositions and a basis for the integration of the various schools of theory. For those interested in critical theory, the acceptance of basic human needs provides a basis for critique. Habermas's (1989) hope for a consensus through talk is probably a hopeless dream for the simple reason that people have needs that they bring with them to such talk and they often cannot see beyond them. This, in addition to the "terror of agreement," which Lyotard (1988) notes in critiquing Habermas's position. Simply put, critique based on human needs would specify that societies that do not provide roughly equal opportunities for the gratification of the needs of the body and the needs of the self should be changed (see Sites 1988, 1990). Scholars have used the former as a basis of critique while neglecting the latter.

Conclusion

It should now be obvious that agents/subjects create and use narratives (stories, texts), including culture, for the purpose of needs gratification since it is only within the framework of narratives that the needs of the self can be gratified. Without narratives there is no basis for security, meaning, or self-esteem and thus no possibility of satisfaction or happiness, and people suffer. There is, then, one truth that can serve as a foundation for reason in the construction of narratives and this is the truth of human suffering, which occurs when the needs of the body and/or the needs of the self go ungratified. The problem, of course, is that even though narratives provide a possible basis for the gratification of needs, many if not most narratives gratify the needs of the few at the expense of the many, thereby creating the terror of which Lyotard has spoken. The few who have the power to control the intellectual and emotional means of production create and perpetuate narratives that gratify their needs while others suffer. Nearly all narratives that frame the social world contain major and minor characters along with heroes and villains. For example, all or most women in human history have been assigned minor roles and all Jews were assigned the role of villain in the narrative created by Hitler. Furthermore, once suffering is produced by a grand narrative, this is often changed or added to in order to valorize such suffering, with religious narratives often serving this purpose. This forestalls challenges to the validity of grand narratives.

Once all such narratives have been deconstructed, new narratives must be put in their place since homo sapiens are and seemingly must be creators and tellers of stories. Once we understand the nature of our species and the *truth of suffering*, we are in a position to judge the validity of any new narratives that might be constructed. Valid narratives will include all people as equal characters making equal needs gratification possible (or see Rawls 1971). Furthermore, stories must permit equal control, which necessitates a wide range of alternatives—a true pluralism. People with different capacities and past experiences cannot be expected to have their needs gratified if alternatives and control possibilities are severely limited; the narrative of bourgeois democracy must be replaced with the narrative of real democracy (MacPherson 1965). If people have no control in a situation, they cannot honestly take credit (nor can they be held responsible) for what transpires and needs go ungratified.

Animals suffer, but because humans are aware of their own experiences and those of others, they experience double suffering when their needs go ungratified. They know the human condition could be otherwise. This is why they often say, along with Job, "Why me? . . . Why do I suffer when others do not?" Since we now know the rain does not necessarily fall on the just and the unjust alike but that narratives determine who suffers, we are in a position to make corrections, to determine our own fate as Touraine (1988) has pointed out. We have deconstructed long enough; it is now time to construct new narratives using as a foundation our knowledge of the human species being. Such narratives will reject the boredom and tragedy of "sameness," which current narratives emphasize, and encourage the celebration of differences; the truth of suffering will give way to the truth of happiness as people are permitted to construct individual self-images consistent with their unique experiences.

References

Abercrombie, Nichols, Stephen Hill, and Bryan S. Turner. 1980. *The Dominant Ideology Thesis*. London: George Allen Unwin.

Ainsworth, Mary D. 1978. *Patterns of Attachment*. Hillsdale, NJ: Basic Books.

Alexander, Jeffery. 1987. "Action and Its Environments." In *The Micro-Macro Link*, edited by J. C. Alexander, B. Gieson, R. Munch, and N. J. Alexander. Berkeley: University of California Press.

Archer, Margaret S. 1988. *Culture and Agency*. New York: Cambridge University Press.

Bashkar, Roy. 1979. *The Possibility of Naturalism*. Atlanta Heights, NJ: Humanities Press.

Bay, Christian. 1958. *The Structure of Freedom*. Stanford, CA: Stanford University Press.

Becker, Ernest. 1968. *The Structure of Evil*. New York: George Braziller.

Becker, Gary S. 1976. *The Economic Approach to Human Behavior*. Chicago: University of Chicago Press.

Becker, Howard. 1955. *Through Values to Social Interpretation*. Durham, NC: Duke University Press.

Berger, Peter L. 1967. *The Sacred Canopy*. Garden City, NY: Doubleday.

Blau, Peter M. 1964. *Exchange and Power in Social Life*. New York: Wiley.

Bourdieu, Pierre. 1986. "From Rules to Strategies." *Cultural Anthropology* I:110–20.

———. 1987. "The Forms of Capital." Pp. 241–258 in *Handbook of Theory and Research for the Sociology of Education*, edited by J. G. Richardson, CT: Greenwood.

Bowlby, John. 1982. *Attachment and Loss*. New York: Basic Books. [This is the last of a three-volume work.]

Burton, John. 1984. *Deviance, Terrorism, and War*. New York: St. Martin's.

Collins, Randall. 1975. *Conflict Sociology*. New York: Academic Press.

———. 1981. "The Microfoundations of Macrosociology." *American Journal of Sociology* 86:984–1014.

———. 1982. *Sociological Insight*. New York: Oxford University Press.

———. 1984. "The Role of Emotion in Social Structure." In *Approaches to Emotion*, edited by K. R. Scherer and P. Ekman. Hillsdale, NJ: Lawrence Erlbaum Associates

———. 1988. *Theoretical Sociology*. New York: Harcourt Brace Jovanovich.

———. 1989a. Reported by Patrick Young in *Sciences News* 135:59.

———. (with Mary Ann Mason and Tom Ekman). 1989b. *Why Kids Lie*. New York: Charles Scribner's Sons.

Ekman, Paul and William V. Frieson. 1978. *The Facial Action Coding System (FACS): A Technique for the Measurement of Facial Action*. Palo Alto, CA: Consulting Psychologists Press.

Emerson, Richard M. 1962. "Power-Dependence Relations." *American Sociological Review* 27:31–41.

Fitzgerald, Ross, ed. 1977. *Human Needs and Politics*. New York: Pergamon.

Foucault, Michel. 1979. *Discipline and Punish: The Birth of the Prison*. Translated by Alan Sheridan. New York: Vintage.

Fox, Nathan A. and R. J. Davidson. 1988. "Patterns of Brain Electrical Activity during the Expression of Discrete Emotions in Ten Month Old Children." *Developmental Psychology* 24:230–36.

Galtung, Johan. 1988. "International Development in Human Perspective." In *The Power of Human Needs in World Society*, edited by R. A. Coate and J. A. Rosati. Boulder, CO: Lynne Rienner.

Garfinkel, Harold. 1967. *Studies in Ethnomethodology*. Garden City, NY: Prentice Hall.

Gazzaniga, Michael. 1985. *The Social Brain*. New York: Basic Books.

———. 1988. *Mind Matters*. New York: Houghton Mifflin.

Gerstein, Dean. 1987. "To Unpack Micro and Macro: Link Small with Large and Part with Whole." Pp. 86–111 in *The Micro-Macro Link*, edited by J. C. Alexander, B. Gieson, R. Munch, and N. J. Smelser. Berkeley: University of California Press.

Gibbs, Jack D. 1989. *Control: Sociology's Central Notion*. Urbana: University of Illinois Press.

Giddens, Anthony. 1984. *The Constitution of Society: Outline of a Theory of Structuration*. Cambridge: Polity.

Goffman, Erving. 1959. *The Presentation of Self in Everyday Life*. Garden City, NY: Doubleday.

———. 1969. *Strategic Interaction*. Philadelphia: University of Pennsylvania Press.

Habermas, Jurgen. 1989. *The Theory of Communicative Action*, Vol. 2. Translated by Thomas McCarthy. Boston: Beacon.

Hanson, Norwood R. 1965. *Patterns of Discovery: An Inquiry into the Conceptual Foundations of Science*. Cambridge: Cambridge University Press.

Harre, Romano. 1979. *Social Being*. Totowa, NJ: Rowman and Littlefield.
——. 1986. *The Social Construction of Emotion*. New York: Blackwell.
Harre, Romano and Edward H. Madden. 1975. *Causal Powers: A Theory of Natural Necessity*. Totowa, NJ: Rowman and Littlefield.
Hechter, Michael. 1989. "Rational Choice Foundations of Social Order." In *Theory Building in Sociology*, edited by J. H. Turner. Newbury Park, CA: Sage.
Hochschild, Arlie. 1983. *The Managed Heart: Commercialization of Human Feelings*. Berkeley: University of California Press.
Jacobson, Edmund. 1967. *Biology of Emotions*. Springfield, IL: Charles C. Thomas.
Kagan, Jerome. 1984. *The Nature of the Child*. New York: Basic Books.
Kemper, Theodore. 1978. *A Social Interactional Theory of Emotions*. New York: Wiley.
——. 1987. "How Many Emotions Are There? Wedding the Social and the Autonomic Components." *American Journal of Sociology* 93:263–89.
Laing, R. D. 1967. *The Politics of Experience*. New York: Ballantine.
Langer, Ellen J. 1983. *The Psychology of Control*. Beverly Hills, CA: Gunn and Hain.
Lyotard, Jean-François. 1984. *The Postmodern Condition: A Report on Knowledge*. Minneapolis: University of Minnesota Press.
——. 1988. *Peregrinations: Law, Form, Event*. New York: Columbia University Press.
MacLean, Paul D. 1973. "A Triune Concept of the Brain and Behavior." In *The Hincks Memorial Lectures*, edited by T. Boag and D. Campbell. Toronto: CBS.
MacPherson, C. B. 1965. *The Real World of Democracy*. Toronto: Canadian Broadcasting Co.
Marcuse, Herbert. 1969. *Eros and Civilization: A Philosophical Inquiry into Freud*. London: Allen Lane.
Marx, Karl. 1964. *Economic and Philosophical Manuscripts of 1844*. Translated by M. Milligam. New York: International Publishers.
Mead, George. 1934. *Mind, Self and Society*. Edited by C. W. Morris. Chicago: University of Chicago Press.
——. 1938. *The Philosophy of the Act*, edited by Charles W. Morris. Chicago: The University of Chicago Press.
Merton, Robert. 1968. "Social Structure and Anomie." Pp. 185–214 In *Social Theory and Social Structure*, edited by R. Merton. New York: Free Press.
Mullins, Nicholas C. 1973. *Theories and Theory Groups in Contemporary American Sociology*. New York: Harper and Row.
Oster, Harriet and Paul Ekman. 1977. "Facial Behavior in Child Development." In *Minnesota Symposia on Child Development, Vol. II*, edited by A. Collins. New York: Thomas A. Crowell.
Parsons, Talcott. 1937. *The Structure of Social Action*. New York: McGraw-Hill.
Parsons, Talcott and E. A. Shills. 1951. "Some Fundamental Categories of the Theory of Action: A General Statement." Pp. 3–29 in *Toward a General Theory of Action*, edited by T. Parsons and E. A. Shills. Cambridge, MA: Harvard University Press.
Rawls, John. 1971. *A Theory of Justice*. Cambridge, MA: Harvard University Press.

Restak, Richard M. 1988. *The Mind*. New York: Bantam.

Rorty, Richard. 1989. *Contingency, Irony and Solidarity*. New York: Cambridge University Press.

Rosenberg, Alexander. 1980. *Sociobiology and the Preemption of Social Science*. Baltimore: The Johns Hopkins University Press.

Scheff, Thomas J. 1988. "Shame and Conformity: The Deference-Emotion System." *American Sociological Review* 53:395–406.

Seligman, Martin. 1975. *Helplessness*. San Francisco: W. H. Freeman.

Sennet, Richard and Jonathan Cobb. 1972. *The Hidden Injuries of Class*. New York: Vintage.

Sites, Danny. 1977. "Power, Exchange and Authority." Unpublished Masters Thesis, Kent State University, Kent, OH.

Sites, Paul. 1973. *Control: The Basis of Social Order*. New York: Dunellen.

————. 1988. "Needs as Analogues of Primary Emotions." In *Conflict: Human Needs Theory*, edited by John Burton. New York: St Martin's.

————. 1990. "Legitimacy and Human Needs." Pp. In *Conflict: Readings in Management and Resolution*, edited by J. Burton and F. Dukes. New York: St. Martin's.

Solomon, Robert C. 1983. *The Passions*. Notre Dame, IN: University of Notre Dame Press.

Springborg, Patricia. 1981. *The Problem of Human Needs in the Critique of Civilization*. London: George Allen and Unwin.

Strauss, Anselm. 1977. *Negotiations*. San Francisco: Jossey-Bass.

Swidler, Ann. 1986. "Culture in Action: Symbols and Strategies." *American Sociological Review* 51:273–286.

Thibaut, John W. and Harold H. Kelly. 1959. *The Social Psychology of Groups*. New York: John Wiley.

Thomas, W. I. 1923. *The Unadjusted Girl*. Boston: Little, Brown.

Touraine, Alain. 1988. *Return of the Actor*. Minneapolis: University of Minnesota Press.

Trevarthen, Colwyn. 1984. "Emotions in Infancy: Regulators of Contact and Relationships with Persons." In *Approaches to Emotions*, edited by K. R. Scherer and P. Ekman. Hillsdale, NJ: Lawrence Erlbaum.

Turner, Jonathan H. 1987. "Toward a Sociological Theory of Motivation." *American Sociological Review* 52:15–27.

————. 1988. *A Theory of Social Interaction*. Stanford, CA: Stanford University Press.

Veblen, Thorstein. 1899. *The Theory of the Leisure Class*. New York: MacMillan.

Weber, Max. 1947. *The Theory of Social and Economic Organization*. Translated by Talcott Parsons. New York: Oxford University Press.

Wippler, Reinhard and Siegwart Lindenberg. 1987. "Collective Phenomena and Rational Choice." Pp. 135–152 in *The Micro-Marco Link*, edited by J. C. Alexander, B. Gieson, R. Munch, and N. J. Smelser. Berkeley: University of California Press.

Wittgenstein, Ludwig. 1972. *Philosophical Investigations*. Oxford: Blackwell.

Wood, James R., Eugene A. Weinstein, and Ronald Parker. 1967. "Children's Interpersonal Tactics." *Sociological Inquiry* 27:129–39.

Wrong, Dennis H. 1961. "The Oversocialized Conception of Man in Modern Sociology." *American Sociological Review* 26:183–193.

Chapter 12

Narration, Reason, and Community

Walter R. Fisher[*]

"What matters at this stage" of the late twentieth century, Alasdair MacIntyre contends, "is the construction of local forms of community within which civility and the intellectual and moral life can be sustained through the dark ages which are already upon us" (1969:245). The conference from which this volume was drawn was, I think, such a construction, however short its duration. Later, I shall refer to it in consideration of the constitution of communities and the modes of communication that enable their existence. To begin, however, a context is necessary. Every story must have its exposition. This one will be synopses of the stories about community and communication told by John Dewey, Martin Buber, Jürgen Habermas, and Hans-Georg Gadamer. Notice will also be given to the notions of certain postmodern storytellers. The argument of this survey is that conceptions of communication imply forms of community, that community depends on particular forms of communication, and that a dialectical tension exists between ideal conceptions of communication and the realization of ideal community beyond the local and ephemeral. When ideal conceptions are applied to ongoing associations, such as society, communication is seen as distorted and community is seen as a distant dream. The burden of the story itself is the argument that a narrational view of communication clarifies the constitution of community and adds an essential consideration, the role of reason in the process. The epilogue is more by way of suggestion than argument; it raises questions, proposes possible answers, and comments on the relationship between local and metanarratives and their communities.

Context

Dewey maintained that there could be "no such thing as community" if people were not interested in others, "in entering into the activities of others and taking part in conjoint and cooperative doings" (1916:24). Because people do have this inclination, along with their private proclivities, community is not only possible, it happens. It comes into being through communication, by which Dewey meant "a process of sharing experience till it becomes a common possession. It modifies the disposition of both parties who partake in it" (ibid.:9). The impetus for and realization of communication is understanding. "Society," for Dewey, "not only continues to exist *by* transmission, *by* communication, but it may fairly be said to exist *in* transmission, *in* communication" (ibid.:4). He did not limit the forms of communication that contribute to community. Everyday discourse counted, as did artistic and scientific expressions. He was, however, concerned about the negative character of public debate, comparing it to a "watered-down version of the Hegelian dialectic" (1935:71). Persuasion, in his view, was an inevitable consequence of genuine communication, but such discourse had to be a nonmanipulative form, a mutual, educative experience.

In regard to community, Dewey held two views: (1) that a real community already exists by virtue of "the infinite relationships of man with his fellows and with nature" (1930:330); and (2) that an ideal community only exists in democratic experience. His conception of communication was tied to this ideal. The connection between ideal community and ideal communication is established clearly in this passage from *Problems of Men*:

> What is the faith in democracy in the role of consultation, of conference, of persuasion, of discussion, in the formulation of public opinion . . . except faith in the capacity of the intelligence of the common man to respond with common sense to the free play of acts and ideas which are secured by effective guarantees of free inquiry, free assembly and free communication. (1958:5)

Given this faith, along with common agreement about common ends sought by conjoint action, understanding would follow and democratic community would thrive. "Consensus," he wrote, "demands communication" (1916:5). And, he maintained, "Democracy is not an alternative to other principles of associated life. It is the idea of community life itself" (1927:148).

Foreshadowing the position of Buber, Dewey held that democracy was not a mode of nation-state governance but a "mode of associated living, of conjoint communicated experience" (1916:87). He anticipated

Habermas's views of communicative action, not only in his stress upon understanding and consensus, but also in his conception of genuine communication as an ideal transaction, one of uncoerced, mutual, educative exchange. And like MacIntyre, Dewey despaired the possibility of community beyond local associations. I share the despair, at least in regard to Dewey's observation that "no government of experts in which the masses do not have a chance to inform experts as to their needs can be anything but an oligarchy managed in the interests of the few" (1927:208). I also believe him when he writes: "no matter how ignorant any person is, there is one thing he knows better than anybody else and that is where the shoe pinches on his own feet" (1958:35; 1927:207). I shall have more to say about experts later.

As I move to the views of Buber on community and communication, I have the feeling of introducing someone to his or her own best friend or loved one. It can hardly be the case that everyone interested in the subject does not know as much or more than I about Buber's thought. This is especially true of Ronald C. Arnett, who has written an excellent book, *Communication and Community: Implication of Buber's Dialogue* (1986; see also Maranhão 1990; Matson and Montagu 1967; Stewart 1978:183–201). So, my purpose here is to touch on essential ideas for this contextualization of my views. The passage that captures Buber's vision of community as well as any, is this one:

> On the far side of the subjective, on this side of the objective, on the narrow ridge, where I and Thou meet, there is the realm of "between." This reality, whose disclosure has begun in our time, shows the way, leading individualism and collectivism, for the life decision of future generation. Here the genuine third alternative is indicated, the knowledge of which will help to bring about the genuine person again and to establish genuine community. (1967:204–05; see also Palmer 1983:99–103)

If another passage is needed to clarify his position, I offer this one: "The real living together of man with man can only thrive where people have the real things of their common life in common; where they can experience, discuss and administer them together, where real fellowship and real work guilds exist" (1958:19). In short, for Buber, genuine community, as an ongoing association, is a commune inspirited by Hasidic and socialist ideals.

It immediately follows from this conception of genuine community that genuine communication cannot be the usual forms of monologic discourse. Whenever communication is strictly monologic, whether in debate, in conversations, in friendly chats, or in lover's talk, real relationship is nonexistent. The same applies to technical communication, which Buber ironically says is "the inalienable sterling quality of 'modern' existence." On rare occasions, at times even in the sorts of communication just enumerated, dialogic communication may emerge. Genuine dialogue appears in those encounters "no matter whether spoken or silent—where each of the participants really has in mind the other or others in their present and particular being and turns to them with the intention of establishing a living mutual relation between himself and them" (1967:19). As with Dewey's notions, Buber's can also lead to despair: waiting for dialogue to occur can be like waiting for Godot.

Consider again the themes that arise from Dewey's and Buber's views. The realization of community in Dewey's thought depends on human intelligence and mutual, educative exchange (Bitzer 1978:67–93; Farrell 1976:1–14; Palmer 1981:71ff.). The actualization of community in Buber's thinking relies on the human capacity to enter the "in-between," to be genuinely in relation to others through dialogic communication. Since the potential for intelligence and authenticity is rarely achieved, mutual, educative exchange and dialogue are rare. Since these forms of communication are seldom in existence, democratic and socialist communities are seldom in existence. When they do exist, they appear in local and short-lived encounters. As ideal achievements, they serve as standards by which ordinary experience and public discourse must be seen as distorted and counterproductive to life as we would want it to be. Reverberations of these themes recur in the writings of Habermas and Gadamer.

Habermas's notion of an emancipated, rational society has strong conceptual affinities with Dewey's construction of democracy. Like Dewey, Habermas stresses human intelligence, the capacity of people to reason and to be rational. This potential is evident in argumentation, which he defines as "that type of speech in which participants thematize contested validity claims and attempt to vindicate them through arguments" (1981:18). "An argument," he writes, "contains reasons or grounds that are connected in a systematic way with the validity claim of a problematic expression" (ibid.:249). The aim of such discourse, in line with Dewey's ideas again, is understanding, or "valid agreement," and consensus. The model underlying Habermas's view of argumentation resembles Buber's notion of encounter. Habermas envisions an "ideal speech situation," a symmetrical and noncoercive transaction. There would be equal opportunity to participate, to criticize, to express personal aims and attitudes, and to perform these acts without regard to power or ideology. The paucity of argumentation based on this model accounts for the lack of an emancipated, rational society, and when the model is used to assess ordinary and public discourse, such discourse must be viewed as distorted.

Gadamer's concept of conversation, also like Buber's view of encounter, leads to the same conclusion when applied to everyday discourse. "It is characteristic of every true conversation," he maintains, "that each opens himself to the other person, truly accepts his point of view as worthy of consideration and gets inside the other to such an extent that he understands not a particular individual, but what he says" (1982:347; see Frentz 1985:1–18). True conversation for Gadamer is dialogue, question and answer, in which there is a "fusion of horizons," an encounter of "transformation into a communion, in which we do not remain what we were" (1982:340). The result is understanding, not just valid agreement. Gadamer privileges linguisticality rather than intelligence, the capacity for authenticity, or argumentative ability. "Language," he insists, "is not just one of man's possessions in the world, but on it depends the fact that man has a world at all" (ibid.:401). From this view, communication is "a living process in which a community is lived. . . . All forms of human community of life are forms of linguistic community: even more, they constitute language" (ibid.:404). Gadamer is talking here about communication and community with their initial "cees" lowercase. When the "cees" are capitalized, when the stress is on true conversation, ordinary, usual communication and community fall short of the ideal, and again, we are left with the local and isolated realizations of what communication and community can be.

A glimmer of hope exists in each of these writer's views: people do have intelligence, the capacity for authenticity, the ability to argue, and a desire for understanding. This is not the case with the leading theorists of postmodernism. Most vocal among them are Foucault, Derrida, and Lyotard. For Foucault, all public discourse is infected with power (1980:109–33); for Derrida, all discourse is condemned to totalization through logocentric distinctions that marginalize people, ideas, institutions, and so on (1976:6–93; 1981:61–171). Lyotard, for his part, declares the end of all metanarratives—the stories that have aspired to universal application and on which dreams of transcendental community have depended (1984:37). Consensus, as conceived by Dewey and Habermas, he says, is "outmoded and suspect" (ibid.:66). Community on any large scale is foreclosed by the fact that communication in society has been reduced, fragmented into language games (ibid.:41). Because this is the case, he thinks that "the idea . . . we need today in order to make decisions in political matters cannot be the idea of the totality, or of the unity, of a body. It can only be the idea of multiplicity or of a diversity" (Lyotard and Thebaud 1985:94; Lyotard 1984:23).

Interestingly, our most adamant antimodernist, MacIntyre, agrees with the underlying observation of Lyotard: ours is a time marked by incommensurate notions of rationality, justice, and ethics. Lyotard accepts the fact; MacIntyre deplores it. Insofar as incommensurability does reign, the dream of community beyond the local must remain a distant, if not impossible, dream. Yet, as I wrote in a recent review of MacIntyre's new book, *Whose Justice? Which Rationality?* there will always be conceptual and/or logical incommensurability between or among people who are certain of their own version of truth and their own particular vocabulary and grammar (MacIntyre 1969:69ff., 1988:326–48). Fortunately, for the world to go on, they do not need to convince or to persuade one another. They must only gain the adherence of a relevant audience, others who are affected by the matter at hand and whose values are fundamental but not beyond discussion and debate. Protesters, as MacIntyre notes in *After Virtue*, talk past one another, as one side grounds arguments in "rights" and the other in "law" (1969:66). He is correct; they do talk past one another. But, they do not talk past those who will decide the outcome of the controversy. The coherence and fidelity of the rival stories told by these factions are assessed and decisions are made and, insofar as these principles are enacted, the assessments and decisions are rational. This sort of rationality will not satisfy those who demand "rational persuasion" or consensus, but then it does comply with another notion of rationality, the idea that rationality is displayed when people are open to argument and have an ability and willingness to participate in it.

To all this—the thinking of pre- and postmodernists alike—our leading neopragmatist, Richard Rorty, says: "We need a redescription of liberalism as the hope that culture as a whole can be 'poeticized' rather than as the Enlightment hope that it can be 'rationalized' or 'scientized.' That is, we need to substitute the hope that chances for fulfillment of idiosyncratic fantasies will be equalized for the hope that everyone will replace 'passion' or fantasy with 'reason' " (1989:53). This new hope, he hopes, will be kept alive by keeping the conversation of humankind going (1979:394, 1989:51–52). Perhaps needless to say, it is not Gadamer's concept of conversation that he has in mind. It is simply talk that recognizes contingency, irony, and solidarity.

In response to these various notions of communication and community, I offer an alternative way of thinking, one that does not deny people's intelligence, the capacity for authenticity, the ability to argue, or the desire for understanding. It is a view that provides a construct that subsumes these human attributes: put succinctly, I argue that human beings are most aptly designated *homo narrans*. This view speaks not only to the idealistic conceptions of communication and community, it also addresses the implications inherent in postmodern theories that privilege ideology, power, desire, and deconstruction in human decision-making and action. To these theories, it says: Decision and action are inevitable; if ideology, power, desire, and indeterminancy are the only features of human decision and action, then the only choice is that of whose domination will prevail, whose oppression shall one submit to and live by. The feature of human decision-making and action left out here is reason. The narrative perspective on human beings restores this feature by reconstructing it in terms of narrative rationality, which I will explain shortly. Narrative reason incorporates traditional logics as they pertain to communicative practices, but reinstates significant questions of values so that intelligence, authenticity, argumentative ability, and understanding are enhanced.

Text

The foundation of my proposal, which is definitely a proposal and not a panacea, is, as I have indicated, the assumption that human beings are essentially storytellers. The assumption derives authority from thinkers as different as MacIntyre and Gregory Bateson. MacIntyre maintains that "man is in his actions and practice, as well as in his fictions, essentially a storytelling animal" (1969:201); that "enacted dramatic narrative is the basic and essential characterization of human actions" (ibid.:194). Bateson opined, "If I am at all fundamentally right in what I am saying, the thinking in terms of stories must be shared by all mind or minds, whether ours or those of redwood forests and sea anemones" (1980:14). The ultimate authority for the belief in the narrative nature of human beings, however, is experiential. Whatever form of communication a person may use, the result will always be an interpretation of some aspect of the world that is historically and culturally grounded and shaped by a fallible human being. There is, in other words, no form of human communication that presents uncontested truths, including this one. Thus, when I use the term narration, I have in mind not the specific individuated forms or genre that we call narrative, but a conceptual frame that would account for the "stories" we tell each other—whether such "stories" are in the form of argumentation, narration, exposition, or esthetic writings and performance. This view is at one with the perspective of Hauerwas and Jones: "Narrative is neither just an account of genre criticism nor a faddish appeal to the importance of telling stories; rather it is a crucial conceptual category for such matters as understanding issues of epistemology and methods of argument, depicting personal identity, and displaying the content of Christian [and, I would add, secular] convictions" (1989:5).

Stories, in my view, are not isolated utterances or gestures but symbolic actions—words and/or deeds—that have sequence and meaning for those who live, create, or interpret them. So understood, they have relevance to real as well as to fictive experiences. Regardless of form, discursive or nondiscursive texts are meant to give order to life by inducing others to dwell in them to establish ways of living in common, in intellectual and spiritual communities in which there is confirmation for the story that constitutes one's life. This presentation is meant to be such a story.

The second component of my proposal is that the material or stuff of stories is "good reasons." By this term, I mean *elements that provide warrants for accepting or adhering to the advice fostered by any form of human communication that can be considered rhetorical.* And it is my view that there is no form of discourse that cannot be so construed. All forms of human communication function to influence the hearts and minds of others—their beliefs, values, attitudes, and/or actions. The concept of good reasons coincides with the assumption that human beings are as much valuing as they are reasoning beings. The fact is that values may serve as reasons, and what we usually call reasons are value-laden.

I call my proposal the narrative paradigm, meaning by paradigm a philosophical representation designed to formalize the structure of a component of experience and to direct understanding and inquiry into the nature and functions of the experience—in this instance, the experience of human communication. In line with the assumptions and definitions just delineated, the paradigm has five presuppositions:

1. Humans are essentially storytellers.
2. The definitive modes of human decision and action are good reasons, which vary in form among situations, genre, and media of communication.
3. The production and use of good reasons are ruled by matters of history, culture, and character along with the specific constraints of time and place of presentation.
4. Rationality is grounded in the nature of persons as narrative beings, in their inherent awareness of narrative coherence—whether or not a story hangs together—and narrative fidelity—whether or not the stories they experience ring true to the stories they know or believe to be true.
5. The world as we live it is a series of stories that must be chosen among in order for us to live life in a process of continual re-creation.

Two features of the paradigm are particularly relevant to the theme of narrativity and community. First is its construction of rationality, narrative rationality, which concerns the quality of stories that entice one to belong to one community or another. As already indicated, narrative rationality has two basic principles: coherence and fidelity.

Before I outline the specific tests used to employ these principles, I would like to note the standards proposed by Hauerwas and David Burrell, from an ethical standpoint, and by Chaim Perelman, from an informal logic perspective. Hauerwas and Burrell hold, "The test of each story is the sort of person it shapes" (1989:135). [I should mention in passing that this is the hallmark of Wayne Booth's recent book, *The Company We Keep: An Ethics of Reading* (1988; see also Beiner 1983:127–28).] Perelman took the position that an argument is as good as the audience that would adhere to it, strongly suggesting that the best such audience would be a universal one (Perelman and Olbrechts-Tyteca 1969:31; Perelman 1979:14, 1984:191). I endorse both of these standards, but I believe that people need more specific guidance than these rules, which are reminiscent of Kant's moral imperative.

In fairness to Hauerwas and Burrell, I want to acknowledge that they do provide criteria by which their standard may be employed. They write:

Any story which we adopt, or allow to adopt us, will have to display:
1. power to release us from destructive alternatives;
2. ways of seeing through current distortions;
3. room to keep us from having to resort to violence;
4. a sense for the tragic: how meaning transcends power.

But, as they go on to say, "It is inaccurate . . . to list these criteria as features a story must display" (1989:135). They concern the effects a story may have, not how it induces us to believe or to act. The position I have taken is that good reasons are the features of stories that persuade us and that by testing their coherence and fidelity, we can discern whether or not they are deserving of our adherence.

Testing for coherence requires attention to three aspects of a story. First, *structural* or *argumentative coherence*. Here the interest is the traditional one of determining whether or not a message is consistent, whether or not it involves a contradiction in form or reasoning. Second, *material coherence*. Here one is concerned about how an immediate story compares with other stories that deal with the same subject. A story may be internally consistent, but important facts may be omitted, counterarguments ignored, and relevant issues overlooked. *There is no story that is not embedded in other stories*. The meaning and merit of a story are always a matter of how it stands with or against other stories. Third, *characterological coherence*. Concern for this third type of coherence is one of the key differences between the concept of narrative rationality and traditional formal and informal logics, and needs some explanation.

Central to all stories is character. Whether or not a story is believable depends on the reliability of characters, both as narrators and actors.

Determinations of one's character are made by interpretations of a person's decisions and actions that reflect values. In other words, character may be considered an organized set of actional tendencies. If these tendencies contradict one another, change significantly, or alter in "strange ways," the result is a questioning of character. Coherence in life and literature requires that characters behave characteristically. Without this kind of predictability, there is no trust, no rational order, no community.

To illustrate the importance of characterological coherence, one may consider the rhetoric of former President Reagan. The question is this: how is it that President Reagan enjoyed a nearly unanimous evaluation as a "Great Communicator" despite the fact that he was also noted for making factual errors, making inconsistent statements, reasoning in only limited fashion, and frequently diverting attention from relevant issues and inquiries? Part of the answer to this question has to do with esthetics, his skill as a performer. Part of the answer has to do with the consistency of his story with the story of America. Part of the answer has to do with his implied audience—the idea that we are all heroes. But, a very important part of the answer has to do with character.

When one has determined that a person—ordinary or presidential— has a trustworthy and reliable character, that his or her heart is in the right place, one is willing to overlook or forgive many things: factual errors if not too dramatic, lapses in reasoning, and occasional discrepancies. These come to be seen as aberrations, probably induced by circumstances but not incompetence. One can see this kind of judgment rendered in obvious forms where friends, loved ones, heroes, and saints are concerned. Those who would criticize such figures become the ones who are criticized. Because President Reagan was considered such a figure, commentators said he had a "Teflon personality." How one achieves this kind of character perception is an interesting question, but now is not the time to pursue it. The point is that character can be a decisive feature of any story and must be assessed carefully.

Testing for fidelity, for the truth qualities of a story, entails two major considerations: weighing the elements of a message usually regarded as its reasons and weighing the values it explicitly or implicitly conveys. In the first instance, one does what one has always been taught to do: determine whether the statements in a message that purport to be fact are indeed facts, that is, confirmed by consensus or reliable, competent witnesses; determine whether relevant facts or arguments have been omitted or misrepresented; determine whether the individuated forms of reasoning in it are sound, that is, assess the sign, cause, definition, analogy, example, and authority arguments—using standards from formal or informal logics; and determine whether the key issues have been addressed, the questions on which decision and action should turn.

In the second instance, one tries to answer the following questions related to values: What are the explicit and implicit values in the story? Are the values appropriate to the nature of the decision or beliefs that the story concerns? What would be the effects of adhering to the values in regard to one's concept of self, to one's behavior, to one's relationship with others and society? Are the values confirmed or validated in one's experience, in the lives and statements of others whom one admires and respects? And even if a prima facie case has been made or a burden of proof has been established, are the values fostered by the story those that would constitute an ideal basis for human conduct? This final question is clearly the paramount issue that confronts those responsible for decisions that impinge on the nature, quality, and continued existence of human life, especially in the fields of medicine and weapons technology and employment.

My intention in developing these questions about values was to offer a scheme to generate a sense of what is good as well as what is strictly logical in the stories that people might adopt. It is a scheme that does not dictate what one should believe, but it does necessarily involve one in considering one's relations with others and the pragmatic consequences of one's choices in regard to self and society.

One answer, then, to the question posed by the title of Stanley Hauerwas and Gregory Jones's book, *Why Narrative?* is that narration, considered as a paradigm, provides a logic consonant with the nature of persons as narrative beings by which the features of stories—good reasons—can be assessed systematically. It is important to note that this logic does not deny the utility of traditional tests of facts and arguments. It differs from formal logic in that it does not presume a world constituted by analytic structures. And it differs from the leading conceptions of informal logic advanced by Stephen Toulmin and Perelman in that it does not presume that the everyday world is analogous to the world of the courtroom, at least as the world of the courtroom is conceived in terms of argument rather than stories. The narrative paradigm presupposes a world constituted by stories and the view that no form of discourse is to be privileged over others because its form is predominantly argumentative. No matter how strictly a case is argued—theologically, scientifically, philosophically, or legally—it will always be a story.

The second feature of the paradigm particularly relevant to the theme of narrative and community is its intrinsic egalitarian bias. This feature answers, again, to the question posed by Hauerwas and Jones's *Why Narrative?* By insisting on the rationality of all normal persons, the paradigm legitimates their membership in the public, that is, the kind of society envisioned by Dewey. That many people forsake or only nominally exercise the privileges of this membership is due, at least in part, to the elitism of traditional conceptions and practices that purport to represent true reason and rationality. These conceptions and the practices that follow from them imply a hierarchical system, a community in which some persons are qualified to judge and to lead and other persons are to follow. Those who are at the top of the hierarchy are experts, persons who know specialized subject matters, and the nature of argumentative issues, forms of reasoning, and rules of advocacy in particular fields of knowledge. Their discourse dominates public decision-making and renders nonexperts spectators of their performances. As Robert N. Goodman has observed: "We have abdicated power over our future to the experts" (1986, Pt. II:5; see also Fischer 1990:40–55). One way to overcome or to move against this reality is to reconceptualize reason and rationality—along the lines I have outlined. Just as literacy—whether conceived in terms of communication competence or cultural knowledge—is prerequisiste to participation in the political, economic, and social life of the society, so is awareness of and sophistication in one's own reason and rationality. Both are essential grounds of social and political empowerment.

I would like to make it clear before I move on to further observations about communication and community that I do not deny the legitimacy (the inevitability) of hierarchy. History records no community, uncivilized or civilized, without key storymakers and storytellers, whether sanctioned by God, a "gift," heritage, power, intelligence, or election. Narration implies, however, that the people do judge the stories that are told for and about them and that they have a rational capacity to make such judgments. To apply a narrative paradigm to communication is to hold, along with Aristotle, that people have a natural tendency to prefer what they perceive as the truth and the just (Aristotle:1.1.1355). It is also to concur with Gadamer, who holds that "there are no people who do not 'think' sometime and somewhere. That means that there is no one who does not form general views about life and death, about freedom and living together, about the good and about happiness" (1981:58). Furthermore, the narrative paradigm does not deny that the people can be wrong. But, then, so can elites, especially when a decision is social or political. There is no evidence that I know of to support the claim that experts know better than anyone else when it comes to such decisions. Nor does the theory behind the narrative paradigm deny the existence and desirability of genius in individuals or the capacity of the people to formulate and adopt new stories that better account for their lives or the mystery of life itself. The sort of hierarchy to which the paradigm is inimical is hierarchy based on the assumption that some people are qualified to be rational and others not.

At the outset of the essay, I expressed my belief that the occasion of the conference from which this volume was drawn marks the existence of a community. It is time that I try to explain, if not prove, the soundness of this conviction. I suggested that there are two considerations in regard to community: the grounds of its constitution and the nature of the communication that provides the forms and fabric of its existence. Since I feel more confident in my views of communication, believing that you will find them less controversial than my notions about community, I shall start with them, that is, with my perspectives on communication and community.

While the principles of coherence and fidelity—narrative rationality—are relevant to all forms of human communication, there are different forms of human communication with different relationships to community. The sort of communication that gives rise to community is what I call *affirmative rhetoric*. It is the kind of discourse that is designed to overcome doubt, to gain unity of belief, attitude, value, and action in accord with a "new" idea, ideology, or practice. Adherence by two or more people to such discourse is tantamount to the creation of a community. When the community's ideas or adherents are attacked for violating the norms of the association, from within or without, there will be what I call *purification rhetoric*, an attempt to rid them of the specter of sin, error, or aberration. And when the community's fundamental tenets are challenged by rival tenets proposing a radically different or new association, what I call *subversion rhetoric* will emerge, discourse meant to undermine the coherence and fidelity of the opposing story.

The clearest evidence of the existence of a community is the presence of what I call *reaffirmative rhetoric*. Its characteristic forms are arguments reasserting the validity of the community's creed or modes of ceremonial, communal transactions. The argumentative form of reaffirmative rhetoric is like the modes of affirmative, purification, and subversion rhetorics. It is meant to remove doubt and uncertainty. The ceremonial, communal modes of reaffirmative rhetoric, on the other hand, presume an identity of heart and mind, a commitment beyond doubt or dispute. Such communication may be verbal or nonverbal, as in such expressions as "I love you" and "I pledge allegiance" and in such acts as participating in communion and in gestures of caring, compassion, wonder, and awe. Where the other forms of rhetoric promote ways of becoming, ceremonial, communal modes of communication signify a way of being, a living presence in relation to an other. In their uncontaminated experiences, they are what others have called dialogic communication. In my view, the other forms of rhetoric only achieve a dialogic dimension when they imply an honored perception of the intended audience: its humanity, divinity, inherent dignity, intelligence, and so on. The one sort of communication that is inimical to community is what I call *evisceration rhetoric*. This is the discourse that asserts nihilism, the absurdity of life itself.

The question at this point is, What informs the forms and modes of rhetoric I have outlined? Here is where I venture my ideas about community. It seems to me that there are two essential sites of community: interpersonal relationships, such as families, friendships, social groupings, and some professional associations—the conference from which this book resulted being an example. The other site is what MacIntyre calls practices, including medicine and law, sport and scholarship. Each of these sites is the home of a set of values that constitute a community, specifying norms of character, role performance, interaction, and ideal aspiration. Put another way, a community is at bottom an ethical construction.

Although the ethical ground of communities is their most important feature, there are others that are also important. First, communities are not constrained by time or place. No doubt communities are enhanced by "physical space which encourages the encounter of strangers," as Parker Palmer has observed (1981:46ff.). And so are they enhanced by face-to-face interactions, whether public or private. But if such contact were a necessary condition of their existence, they would not only always be local, they would also always be ephemeral. That communities are not always local or ephemeral is demonstrated by the existence of tradition and the aforementioned conference, in which we enact the values I cited from MacIntyre at the outset: civility, intellect, and morality. Adherence to these values did not begin, nor will it end here. Moreover, these values coincide with the values celebrated long ago, in the representation of Socrates, who spoke for the good, beauty, health, wisdom, courage, temperance, justice, harmony, order, friendship, and a oneness with the meaning of life here and hereafter. At the same time that these values affect our lives, there is another set of values that persists as well. There is a community, largely outside the conference, that adheres to the values of Callicles: pleasure, expediency, self-aggrandizement, strength, political acumen, material success, and power. And yet, these values are not unknown to us, or at least to me, and this raises a second observation.

We belong not to one community but several, and the values that constitute them can well be in conflict. A case in point is the "American dream," which is the embodiment of values that define what it means to be a citizen in the American community. In writing about the 1972 presidential election, I proposed the idea that the American dream is actually two dreams, or better yet, two myths, a materialistic one and a moralistic one. The materialistic myth is expressed in the "rags to riches" story; it espouses a work ethic and endorses such values as effort, persistence, "playing the game," initiative, self-reliance, achievement, and success. Competition is its presumed way of pursuing the dream. Unlike the moralistic myth, the materialistic myth does not require a regeneration or sacrifice of self; rather, it promises that if one employs one's energies and talents to the fullest, one will reap the rewards of status, wealth, and power. In naked form, the materialistic myth is compassionless and self-centered; it encourages manipulation and exploitation.

The moralistic myth gains authority from the Declaration of Independence, which states that "all men are created equal"; they are "endowed by their Creator with certain inalienable rights"; "among these are life, liberty and the pursuit of happiness." Cooperation is its favored way of being, and its principal values are tolerance, charity, compassion, and true regard for the dignity and worth of each individual. One who stresses these values too much runs the risk of being considered self-righteous and unrealistic.

My point here is that adherence to both myths is what defines one as being American. No American can escape the whole dream. When one of the myths dominates, whether in the polity at large or in a particular individual, the other myth is hauntingly there in the background. Robert Bellah and his coauthors may be correct, in their book *Habits of the Heart*, when they maintain that it is "individualism, and not equality, that has marched inexorably through our history" (1985:viii), but I would maintain it has not done so without equality taunting its every step. As Kenneth L. Karst observed: "At some deep level Americans have always understood: equality among citizens is essential to the community of meaning that defines the American nation" (1989:196).

This brings me to a third observation. Not only do people belong to multiple, competing communities, it has always been so. I agree with MacIntyre that there are distinct traditions that transcend time and place (I have said as much already), but I disagree with the notion that there was a time or place when communities were not local, that is, circumscribed by limited groups of adherents of certain values or arguments within any given polity (MacIntyre 1988:349ff.). I also agree with Jeffrey Stout's analysis of how communities related to practices, such as medicine and law, become corrupt when their practitioners pursue values external to them (1988:267ff.). When doctors and lawyers pursue money, power, and prestige to the detriment of health and justice, their professions suffer and so do their characters, at least within those professions by those who still adhere to the ideals that constitute the practice. In other communities, however, their behavior may be hailed as a model. One's membership in multiple, competing communities means that one can be an upstanding character and a rogue at the same time.

Epilogue

The most obvious question to be raised now is, How do people come to be members of a community, or, put another way, how are they induced to recognize that they are, in fact, members of a community? Given urbanization and the breakdown of neighborhoods, given the fragmentation of society and the problems of legitimation, given the renascence of nationalism and the struggle among people within and among nations over economic, ecological, and military enterprises, and given the control of media by commercial interests and power elites, the question might even be better put this way: How can dissociated, or unhappily associated, or unreflectively entangled people be brought to a sense of interdependence and common fate that leads to joint actions, to a sense of community, without individuals being homogenized into conformist or repressive collectivities (Williams 1989a:19–38, 111–19, 1989b:177–97)? One answer, perhaps the dominant one today, is to give up on the idea of community beyond the local and ephemeral, to celebrate diversity, difference, and democracy in its limited moments of realization. For my part, I have no answer beyond the one I have offered: Communities are co-constituted through communication trans- actions in which participants coauthor a story that has coherence and fidelity for the life that one would lead. One may adhere to a story because it sanctions a life one must live in order to survive or to succeed. This sort of adherence creates communities by concession or conformity. One may also adhere to a story because one senses in it an honored perception of oneself. Such adherence creates communities by election or conversion. From this view, truly transcendental stories are those that show or reveal us to ourselves ontologically, they account for our Being—what we are and what we can be (Scult 1989). As I have maintained elsewhere: "Any story, any form of rhetorical communica- tion, not only says something about the world, it also implies an audience, persons who conceive of themselves in very specific ways" (Fisher 1987:75, 187). The task, as Perelman clearly saw, "is not, as often assumed, to address *either* a particular audience *or* a universal audience, but in the process of persuasion to adjust to and then to transform the particularities of an audience into universal dimensions" (1984:192).

The point I would stress is that embedded in some local narratives are narratives with potential universal application. For instance, in the example MacIntyre cites of protesters arguing past one another: At the same time that they tell rival stories about a given issue, they also participate in a story about how dispute in a democratic society should be conducted. The basic plot line of this story is respect for the dignity and worth of all people. Acting in accord with this story would transform the dispute into dialogue. And, it should be noted, this story, regarding the dignity and worth of all people, like other metanarratives, began as a local narrative.

Finally, it seems to me that the calls for community today are like the parallel calls for a return to values. The fact of the matter is that there has never been a time without communities and never a human decision or action that did not reflect values. So, in a sense, these calls bounce against reality. They are, in effect, calls for a particular but transcendental community and a specific but unifying set of values. What is desired, in short, is an ideal—a true democracy, a socialist commune, an emancipated society, or a civil, intellectual, moral enclave. The realization of these ideals, or their closer approximation, depends, I think, on having realistic conceptions of communication and the material conditions that mitigate them. The narrative paradigm is one such conception: it sees people as they are and as what they can be—with reason.

Acknowledgments

Portions of this essay are taken from my book, *Human Communication as Narration: Toward a Philosophy of Reason, Value, and Action* (Columbia, SC: University of South Carolina Press, 1987). I am grateful to Thomas A. Hollihan, Stephen D. O'Leary, Peter J. Marston, Allen Scult, and John R. Stewart for constructive readings of this essay.

References

Aristotle. 1954. *Rhetoric*. Translated by W. Rhys Roberts. New York: Modern Library.

Arnett, Ronald C. 1986. *Communication and Community: Implications of Buber's Dialogue*. Carbondale, IL: Southern Illinois University Press.

Bateson, Gregory. 1980. *Mind and Nature: A Necessary Unity*. New York: Bantam.

Beiner, Ronald. 1983. *Political Judgment*. Chicago: University of Chicago Press.

Bellah, Robert, Richard Madsen, William Sullivan, Ann Swidler, and Stephen M. Tipton. 1985. *Habits of the Heart: Individualism and Commitment in American Life*. Berkeley: University of California Press.

Bitzer, Lloyd F. 1978. "Rhetoric and Public Knowledge." In *Rhetoric, Philosophy, and Literature: An Exploration*, edited by Don Burks. West Lafayette, IN: Purdue University Press.

Booth, Wayne C. 1988. *The Company We Keep: An Ethics of Reading*. Berkeley: University of California Press.

Buber, Martin. 1958. *Paths to Utopia*. Translated by R. F. C. Hull. Boston: Beacon Press.

———. 1967. *Between Man and Man*. Translated by Roger G. Smith. New York: Macmillan.

Derrida, Jacques. 1976. *Of Gramatology*. Translated by Gayatri C. Spivak. Baltimore: The John Hopkins University Press.

———. 1981. *Dissemination*. Translated by Barbara Johnson. Chicago: University of Chicago Press.

Dewey, John. 1916. *Democracy and Education*. New York: Macmillan.

———. 1927. *The Public and Its Problems*. Chicago: The Swallow Press.

———. 1930. *Human Nature and Conduct*. New York: Modern Library.

———. 1935. *Liberalism and Social Action*. New York: Capricorn.

———. 1958. *Problems of Men*. Totowa, NJ: Littlefield, Adams.

Farrell, Thomas B. 1976. "Knowledge, Consensus, and Rhetorical Theory." *Quarterly Journal of Speech* 62:1–14.

Fischer, Frank. 1990. *Technocracy and the Politics of Expertise*. Newbury Park, CA: Sage.

Fisher, Walter R. 1987. *Human Communication as Narration: Toward a Philosophy of Reason, Value, and Action*. Columbia: University of South Carolina Press.

Foucault, Michel. 1980. *Power/Knowledge: Selected Interviews and Other Writings, 1972–1977*. Edited by Colin Gordon; translated by Colin Gordon, Lee Marshall, John Mepham, and Kate Soper. New York: Pantheon.

Frentz, Thomas S. 1985. "Rhetorical Conversation, Time, and Moral Action." *Quarterly Journal of Speech* 71:1–18.

Gadamer, Hans-Georg. 1981. *Reason in the Age of Science*. Translated by Frederick G. Lawrence. Cambridge, MA: MIT Press.

———. 1982. *Truth and Method*. New York: Crossroad.

Goodman, Robert N. 1986. "Technological Arrogance, Plus Ignorance, Spells Disaster." *Los Angeles Times*, Part II, 5.

Habermas, Jürgen. 1981. *The Theory of Communicative Action, Vol. 1: Reason and Rationalization of Society*. Translated by Thomas McCarthy. Boston: Beacon.

Hauerwas, Stanley and David Burrell. 1989. "From System to Story: An Alternative Rationality." Pp. 158–90 in *Why Narrative?*, edited by Stanley Hauerwas and L. Gregory Jones. Notre Dame, IN: Notre Dame University Press.

Hauerwas, Stanley and L. Gregory Jones, eds. 1989. *Why Narrative? Readings in Narrative Theology*. Notre Dame, IN: Notre Dame University Press.

Karst, Kenneth L. 1989. *Belonging to America: Equal Citizenship and the Constitution*. New Haven, CT: Yale University Press.

Lyotard, Jean-François. 1984. *The Postmodern Condition: A Report on Knowledge*. Translated by Geoff Bennington and Brian Massumi. Minneapolis: University of Minnesota Press.

Lyotard, Jean-François and Jean-Loup Thébaud. 1985. *Just Gaming*. Translated by Wlad Godzich. Minneapolis: University of Minnesota Press.

MacIntyre, Alasdair. 1969. *After Virtue: A Study in Moral Theory*. Notre Dame, IN: Notre Dame University Press.

——. 1988. *Whose Justice? Which Rationality?* Notre Dame, IN: Notre Dame University Press.

Maranhão, Tullio, ed. 1990. *The Interpretation of Dialogue*. Chicago: University of Chicago Press.

Matson, Floyd W. and Ashley Montagu, eds. 1967. *The Human Dialogue: Perspectives on Communication*. New York: Free Press.

Palmer, Parker J. 1981. *The Company of Strangers: Christians and the Renewal of America's Public Life*. New York: Crossroad.

——. 1983. *To Know as We Are Known: A Spirituality of Education*. San Francisco: Harper and Row.

Perelman, Chaïm. 1979. "The New Rhetoric: A Theory of Practical Reasoning." In *The New Rhetoric and the Humanities: Essays in Rhetoric and Its Applications*. Dordrecht, Holland: D. Reidel.

——. 1984. "The New Rhetoric and the Rhetoricians." *The Quarterly Journal of Speech* 70:188–96.

Perelman, Chaïm and L. Olbrechts-Tyteca. 1969. *The New Rhetoric: A Treatise on Argumentation*. Translated by John Wilkinson and Purcell Weaver. Notre Dame, IN: Notre Dame University Press.

Rorty, Richard. 1979. *Philosophy and the Mirror of Nature*. Princeton, NJ: Princeton University Press.

——. 1989. *Contingency, Irony, and Solidarity*. Cambridge: Cambridge University Press.

Scult, Allen. 1989. "Deconstructed Discourse and Rhetorical Truth: The Journey of a Narrative in Time." Paper presented at the International Society for the Study of Rhetoric Biennial Congress, Ottingen, Germany.

Stewart, John R. 1978. "Foundations of Dialogic Communication." *Quarterly Journal of Speech* 64:183–201.

Stout, Jeffrey. 1988. *Ethics After Babel: The Languages of Morals and Their Discontents*. Boston: Beacon.

Williams, Raymond. 1989a. *Resources of Hope: Culture, Democracy and Socialism*. Edited by Robin Gable. London: Verso.

——. 1989b. *The Politics of Modernism: Against the New Conformists*, edited by Tony Pinkney. London: Verso.

Chapter 13

From Suspicion to Affirmation: Postmodernism and the Challenges of Rhetorical Analysis

Richard Harvey Brown

During the past decade the "rhetorical turn" has become an important intellectual movement in the social sciences. It is now a commonplace that social and cultural reality, and the social sciences themselves, are built up through practices of communication. Not only is society increasingly viewed as a text, as we have seen, but scientific texts themselves are viewed as rhetorical constructions. In such a view, the distinction between facts and fictions becomes blurred, since both are seen as products of and sources for communicative action; both are viewed as representations of reality that also represents various groups, interests, and ideologies.

While such a postmodern relativization can be exhilarating, it also undermines the intellectual authority of its very proponents, as well as that of anyone who would advance a moral or political position in the name of facts or reasons. Textual criticism subverts dogmatic claims in science and in politics. But as scholars and as citizens we still need to justify the truth of our scientific statements and the morality of our political actions. Indeed, both these challenges must be met if we are to establish rational and ethical standards for our collective life. Thus rhetorical analysis of scholarly and social texts has a positive constructive task as well as a negative deconstructive one. This positive task is to imagine more adequate narratives for our political community, and to show how academic writing can help create these narratives.

Skepticism about texts and commitment to social justice have led social theorists and rhetoricians to show how forms of knowledge are infused with power. Such theorists uncovered the social and historical emergence of institutionalized forms of knowledge, thus revealing the moral and political dimensions of what appear to be purely natural or technical processes. In particular, postmodern challenges to prevailing orthodoxies have prompted intensified critical attention to the language and logic of the human sciences, and ultimately to their rhetoric. By "decentering" and "defamiliarizing" scholarly texts, it is hoped that critics might better practice what Ricoeur (1983) has called a "hermeneutics of suspicion."

In addition, however, some scholars, like those gathered in this volume, have also struggled towards a new "hermeneutics of affirmation." These thinkers largely reject positivist and foundationalist views of language and reality, but they also find in rhetoric or deconstruction a potential affirmation of the human authorship of social life, and a possible antidote for discourses of elitism, technical exclusivity, and political domination. For example, it is argued that rhetorical deconstruction can make elite and technical discourses amenable to popular understanding and available for moral interpretation. This rhetorical turn deserves celebration. It is important to remember, however, that all this is not purely a product of textual criticism. Interpretive openness and moral sensibility through critical rhetorical methods are possible only within the context of certain social and historical conditions. Rhetorical analysis may broaden text interpretation to include aspects of civic life, but this does not guarantee that the right stories and social dramas will be enacted. Words still can repress, dramas still can do damage (Lewis 1990:1).

By the same token, to reform the self-image and practice of social inquiry requires more than the replacement of positivistic constructions with rhetorical deconstructions. More importantly, it requires a new vision and new practices of the public space. Thus, the apparently arcane struggle over postmodernism in the halls of academe also implies a struggle for the soul of democratic peoples. Traditional social science gave an implicit account of the public space and a model of the ideal citizen. Disciplined inquiry into the laws of society provided an ideal of general political discussion; the scholar's suspension of self-interest provided a model of the citizen, who would make judgments about the social whole according to general reason, not partisan passions. Science, in the words of Walter Lippmann, was "the discipline of democracy."

Thus, however brilliantly positivism and foundationalism have been criticized by academics, they remain powerful supports for institutions and practices that few of us are willing to abandon: academic freedom, professional judgment, civil liberties, and due process of law (Peters 1990). As a child of liberalism and the Enlightenment, social science has been a major ideological force in the victory of civility over violence, reason and evidence over passion and prejudice, clear communication over cloudy commitment. Thus, we should not dismiss positivist social science too blithely, nor imagine with Richard Rorty that all one needs is a more congenial vocabulary. Instead, if we are to make critical social theory consequential in the public and political arenas, we must consider its ramifications outside the halls of academe. Social inquiry has been more than a conversation in a philosopher's salon; it also helps turn the wheels of state (ibid.).

As this whole volume seeks to show, we have no wish to defend positivist or traditional social science per se. But in order to launch a new kind of critical, rhetorical, postmodern social theory, we need to appreciate the profound achievements of our orthodox opponents. The social sciences in Europe and the United States answered urgent political and public questions by providing models of the task of the scholar, the nature of knowledge, the workings of the public sphere, the conduct of discussion, and the education of the citizenry. Ideals implicit in social science, in short, became interwoven with the very fabric of the liberal polity.

For these reasons the claim that reality and knowledge are social constructions has important results not only for epistemology but also for the relation of social theory to a moral civic life. What, then, can be a substitute way of conceiving the nature and functions of social science now that foundationalism has been rejected and liberalism is exhausted? Clearly, any response entails relativism and, with this, the fear that usually accompanies the view of the world as uncertain. Acceptance of rhetoric, social constructionism, and relativity undermines absolutisms and invites a broader tolerance for alternative perspectives. In an increasingly diverse and conflictival world, the need for such an openness of discourse is greater than ever. But politics is about closure, and power about exclusion. We still need moral criteria to make and measure actions and decisions. But whose discourse and which moral criteria shall we use?

Several answers to the fear of relativism in the relation of rhetorical theory to a moral political practice can be made. First, fewer atrocities in the history of the world have happened as a result of excessive tolerance than as a result of absolutism. Which is worse, the possibility that evil will be tolerated in the name of cultural relativism, or the promise that future atrocities will be justified by some group's assurance that they are absolutely right? Second, relativism does not entail a society without standards. Rather, the inclusion of rhetoric in epistemology helps us to recognize when, where, and how the standards are to be established cooperatively, constantly renewed, and periodically reshaped. Hence, unlike absolutism, relativism is reflective about its own limits.

A third response to the fear of relativism deserves elaboration. This response is to shift from a conception of truth as discovery or product, toward a view of truth as invention or process. In their different ways, this shift characterizes the writings of Chaim Perelman (Perelman and Olbrechts-Tyteca 1969), Jürgen Habermas (1983), and Richard Rorty (1982, 1987). For example, Rorty has argued that it "is the vocabulary of practice rather than of theory, of action rather than contemplation, in which one can say something useful about truth" (1982:162). Rorty establishes the centrality of language, allowing the "text" and conversation to become loci of inquiry. He thereby orients us toward communicative *process* with respect to the practical life of a civic or scholarly community. In this sense, pragmatism does not collapse into relativism, but "the pragmatist knows no better way to explain his convictions than to remind his interlocutor of the position they both are in, the contingent starting points they both share, the floating, ungrounded conversations of which they are both members" (Rorty 1982:173–74; see also Cheney 1987). Even if we accept Rorty's deconstruction of epistemology, however, the consequences of such a move are open and, for better or worse, it does make it harder to isolate any universal or transcultural standards of judgment (Hacking 1986; Rabinow 1986:236).

Michel Foucault explored this problem by showing how Western notions of reason and identity are historically embedded in institutionalized patterns of discourse. Thus, despite pressures from the French Left, Foucault was reluctant to designate utopian goals or even a particular social arrangement as *the* ideal implied by his historical and social criticism. Instead, Foucault argued for an institutionalized social criticism. In his historical genealogies of major institutions of society, such as mental health, criminal justice, and the human sciences, and in his later analyses of power, Foucault sought to expose various modes of domination. Foucault conceived of power as fundamentally interactive, and best understood through analysis of points of real and potential resistance. In this sense, Foucault promoted a critique of knowledge/power that would treat it *in action*, for that is the only place it truly exists (Foucault 1980; see Dallmayr 1984; Cheney 1987). Thus Foucault also responds to relativism by focusing on the how rather than the what of truth or virtue.

Additional and important insight into the power of rhetorical criticism and its role in praxis can be derived from Kenneth Burke. Unlike most literary theorists, Burke never separated action from contemplation, willing from imagining, or poetry from power. Instead, Burke held that all intellectual activity (even the most theoretical sort that disdains politics) is itself a kind of praxis, first and foremost an *act* (Lentricchia

1983:87; Cheney 1987). Burke thereby helps us to recover the classical relationship of *theoria* and *praxis* through a realization of criticism's practical power. By concerning itself with the ways we make and change allegiances to key symbols of authority such as family, employer, religion, or nation, rhetorical criticism participates in the ongoing moral and practical re-creation of society. As early as 1937, Burke acknowledged this dimension of his activity:

> Our own program, as literary critic, is to integrate technical criticism with social criticism . . . by taking the allegiance to the symbol of authority as our subject. We take this as our starting point and "radiate" from it. Since the symbols of authority are radically linked with [social and material] relationships, this point of departure automatically involves us in socio-economic criticism. And since the whole purpose of a "revolutionary" critic is to contribute to a change in allegiance to the symbols of authority, we maintain our role as "propagandist" by keeping this subject ever uppermost in our concerns. (1937:Vol. II, 234–35)

More specifically, as Cheney has noted, what Burke seeks is a continual shift toward humane symbols of authority, as devices "for spreading the areas of allegiance" (Burke 1935:89; see 1938, 1961). Such symbols must enlist our sympathies and hopes by articulating ideals "which we should like to share" (1937:Vol. II, 78). Consequently, for Burke the ideal society is one of *communion*, where the reciprocity of identification is maximized, where all have a "common stake in both cooperative and symbolic networks" (ibid.:247–48), where "we the people" means the entire human race (ibid. 1935). With the broadening of loyalties, a new kind of transcendence might be achieved in which opposing groups would stress and enhance their similarities and not their differences. This is the locus of social praxis for Burke—one in which ethics and politics meet on rhetorical ground (Cheney 1987).

To the extent that modern social science ignores this critical perspective and remains linguistically unreflective, it becomes part of society's mechanisms for legitimation, marginalization, and punishment. In reproducing prevailing discursive practices, an unreflective social science helps to fix persons, objects, and relations in the categories already established through institutionalized social control. By contrast, a rhetorically reflexive social science would make it evident that objects, persons, and events are inseparable form the processes of representation by which they are formed. The activities of the imagination that produce facts and meanings are not simply acts of a disembodied cogito; instead, they are historically developed practices that reside in the very style in which statements are made, in the grammatical and narrative structures that compose even the discourses of science. The *what* of any knowledge system is radically entangled in the *how* of its writing and speaking. For this reason, the text that is self-conscious about its own rhetorical structure is the exemplar of a nondelusional mode of writing for social scientists (Shapiro 1989:7–8) and, by extension, for citizens as well.

Thus the tensions between rhetorical reflexivity and political relevance can be fruitfully exploited by viewing the rhetoric of the social sciences as a critique that empowers peoples and enables actions. The notorious Derridean aphorism, *"il n'ya pas de hors-texte,"* may be invoked to abet an escape from the determinate necessities of history, a self-abandonment to the indeterminate pleasures of the text; however, it may also be construed as an insistence upon the ideological force of discourse in general and especially of those discourses that claim to reflect an essential pregiven truth (Montrose 1989). Thus a rhetorically reflexive social theory is no longer "merely theoretical." Instead, it makes something happen: It disables the power of the words to go on blindly proliferating the ideologies and the canonical readings that they impose. In this way a critical rhetoric earns its adjective of "critical." It becomes an indispensable means of unmasking ideological assumptions (Miller 1982:89).

These observations also suggest that critical rhetorical practice has an uneasy relation to its own institutionalization. This is because rhetorical criticism is transgressive, more profane than pious. It demands a generalized displacement and rearticulation of established discourses or disciplines, not a quarantined place at their margins (LaCapra 1987:236). Thus the relativity of rhetorical deconstruction and its ambiguous relation to practice does not imply the endless proliferation of variety, but the agonistic elimination of error, the marginalization of trivial contentions, and the clarification of fundamental and irreducible differences. It is not a "liberal toleration of opposing views from a neutral ground, but transformation, conversion, or at least, the kind of communication which clarifies exactly what is at stake in any critical conflict" (Mitchell 1982:613–14).

For all these reasons, critical rhetorical analysis is more than a game of "the emperor has no clothes." It does not rest in smugness or unease, having dispatched the philosophic problems of essences, universals, and foundations. Instead, rhetorical criticism can be the starting point for affirmation. We still can be as knights in search of a Holy Grail of truth, but now we do so ironically, knowing that the quest itself is our telos, because the "Holy Grail" is realized only in this quest.

I believe that this is how postmodernist, rhetorical, deconstructive discourse can be a discourse both of resistance and of affirmation. What is affirmed is the will to truth, and this affirmation is contained in the practice of resistance, including resistance to that easy postmodernism of either complacent self-endorsement or nihilistic "anything goes." Resistance will always have to be specific and contingent upon the cultural field within which it operates. It cannot be defined simply in terms of negativity or nonidentity, a la Adorno, nor will the litanies of a totalizing, collective project suffice. At the same time, the very notion of resistance may itself be problematic in its simple opposition to affirmation. After all, there are affirmative forms of resistance and resisting forms of affirmation. The space of fruitful tensions between a hermeneutics of suspicion and a hermeneutics of affirmation is always shifting. But this problem cannot and should not keep us from making judgments. We need neither to suppress nor to overcome the tensions of rhetorical deconstruction. Instead, we should heighten these tensions, continually rediscover and refocus them in criticism and in practice (Baker 1990). No matter how troubling it may be, the landscape of the postmodern surrounds us. It simultaneously delimits and opens our horizons. It is our problem and our hope.

This leaves us with a final response to the fear of relativism engendered by a critical rhetoric: In a democratic polity, we are and must be relativists in practice because we exercise judgments as citizens in shaping or finding ethical truth. Democratic practice requires prudent judgment, and such judgment presupposes rhetorical reflection on political experience that is inherently contingent.

This conception of judgment and rhetoric in the creation of truth was adumbrated by Vico, who saw that the ethical use of reason required judgment in order to relate principles to particular circumstances. Vico opposed Descartes's conception that knowledge is the consciousness of universal laws. Instead, he showed that certainty does not have universal validity. The Latin term *certum* meant the particular or individual (Vico [1744] 1972:par. 321). The only knowledge that the Cartesian cogito can have is knowledge of itself. By contrast, knowledge of the world requires a reflective judgment in which the particular case is related to the general context, and the actions of individuals are seen as part of a shared making of history through language (Makkreel 1980:100). Thus for Vico ([1744] 1972:34) the mistake of Cartesian rationalists was to abandon this Renaissance conception of prudence or reflective judgment in favor of technical decision-making based on supposedly universal laws.

In the spirit of Vico, the essays in this volume show that both theories and representations of truth can be seen as linguistic constructions. The logic of science is itself a kind of rhetoric; conversely, rhetorical construction itself can be a mode of making truths to guide our common life.

References

Baker, Scott. 1990. "Reflection, Doubt, and the Place of Rhetoric in Postmodern Social Theory." Pp. 232–245 in *The Postmodern in Sociological Theory*, edited by Richard Harvey Brown. A special section of *Sociological Theory* 8, 2 (Fall).

Burke, Kenneth. 1935. "Revolutionary Symbolism in America." Pp. 87–94, in *American Writers' Congress*, edited by H. Hart, New York: International Publishers.

———. 1937. *Attitudes Toward History*. New York: New Republic.

———. 1938. "Twelve Propositions by Kenneth Burke on the Relation between Economics and Psychology." *Science and Society* 2:242–52.

———. 1961. *The Rhetoric of Religion*. Berkeley, University of California Press.

Cheney, George. 1987. "On Communicative Praxis and the Realization of Our Discipline's Potential." Paper presented to the Speech Communication Association Meeting, Columbus, Ohio.

Dallmayr, Fred R. 1984. *Polis and Praxis: Exercises in Contemporary Political Theory*. Cambridge, MA: MIT Press.

Foucault, Michel. 1980. *Knowledge/Power. Selected Interviews and Other Writings, 1972–1977*, edited by Colin Gordon. New York: Pantheon.

Habermas, Jürgen. 1983. "Modernity—An Incomplete Project." In *The Anti-Aesthetic: Essays on Postmodern Culture*, edited by Hal Foster. Port Townsend, WA: Bay Press.

Hacking, Ian. 1986. "Making Up People." Pp. 222–36 in *Reconstructing Individualism: Autonomy, Individuality, and the Self in Western Thought*, edited by T. C. Heller, M. Sosna, and D. E. Wellberg. Stanford, CA: Stanford University Press.

LaCapra, Dominik. 1987. "Criticism Today," Pp. 235–255 in *The Aims of Representation: Subject/Text/History*, edited by Murry Krieger. New York: Columbia University Press.

Lentricchia, Frank. 1983. *Criticism and Social Change*. Chicago: University of Chicago Press.

Lewis, Bill. 1990. "Limiting Legal Narratives: The Case of Baby M." Paper presented to the Conference on Narrative, Iowa City.

Makkreel, Rudolf A. 1980. "Vico and Some Kantian Reflections on Historical Judgment." *Man and World* 13:99–120.

Miller, J. Hillis. 1982. "The Function of Rhetorical Study at the Present Time." In *Teaching Literature: What Is Needed Now*. Cambridge, MA: Harvard University Press.

Mitchell, T. J. 1982. "Critical Inquiry and the Ideology of Pluralism," *Critical Inquiry* 8(3, Summer):604–18.

Montrose, L. A. 1989. "Professing the Renaissance: The Poetics and Politics of Culture." In *The New Historicism*, edited by H. A. Yesser. New York: Routledge.

Perelman, Chaim, and Lucie Olbrechts-Tyteca. 1969. *The New Rhetoric: A Treatise on Argumentation*. Notre Dame, IN: University of Notre Dame Press.

Peters, John. 1990. "Rhetorics Revival, Positivism's Persistence: Social Science, Clear Communication, and the Public Space." Pp. 224–231 in *The Postmodern Turn in Sociological Theory*, edited by Richard Harvey Brown. A special number of *Sociological Theory* 8, 2 (Fall).

Rabinow, Paul. 1986. "Representations Are Social Facts: Modernity and Postmodernity in Anthropology." In *Writing Culture: The Poetics and Politics of Ethnography*, edited by James Clifford and George Marcus. Berkeley: University of California Press.

Ricoeur, Paul. 1983. *Time and Narrative*, Vol. 1. Translated by Kathleen McLaughlin and David Pellaner. Chicago: University of Chicago Press.

Rorty, Amelie Oskenberg. 1987. "Persons." *Social Research* 54 (1, Spring) 55–72.

Rorty, Richard. 1982. *The Consequences of Pragmatism*. Minneapolis: University of Minnesota Press.

Shapiro, Michael. 1989. *The Politics of Representation: Writing Practices in Biography, Photography, and Policy Analysis*. Minneapolis: University of Wisconsin Press.

Vico, Giambattista. [1744] 1972. *The New Science of Giambattista Vico*. Translated by Thomas Goddard Bergin and Max Harold Frisch. Ithaca, NY: Cornell University Press.

INDEX

Acting, 135
Afghanistan
  conclusions of studies, 107–111
  north-west frontier studies, 93–94,
    96–97
  record as social product, 104–107
  structural settings, 97–100, 102–104
Agency
  as human control, 187–188
  as human need, 179–183
Alcoholism
  deviant in, constructing, 123–125
  field of, 121
  movement of, 121–123
American Psychological Association,
  81
American Society for Psychical
  Research (ASPR), 79–80
Anthro-apologists, 41–42
Argumentative techniques, 145,
  148–149
ASPR. *See* American Society for
  Psychical Research

Colonial ethnography. *See*
  Afghanistan
Community
  context, 200–204
  membership, 214–215
  text, 210–214
Culture, primacy of, 188–192

Depoliticization, social sciences as
  planning mission, 141–143
  political as rhetorical situation,
    135–138
  social science knowledge and
    public administraton, 138–141
Disciplinary writing
  and hermeneutics, 32–33
  and meaning, 33, 35
  and reflexive examination of
    language, 37–38
  and social sciences, 36–37

studies of, 31–35
and text, 31–33, 34
Discursive form, 53–57
Dormant metaphor, 148–149

Efficiency, 148–149. *See also* Housing
  policy planning
Ethnography
  Afghanistan
    conclusions of studies, 107–111
    north-west frontier studies,
      93–94, 96–97
    record as social product, 104–107
    structural settings, 97–100,
      102–104
  attention to, 91
  for social theory, 166–171
  and *Tristes Tropiques*, 63–68
Experimental moment, 39–40

File, 157
Filemaking
  and Lang, 157–158
  as social theory, 162–166
  term of, 156
Flexibility, 149

Hermeneutics, 32–33
Housing policy planning, and
  rhetoric of efficiency
  administrative rhetoric, 149–151
  dormant metaphor, 148–149
  examination of argumentative
    strategy, 144–146
  policy planning as argumentation,
    143–144
  quantitative justification, 146–148
  quasi-logical arguments, 145,
    146–148
Human needs and control
  agency as control, 187–188
  agency as needs, 179–183
  conclusions of, 192–193
  primacy of, versus primacy of
    culture, 188–192